THE
KNITTER'S
BOOK OF
KNOWLEDGE

THE KNITTER'S BOOK OF KNOWLEDGE

A Complete Guide to Essential Knitting Techniques

DEBBIE BLISS

Illustrations by Cathy Brear
Photography by Kim Lightbody

LARK
LARKCRAFTS.COM

CONTENTS

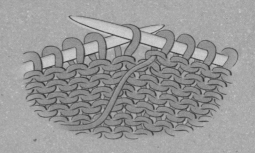

INTRODUCTION

One of the many things I love about the knitting community is their incredible generosity when it comes to sharing their knowledge and passing on their skills to others. I have taught on many workshops where, if I am busy with one knitter, there will always be someone in the group who will offer to help someone who is struggling or who is a beginner. As knitting circles grow in popularity, information and tips are exchanged that not only benefit those on the receiving end in a particular group, but which will be passed on to other groups and to future generations, ensuring that the craft we love will stay alive and continue to grow and grow.

As I feel so passionately about the value of sharing skills, I was delighted to be given the opportunity to share my own knitting knowledge and methods of working by putting together a book of the many, many knitting techniques that I have come across in over forty years as a knitwear designer with my own brand of hand-knitting yarns. As readers become more familiar with ways of improving their skills, I am sure they will want to put them into practice when knitting from commercial patterns, and I hope they will also be inspired to start creating original projects. So, I have included a chapter where I talk about my own design journey, from finding inspiration and working with texture and color, to tackling the practical math that translates the original idea into the finished item. There are also pointers to designing flattering garments to suit your body shape, and the different elements to take into consideration when designing for babies and children.

Ways of doing things can be subjective, and after trying many different methods over the years to improve my own technical abilities, I have my personal favorites, but I am aware that other knitters may be equally passionate about the techniques they prefer. With this in mind, I have included here variations of methods, so you can try them out yourself and decide which one suits you best.

As this book was being put together it became a journey of discovery for myself, too, and I realized how easy it was to become stuck in a rut and always work the methods I was the most familiar with. I hope that this book will also be full of surprises for you as well, and that it will help you along on the path to producing garments, accessories, and homewares that are beautifully knitted and skillfully put together.

DEBBIE BLISS

YARNS, NEEDLES, & OTHER THINGS

The only things you need to start knitting are a pair of knitting needles, a ball of yarn, and small scissors to cut the yarn with; nothing more, nothing less. But as you fall in love with the craft and want to knit more and more projects, you will want a bit more equipment.

And, of course, you will need to buy yarn. There is an absolutely huge selection to choose from, and on the following pages you'll find information on popular types, weights, and fibers.

YARNS

Yarn is the long, continuous length of interlocked fibers that is mostly used in knitting, although knitters have experimented with wire, plastic, and many other materials. Yarn is made from single spun threads called "plies," which are twisted together to add strength.

YARN TYPES

There is a huge variety of yarns available now, and what's shown here is a selection, not a complete list. Each type of yarn has its own strengths and weaknesses, and there will be some that are not suitable for knits that have been designed with the attributes of a particular fiber in mind: one yarn may have lovely drape whereas another has great stitch definition. If you are thinking of substituting a yarn (see page 70), always take on board the characteristics of the original and the new yarn.

Back row: fluffy, self-striping, heather tweed, ribbon (which is also an ombre).

Second row: tweed, smooth, variegated.

Third row: fur, chenille.

Fourth row: variegated, metallic, tweed.

SMOOTH

The most commonly used yarns are smooth, and one solid color. They can be made of various fibers (see page 16), and be different weights (see page 14), and have different amounts of twist (see page 15). Depending on these qualities, smooth yarns can knit up to produce fabric that is crisp and stiff, or silky and fluid, or soft and cozy... These may be the most commonly used yarns, but they are also the most versatile.

FLUFFY

These yarns vary from having a slightly fluffy halo, to being deeply furry. They usually contain angora or mohair—which provide the fluff—and another fiber—usually wool—for strength (see page 16). These yarns can be forgiving for beginner knitters as the fluff can disguise uneven stitches, and even small mistakes, but they are notoriously difficult to unravel if need be. Fluffy yarns aren't good for knitting textured patterns such as cables (see page 122), because the fluff tends to obscure the stitch patterns.

TEXTURED

You can create textural surface effects with plain stockinette stitch using these yarns, but some caution is advised. Yarn that looks very tempting in a ball can knit up to produce a surprisingly unattractive fabric, so always buy a single ball and knit a decent-sized swatch to check that you like the result.

At one end of the textural scale there are yarns such as chenille, which has a short pile and creates a velvety fabric; and bouclé, which has a twisted structure with little loops; and ribbon, which comes in various widths and thicknesses. At the other end of the scale are the very textured yarns that are often called "novelty yarns," including eyelash, which has filaments branching off a central core; fur, which can knit up to be very dense and hairy; and railroad, which has a ladder-like structure and can be very difficult to knit with.

METALLIC

Sometimes called "Lurex" yarns after one of the leading manufacturers, these yarns are bright and shiny, and can be very scratchy against the skin. Yarns made from other fibers but with metallic strands or flecks in them can provide some sparkle, and less scratchiness.

TWEED

Designed to resemble tweed cloth when knitted up, there are different types of tweed yarn, as there are of tweed cloth. Some tweeds are heavily flecked with contrasting colors and are also quite textural, while others are more softly mottled and are sometimes called "heather" yarns.

MARLED

Made from two different-colored plies spun together, these can be subtle—if the plies are similar colors—or vivid—if the plies contrast. The plies can be one color, or either or both can change color along their length.

COLOR–EFFECT

These yarns create color patterning using plain stockinette stitch, and there's a range of different types. Variegated yarns have short lengths of the yarn dyed in different colors so that when it's knitted up patches or streaks of color appear. The patterning will depend on the width of the fabric, and it can be alarming; a full-width swatch is always a good idea. Ombre yarns work on the same principle, but are dyed in shades of one color, and tend to be less startling than variegated yarns. Self-striping yarns have longer lengths of dyed color, so when they are knitted up, stripes are created. The depth of the stripes depends on the width of the knitting. Primarily designed for knitting socks, self-patterning yarns are dyed in flecks and lengths of color and when knitted up create a fabric that looks (a little bit) like a Fair Isle pattern.

YARN WEIGHTS

This term refers to the thickness of the yarn, not the weight of the ball. The size of knitting needle used will depend on the weight because—unless a different effect is required—fine yarns will need smaller stitches and chunkier yarns larger ones. A too-large needle for a sport-weight yarn, for example, will produce a loose stitch and make the fabric more transparent. The stitches should form a solid but not stiff fabric; this is referred to as "stitch fill."

The names for different weights of yarn are not globally consistent, or consistent between spinners, and not all yarns that are described as a specific weight will be exactly the same thickness. However, there are some widely recognized weights, and most commercially available yarns fall into one of them.

Clockwise from top left: worsted, baby, 4-ply, lace weight, sport-weight, bulky. In the center: chunky.

LACE WEIGHT

The finest yarn, primarily used—as the name suggests—for knitting lace. These yarns are usually made in high-quality wool (see page 16), to make them strong as well as fine. Expect to cast on about 33–40 stitches to 4 inches using US size 000–1 knitting needles.

FINGERING OR 4-PLY OR SOCK

A fine yarn that gives about 27–34 stitches to 4 inches using US size 1–3 knitting needles. If a yarn is specifically labeled as sock yarn, it will usually be made from a blend of wool and man-made fiber, for strength.

LIGHT SPORT-WEIGHT OR BABY

A popular weight that gives 23–26 stitches to 4 inches using US size 3–5 knitting needles. Although it is ideal for baby clothes, it's also great for lighter adult garments.

SPORT-WEIGHT OR DOUBLE KNITTING OR LIGHT WORSTED

Probably the most popular weight of yarn, and the most versatile as it is available in a variety of fibers (see page 16), and is suitable for a wide range of types and styles of knitting. Expect to cast on about 21–24 stitches to 4 inches using US size 5–7 knitting needles.

WORSTED-WEIGHT OR ARAN

An excellent weight for home furnishing projects, and for heavier adult garments, this weight of yarn knits up fairly quickly without having to use very thick needles. There will be about 16–20 stitches cast on to 4 inches using US size 7–9 knitting needles.

CHUNKY OR CRAFT

Very popular with beginner knitters as the project will "grow" quickly, chunky yarns give about 12–15 stitches to 4 inches using US size 9–11 knitting needles. But be aware that thick needles can actually be more difficult to handle than thinner ones if you are a knitting novice.

BULKY OR SUPER-CHUNKY

A thick yarn that works best for heavier sweaters and jackets and for home furnishing projects. Expect to cast on about 7–11 stitches to 4 inches using US size 11–17 knitting needles.

STRUCTURE OF YARN

The most common yarn structure is twisted, or plied, strands; if you untwist the cut end of a strand of yarn, you can usually see how many finer threads have been twisted together to make the yarn. However, there are other yarn structures, most of which use plies in one way or another, but some of which don't.

No matter what fiber is used (see page 16), it is spun into strands called plies. The plies are spun in a "Z" direction—where the twists run up to the right—and then plied together in a "S" twist—where the twists run up to the left—to create a yarn. With a balanced twist, a yarn does not twist against itself.

However, the number of plies does not determine the weight of a yarn (see page 14). Chunky yarns can be made from just one ply, or fingering yarns from four plies. Plied yarns are more resilient than non-plied ones, such as roving, which is single-strand, loosely twisted yarn.

Most yarns are made from plies of the same thickness, but some textural yarns use plies of different thicknesses to create an effect. Spiral yarn has a thin ply twisted around a thick one, while nub yarn has two plies that are twisted at different tensions so that bumps appear. Bouclé yarn also has two plies at different tensions, but the twisting creates loops of fiber, while chenille yarn has two plies twisted tightly around strands of short pile. Slub yarn is made from one ply that varies in thickness along its length.

Ribbon yarns are woven, like fabric, and chainette yarns look rather like loose-knit i-cords (see page 115).

Clockwise from top left: roving, slub, chainette, 4-ply, bouclé, chenille, spiral, ribbon, 3-ply, 2-ply.

DIFFERENT FIBERS

There are many different fibers used in knitting yarns, but they are usually classified as either animal fibers, plant fibers, or synthetic fibers. Some fibers can feel beautiful in the ball, but can be disappointing when knitted up. Other fibers need to be blended to make them more suitable for a knitted fabric. Listed here are some of the fibers most often used to make yarns.

WOOL

This is the most popular knitting fiber in the world, and indeed many people still refer to yarn as "wool." However, there are many types of wool, including lambswool, which comes from the first shearing of a sheep and is very soft and warm, and the wools from specific breeds of sheep, such as Merino, or Shetland sheep.

The qualities that make wool so popular are its combination of warmth and light weight, and the fact that it can "breathe." However, it can be itchy on the skin, and some people are allergic to it. Pure wool needs to be carefully laundered to prevent it shrinking, but many modern wools are treated to make them machine-washable.

Wool is relatively elastic to knit with, making it easy for beginners to use, and quite forgiving of uneven stitches.

OTHER ANIMAL FIBERS

As well as sheep's wool, the fleeces or fur of goats, llamas, possums, alpacas, camels, and rabbits can also be spun into yarn, though very often the fibers need to be mixed with sheep's wool to create yarn that is strong enough to knit with. Angora comes from the Angora rabbit and mohair comes from the Angora goat, while cashmere is made from the finest fibers combed from the fleeces of Kashmir goats. Alpacas give alpaca yarn, and their relatives, llamas, camels, and vicunas, also have fleeces that produce good fibers for making yarns.

Yarns made from these fibers have the attributes of sheep's wool, plus whatever individual qualities they offer, such as softness or fluffiness.

COTTON

Cotton comes in different grades, with Egyptian cotton being the softest, and organic cotton coming from plants that have been grown organically. Cotton yarn takes dye well, is easy to look after, and knits up into cool and easy-to-wear fabric that most people find comfortable against their skin.

Pure cotton yarn shows up stitch detail beautifully, but that quality also makes it quite unforgiving of imperfect knitting. It's stiffness can also make it a bit tricky for beginners to work with, but that is improved by mixing it with other fibers.

OTHER PLANT FIBERS

Linen is another popular yarn fiber and is made from the flax plant. Similar in many ways to cotton in terms of its attributes, linen can be scratchy at first, but it ages very well, becoming wonderfully soft the more it is washed.

Other types of plant fiber used in yarn-spinning include bamboo, which makes a soft yarn that drapes fluidly, and soya, which makes a silky yarn that's easy to wear.

SILK

The cocoon of the mulberry silkworm is the primary source of silk fiber, which is unrolled as one continuous thread. The high labor cost of raising, harvesting, and spinning the silk make it expensive, which is why it's often mixed with other fibers to create yarn. Knitted silk is soft and drapes well, but is relatively inelastic and unforgiving for beginners to work with.

MAN-MADE FIBER

Acrylic, nylon, and rayon are the three man-made fibers mainly used to make yarn. They have different qualities, but all wash well, are easy to care for, and are relatively inexpensive, which is why they remain popular. Man-made fiber yarns vary enormously in quality, so choose yarns with care.

MIXED FIBERS

This term can cover any blend of fibers, from luxurious silk/mohair to practical wool/acrylic. Adding man-made fibers to natural ones can make a lighter, easy-care, more elastic yarn that still has the feel of the natural fiber. And mixing natural fibers can make expensive ones such as cashmere more affordable. Mixed cotton and wool creates a yarn with many of the qualities of wool, but without the itchiness that can make it difficult to wear against the skin for some people.

Clockwise from top left: recycled, silk, bamboo, man-made fiber, alpaca, merino, cotton, wool/cotton, linen, lamb's wool.

In the center from the top: Shetland, super-wash, angora.

On the right: mohair and silk blend.

LAUNDERING

These days most yarns are colorfast, but you can check by wetting a length of the yarn and wrapping it tightly around a piece of white paper kitchen towel. Leave it to dry then unwind the yarn and if it has marked the towel then the yarn is not colorfast.

Many wool yarns especially are treated to make them machine washable; look for the phrase "super-wash." If you are concerned, then machine wash your gauge swatch before washing the project.

WINDING A BALL

If the yarn you choose comes in a hank, then you have to wind it into a ball before you can knit with it. You can place the hank on a chair back or ask someone to hold it, stretching it out between their hands so you can wind off easily. It's best to make a center-pull ball—one where you pull out the working yarn from the middle of the ball rather than from the outside—as then the ball won't roll around and escape while you are knitting from it, which is not only annoying but also can affect your gauge. Even if your yarn comes in a ball rather than a hank, it is always good to take your working yarn from the inside; pull out the center of the ball and find the end.

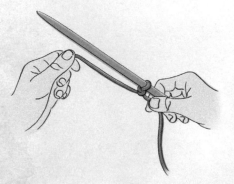

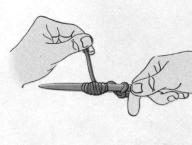

2. Start winding the yarn around the needle, quite loosely at first. Make sure you don't wind over the slip knot. Don't try and work too quickly; unloop the yarn from your friend's wrists, or the chair, slowly and smoothly to avoid getting it tangled.

1. Make a slip knot (see page 34) in one end of the yarn and slide it down to the head of a knitting needle.

3. Continue winding, keeping the yarn taut but not pulling on it, and making sure the knot remains free.

4. Slide the wound ball off the needle. Then slide the knot off. Pull on the knot to use the yarn from the center of the ball.

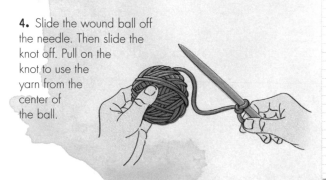

WITH A SWIFT AND BALL-WINDER

These are not inexpensive pieces of equipment, but they do make the winding process quick and easy. The equipment you buy should come with instructions, but the basic principle is as follows. Clamp the swift and the ball-winder to a table, close together, but not touching. Untwist the hank and undo the ties at each end, then expand the swift (rather like an umbrella), and drape the hank over it. Make sure one end of the yarn is free and that the hank is not twisted, then expand the swift further until the hank is held taut, and tighten the knob to prevent the swift collapsing (see photograph opposite).

Thread one end of the yarn through the yarn guide on the ball-winder and anchor it in the slot in the top or side. Then turn the handle on the ball-winder and watch with delight as the hank turns into a ball. Don't wind too fast, and don't stop suddenly halfway through, and watch out at the end because as the last loop of yarn is wound off, the swift will suddenly expand.

Slip the end of yarn out of the anchoring slot and take the ball off the winder. Pull on the end that was anchored to pull the yarn from the center of the ball.

BALL BANDS

The ball band is the label wrapped around a ball of yarn; on a hank it will be a tag. The information on a ball band is crucial, although the way it is set out will vary depending on the manufacturer. Keep one of the ball bands as you work on a project so that if you have a query, or need an extra ball of yarn, you can go back to your retailer with as much information as possible.

Country of origin This is where the yarn was made, not necessarily where the fiber came from.

Gauge and recommended needle size These are the yarn manufacturer's recommendations and may not be the same as those suggested in the pattern you are following. If they do vary, always use the recommendations in the pattern.

Name The name of the manufacturer and the name of the yarn.

Weight The weight of the ball of yarn in grams or ounces.

Yardage The approximate length of the yarn in the ball. This is important if you are substituting yarn (see page 70), or if you are designing a project yourself.

Fiber What fiber/s the yarn is made from.

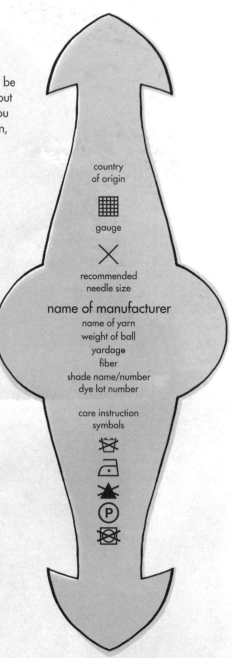

country of origin

gauge

recommended needle size

name of manufacturer
name of yarn
weight of ball
yardage
fiber
shade name/number
dye lot number

care instruction symbols

Above: a swift and ball-winder.

Shade and dye lot numbers Yarn is dyed in huge batches, and each batch has a unique number. It is important that all the balls of yarn you buy for a project have the same dye lot number because the dye mixes do vary a little from batch to batch, and the smallest color variation can show a lot in a garment. To avoid disappointment, it is a good idea to buy one extra ball or hank.

Care instruction symbols How to care for the finished project.

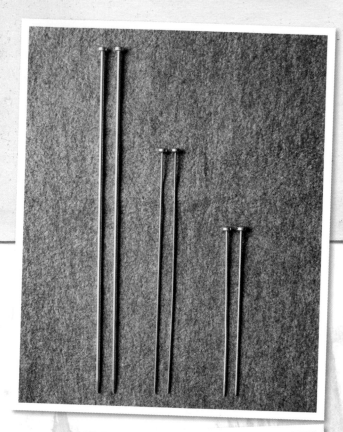

EQUIPMENT

Buy items as you need them; there are so many gizmos available that it can be confusing as to what you really need, and what just has attractive packaging. As well as actual knitting equipment, you could argue that great lighting and a chair with good back support are pretty essential, too.

KNITTING NEEDLES

There is a huge variety of knitting needles to choose from, but the three basic types are straight, circular, and double-pointed. The preference for a type and material is personal to every knitter, but some types may be better suited to different projects; you may prefer a needle with a sharper point with a particular yarn, or shorter needles for knitting small projects.

STRAIGHT KNITTING NEEDLES

Knitting needles are available in different materials; steel, aluminum, wood, bamboo, and plastic, and the choice is down to personal preference. Wood and bamboo needles are good if you are a beginner as they are less slippery than metal or plastic and the stitches won't slide off them easily.

Needles are sized by thickness according to the US or the metric system, though if you buy vintage needles they may well use the old UK system of sizing. You will find a chart of needle sizes on page 22.

As well as thickness sizing, knitting needles come in different lengths, and while it won't make a difference to the knitting, you'll find it easier to handle needles that aren't too long or too short for the number of stitches you have cast on.

Left: metal needles of different lengths.

Below: wood, bamboo, plastic, and metal knitting needles.

DOUBLE-POINTED NEEDLES

These needles have a point at each end and are used for working in the round on smaller projects, such as socks (see page 116). They come in sets of four or five and are available in the same materials as straight needles.

The set of five needles shown are square in profile, rather than round. Although this sounds very odd, they are actually easy to hold and produce beautifully even knitting.

Right: sets of double-pointed knitting needles.

Below: metal needles with plastic flex extensions.

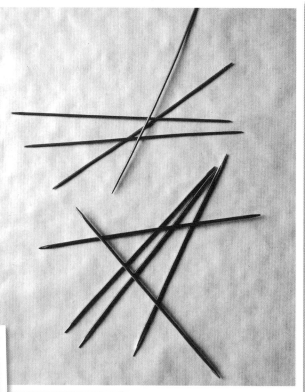

STRAIGHT NEEDLES WITH EXTENSION CABLES

These are short straight needles with nylon or plastic cables coming off the ends; the knitting slides down to sit on the cables and will rest in your lap rather than needing to be held on the needles. So these needles are great if the project is large, or if you have wrist problems.

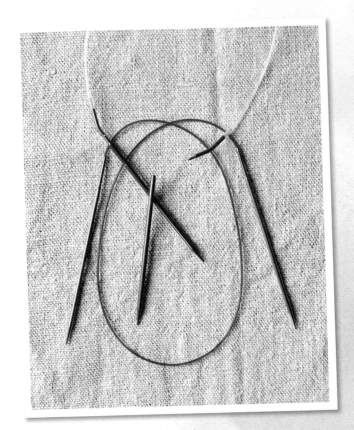

CIRCULAR NEEDLE

This is a nylon or plastic cable with a short straight needle at each end. They are used for working larger projects in the round (see page 108). Circular needles come in different lengths as well as different needle sizes and it's important to use the right length. You can also work backward and forward on circular needles, which is useful for very large projects such as throws or afghans, or for the long front bands on a cardigan. It's also a neat and easy way to knit when traveling.

A circular needle can be fixed, with the needle fused to each end of the cable, or interchangeable, so the needles can be unscrewed and attached to different-length cables. The latter are very versatile, but part of the success with a circular needle depends on the join between needle and cable being very smooth, and with interchangeable needles it may not be.

Left: fixed circular needle (with the red cable), and interchangeable circular needle (with one needle unscrewed).

NEEDLE SIZES

This chart gives needle sizes across the three sizing systems.

US	Metric	Old UK & Canadian	US	Metric	Old UK & Canadian
000	1.5	–	9	5.5	5
00	1.75	–	10	6	4
0	2	14	10½	6.5	3
1	2.25	13	10½	7	2
2	2.75	12	11	7.5	1
2–3	3	11	11	8	0
3	3.25	10	13	9	00
4	3.5	–	15	10	000
5	3.75	9	17	12	–
6	4	8	19	16	–
7	4.5	7	35	19	–
8	5	6	50	25	–

OTHER EQUIPMENT

There are some very appealing products around, but the basics are just as efficient: a scrap of spare yarn makes a good stitch marker, and pen and paper work as well as a row counter. I like to use vintage equipment, too, so my priority would probably be a needle size gauge, as I often have needles that the size has rubbed off, or they have old sizing numbers: look for one that has both US and metric sizes.

STITCH HOLDERS

These are used to keep some stitches separate from others that are being worked on. A safety pin is ideal to hold two or three stitches, but a larger holder will be needed for more stitches. A double-ended stitch holder allows you to knit straight off either end of it. If you need to hold a lot of stitches and don't want a big holder getting in the way, you can thread the stitches onto a strand of yarn in the same way as you would put in a lifeline (see page 73). Remember to tie the ends of the strand of yarn firmly together to stop the stitches slipping off it.

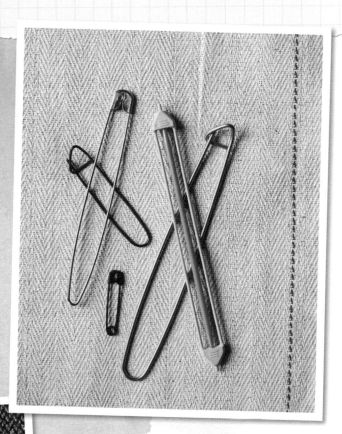

Right: metal stitch holders (red and gold), vintage holder (silver), safety pin, and double-ended stitch holder.

Below: round markers (threaded on needle), hook-in stitch markers, and lock-in (green) stitch markers.

MARKERS

Stitch markers are slipped into or clipped onto a specific knitted stitch so that you can refer back to that stitch later on in the knitting, or to mark off a repeat to help you keep track of a pattern (see page 73).

Round markers are threaded onto the needle and are used to mark the beginning of a round in circular knitting (see page 73). They can also be used on straight or circular needles to mark increase or decrease positions, or stitch repeats in complex patterns. Round markers can be very decorative, or just plain plastic or metal rings. You can use a loop of yarn instead of a solid marker, but be careful not to get distracted and knit it as if it were a stitch.

CABLE NEEDLE

These needles are used for working cables (see pages 122–125) and they come in different sizes and styles. Always use a cable needle that is a similar size to the knitting needles you are using. A cranked needle or U-shaped cable is a good choice for beginners to cabling, as it makes it almost impossible to drop the stitches that are being moved.

Right, from the left: thick and thin cranked cable needles, wooden cable needle, and U-shaped cable needle.

Below, from the left: easy-grip crochet hook, wooden hook, thick and thin metal hooks.

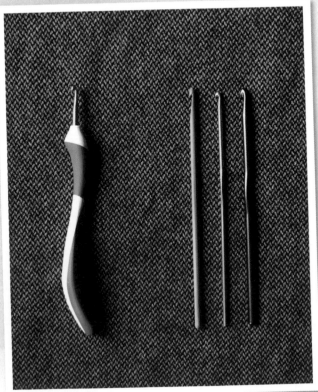

CROCHET HOOKS

As well as being vital for adding crochet edges to knitting (see page 214), crochet hooks can be used to pick up stitches (see page 75), or to retrieve dropped stitches (see page 298). Like knitting needles, they come in various sizes and are available in different materials. They also have different-shaped handles, so try a few in a store before buying one to see what you find most comfortable to hold.

POINT PROTECTORS

These serve two purposes; to stop your knitting needles punching holes in your project bag, and to stop the knitting falling off the needles when you set it aside. However, if you are setting a piece of knitting aside for more than a couple of days, you shouldn't leave it on the needles as the stitches on the needle will often distort a little and leave a visible line in the finished knitting. Thread the stitches onto a length of yarn instead, in the same way as you would put in a lifeline (see page 73). Remember to tie the ends of the length of yarn firmly together to stop the stitches slipping off it.

ROW COUNTER

This little gadget threads onto your knitting needle and you turn the dial every time you complete a row to keep track of where you are in a pattern.

Above: row counter and point protectors.

Right: thread snips and small, sharp scissors.

SCISSORS

Even when patterns say "Break yarn," they don't really mean it. Always cut yarn using scissors or snips to avoid stretching it or pulling on stitches.

PINS

For blocking projects (see page 219) you will need pins: the types with glass or metal heads are best as they are easy to see and will withstand the heat of the iron. For pinning knitted pieces together before sewing them up, use curved safety pins or seams clips, which won't distort the length of an edge, or stab you while you sew.

SEWING NEEDLES

When sewing up seams, use a blunt-tipped tapestry or knitter's sewing needle so that you sew between the knitted stitches without piercing the yarn. A sewing needle with a bent tip is useful for mattress stitch as it makes it easy to see the tip when you push it up between the stitches.

Right, from the top: seam clips, sewing needles with bent tips, knitting pins, curved safety pins.

Below, clockwise from top left: tape measure, measuring gauge, two styles of needle size gauge.

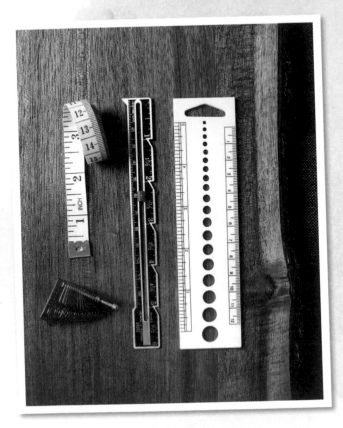

BLOCKING BOARD

You will need to pin out a piece of knitting to block it (see pages 218–219). You can do this on a padded board you make yourself, a commercially bought board, or your ironing board.

NEEDLE SIZE GAUGE

You need one of these if you are using vintage needles or ones marked in a system you are not familiar with, or if the sizing numbers have rubbed off the needle.

MEASURING

You need a tape measure for measuring people and the length of a piece of knitting, and a ruler or measuring gauge for measuring gauge in a swatch (see page 68).

BALL HOLDER

These are useful for single balls of yarn to prevent them rolling away while you work, or when using two or more balls in color knitting (see page 156). A yarn bowl can be decorative as well as practical, and the vintage plastic beehive holders are charming. You can also use a jam jar with a crocheted lid, or one with an eyelet inserted in the metal lid, or a plastic juice cup (see page 169).

BOBBINS

You can make butterfly bobbins for color knitting, or wind yarn around purchased bobbins (see page 168). Purchased bobbins can be simple flat plastic shapes to wind yarn around, or be able to grip yarn so you can control how much is released.

YARN RING

For color knitting you can wear this on the finger you are controlling the yarns with and so control two strands with one finger (see page 183).

Above: yarn bowl (made as a chopstick bowl) and vintage beehive yarn holder.

Below left: butterfly bobbin (top), and two styles of purchased bobbins.

Below right: yarn ring.

FIRST STEPS

If you have never even held yarn and knitting needles before, let alone done any actual knitting, then this chapter will get you started. One of the great things about knitting is that there isn't much to learn to begin with: there are only two stitches to master, the knit stitch and the purl stitch; everything you knit will be based on them. There are various ways you can hold the yarn and needles, so choose what feels most comfortable.

Even if you are already a knitter, don't skip this chapter as there are some cast-ons and bind-offs that you might not be familiar with, but may well find very useful.

HOLDING THE YARN & NEEDLES

If you have never knitted anything at all then before you start, spend a bit of time getting familiar with the tools you are going to use. It'll be much easier to make stitches smoothly and consistently when the needles and yarn feel comfortable in your hands.

HOLDING THE YARN

For neat knitting, it is important to control the flow of the yarn to the needles in a smooth way that is neither too tight or too loose. There is no right or wrong way to do this; it is the end result that matters. Here are the most common methods, including the one that I use.

IN YOUR RIGHT HAND

Hold the yarn in your right hand if you are going to knit using the US/UK way of holding the knitting needles (see page 32). Looking at the palm of your hand, wind the yarn around your fingers in one of these three ways.

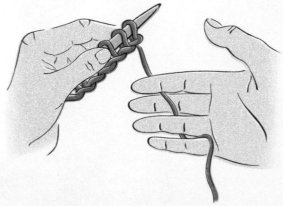

1. Wind the yarn over your little finger, under your third finger, over your center finger, and under your index finger. Use your index finger to wrap the yarn around the tip of the needle. Of the three arrangements shown here, this one puts the least amount of tension on the yarn.

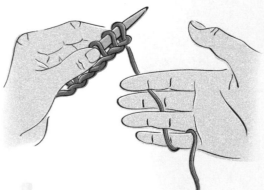

2. Wind the yarn right around your little finger, under your third finger, over your center finger, and under your index finger. Use your index finger to wrap the yarn around the tip of the needle. Of the three arrangements shown here, this one puts the most amount of tension on the yarn.

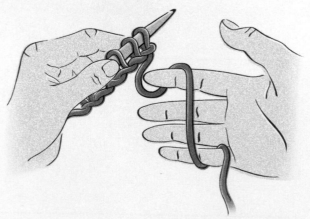

3. Wind the yarn right around your little finger, over your third and center fingers, and around your index finger. Use your index finger to wrap the yarn around the tip of the needle. This is the way I hold the yarn.

IN YOUR LEFT HAND

Hold the yarn in your left hand if you are going to knit using the Continental method (see page 33), or the left-handed method (see page 48). Wind the yarn around your fingers in one of the following ways.

(see page 33) (see page 48)

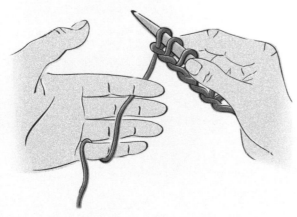

1. Wind the yarn right around your little finger, over your third finger and center fingers, and under your index finger. Use your index finger to wrap the yarn around the tip of the needle. This arrangement works well if you are holding the needles in the Continental way.

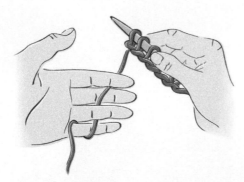

2. Wind the yarn right around your little finger, under your third finger, over your center finger, and under your index finger. Use your index finger to wrap the yarn around the tip of the needle. You can also just pass the yarn over your little finger, rather than wrapping around it, if you need less tension.

HOLDING DIFFERENT YARNS

You might find that you need to hold different types of yarns in different ways. For example, a smooth mercerized cotton yarn might need more tension to knit up evenly than a soft wool yarn does. Experiment with holding new-to-you yarns in different ways before you knit a gauge square.

HOLDING THE NEEDLES

Knitters tend to hold the needles the way they were taught when they first learned to knit, but it can be useful to try another way to see if it improves your speed or neatness. I hold my needles like a pencil, but if I am working on a large project with many stitches on the needles, I sometimes change to the knife position just to vary the position of my fingers and loosen them up.

LIKE A PENCIL

LIKE A KNIFE

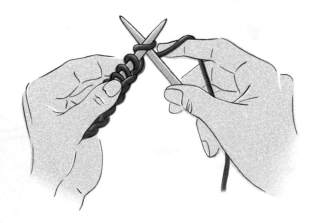

Hold the right-hand needle in the crook of your thumb, in the same way as a pencil. When casting on and working the first few rows, the knitted fabric will pass over your hand, between your thumb and index finger. As the work grows, slide your thumb under the knitted fabric and hold the needle from below. The right index finger is going to control the tension of the yarn, so it is important to keep the yarn slightly taut around this finger.

The left-hand needle, the one with the stitches on at the start of a row, is held from above, using your thumb and index finger to control the tip of the needle.

Hold the right-hand needle from above, in the same way as a knife. This method tends to mean you have to let go of the right needle to wrap the yarn around the tip of it, so knitting will be slower than if you hold the needle like a pencil. The right index finger is going to control the tension of the yarn, so it is important to keep the yarn slightly taut around this finger.

The left-hand needle, the one with the stitches on at the start of a row, is held from above, using your thumb and index finger to control the tip of the needle.

CONTINENTAL METHOD

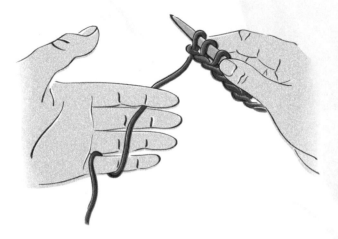

1. Holding the needle with the stitches on in your right hand, wrap the yarn around the fingers of your left hand in the arrangement you prefer (see page 31). Then move the needle with the stitches on into your left hand. The left index finger is going to control the tension of the yarn, so it is important to keep the yarn slightly taut around this finger.

2. Transfer the needle with the stitches on into your left hand. Hold the right-hand needle from above, gripping it between your thumb and center finger.

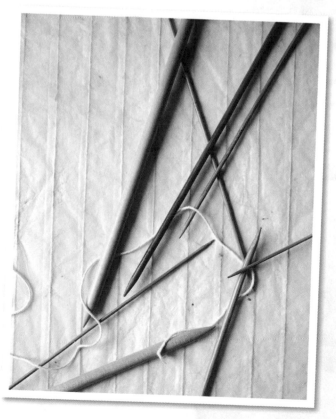

CASTING ON

The cast-on row is the start of any knitting project. Different methods are useful for different types of edge, but you will develop a favorite: mine is the thumb method (see page 36).

MAKING A SLIP KNOT

The slip knot, sometimes called a "slip loop," creates the very first stitch of a cast on, and almost all cast on methods begin with this knot. The "tail end" is the loose end of the yarn, and the "ball end" is the end running to the ball.

1. Make a loop as shown, taking the tail end of the yarn over the ball end and then under the loop.

2. Slip a knitting needle under the tail end of the yarn. The tail should be at least 10cm, but you can leave a longer tail and use it to sew up a seam, see pages 220–225.

3. Holding both ends of the yarn in one hand, pull the needle upward to tighten the knot. Cast on stitches as required (see pages 36–43) and work the first row, then pull gently on the tail of yarn to tighten the knot as needed.

CASTING ON WITHOUT A SLIP KNOT

I usually cast on using the thumb method (see page 36) and over the years have found that it is not always necessary to work a slip knot. Without it you produce a neater edge, which is useful if that part of the garment is not going to be sewn up; for example, at the hem of a side vent.

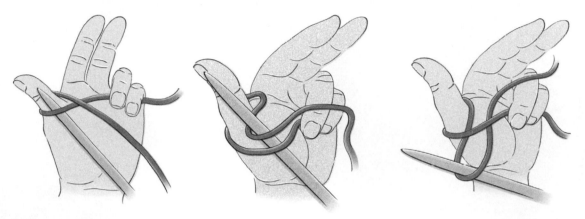

1. Measure out the required length of yarn (see page 36). Wrap the tail end of the yarn around your left thumb from front to back, then hold that end under your fingers, as shown. Using your right hand, slip the point of a knitting needle under the yarn wrapped around your thumb.

2. With your right index finger, wrap the ball end of the yarn over the point of the needle.

3. Pull the needle, and the loop of yarn around it, under the yarn wrapped around your thumb.

4. Slip your left thumb out of the yarn wrapped around it. The yarn is simply twisted around the needle, but when you make the next stitch using the thumb method (see page 36), this twist is locked in place and becomes the first stitch.

THUMB CAST ON

I tend to be rather a tight knitter and I find that with this method I can control the gauge more easily than with the cable method. Because the thumb method is a looser cast on, it is good when you need some elasticity; for example, when a cuff or brim of a hat is turned back so the fabric is doubled. On garter stitch it creates a very neat edge that looks like the rest of the fabric (for the same neatness when using the cable method with garter stitch, work an extra row). The down side can be that you are working toward the end, or tail, of the yarn, so you need to estimate the length needed to cast on all the stitches required: a simple formula is to allow ¾in per stitch.

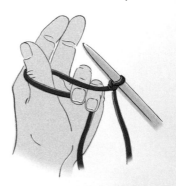

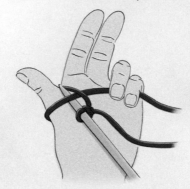

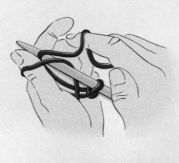

1. Measure out the required length of yarn and make a slip knot (see page 34), or use the no-knot method (see page 35) to start the cast on. Hold this needle in your right hand. *Wrap the tail end of the yarn around your left thumb from front to back.

2. Using your right hand, slip the point of a knitting needle under the yarn wrapped around your thumb, as shown.

3. With your right index finger, wrap the ball end of the yarn over the point of the needle.

4. Pull the needle, and the loop of yarn around it, under the yarn wrapped around your thumb.

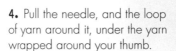

5. Slip your left thumb out of the yarn wrapped around it. Pull gently on the tail end of the yarn to tighten the stitch. Repeat from * until the required number of stitches have been cast on.

TIGHT CAST ON?

If you find that you tend to cast on too tightly, try working the cast on on two needles held together. You can do this for the thumb cast on, long-tail cast on (see page 38), or backward loop cast on (see page 39), as shown.

When you have cast on all the stitches, slip one needle out of them before knitting the first row. Alternatively, work the cast on on a larger size needle than you will use to knit the project with.

CABLE CAST ON

This cast on uses two needles and follows the same technique as the knit stitch (see page 44). It has the advantage of not needing to estimate the amount of yarn needed as you are working using the yarn from the ball. As it is not as elastic as the thumb method, the cable cast on can be useful in areas where some sturdiness is required such as the cuff of a sleeve, which can get a lot of wear.

1. Make a slip knot about 4in from the end of the yarn. Hold this needle in your left hand. Insert the right-hand needle through the front of the slip knot, below the left-hand needle.

2. Bring the working yarn up and then over the point of the right-hand needle.

3. *Pull the right-hand needle, and the yarn wrapped over it, through the slip knot to make a new loop on the right-hand needle.

4. Place this loop on the left-hand needle, as shown. Gently pull the working yarn to tighten the stitch.

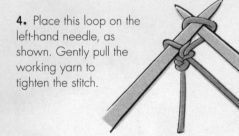

5. Insert the right-hand needle between the slip knot and the first stitch on the left-hand needle. Wrap the yarn over the point of the right-hand needle. Repeat from * until the required number of stitches have been cast on, inserting the needle between the last two stitches each time.

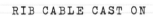

LONG-TAIL CAST ON

This method is very similar to the thumb cast on method (see page 36), but uses the finger as well as the thumb, plus a needle. It creates a firm but fairly elastic cast on, so it is good for children's garments, which have to take a fair amount of wear as well as needing to be wearable. This method is also known as "double thumb cast on."

1. Measure out the required length of yarn (see page 36) and make a slip knot (see page 34). Hold this needle in your right hand. *Wrap the ball end of the yarn around your left index finger and the tail end around your left thumb, making a V-shape as shown. Hold both ends in place with the other fingers of your left hand.

2. Using your right hand, slip the point of the knitting needle under the yarn wrapped around your thumb, as shown.

3. Then take the needle down through the loop around your index finger.

4. Bring the needle back up through the loop around your thumb.

5. Slip your thumb out of its loop, and pull the new stitch on the needle tight. Repeat from * until the required number of stitches have been cast on.

BACKWARD LOOP CAST ON

This cast on is most commonly used when stitches need to be added when in the middle of a row, as for buttonholes (see pages 253–255), or when you need to increase or cast on at the sides (see page 88). It is a quick and easy method of casting on, but is not stable enough to be used to begin a garment.

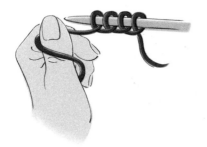 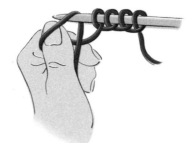 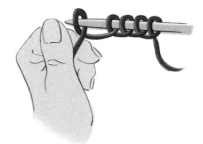

1. Hold the needle in your right hand. *Wrap the working yarn around your left thumb from front to back.

2. Slip the needle under the loop around your thumb.

3. Slide your thumb out of the loop and pull the new stitch tight on the needle. Repeat from * until the required number of stitches have been cast on.

KNIT LACE CAST ON

This method is very similar to the cable method (see page 37), but instead of putting the needle between the stitches, you put it into the loop of the previous stitch. It creates an elastic, flexible cast on that is particularly good for lace edgings, especially where the width of the knitting is going to be wider than the original cast-on edge. For example, on a scalloped edge the elasticity of the cast on means that the shape doesn't pull or distort.

1. Work Steps 1–4 of a cable cast on, placing the stitch onto the left-hand needle and pulling it taut.

2. Then instead of putting the tip of the right-hand needle between the slip knot and the stitch just made, put the needle into the stitch from left to right. Wrap the yarn over it as for a cable cast on, bring the new stitch loop through the old one and place it on the left-hand needle. Cast on all the required stitches in this way.

TUBULAR CAST ON

This cast on creates an elastic edge for rib and also makes for a very neat, satisfying hem that is hardwearing, which, like the long-tail cast on (see page 38), makes it particularly good for childrenswear. A tubular cast on looks a bit complicated, but is actually very easy to knit. This method produces an odd number of stitches, so if an even number is needed either cast on enough stitches to make one extra stitch then work two stitches together when the rib is completed, or cast on enough for one fewer stitches and increase once the rib is completed.

1. Using a contrast color yarn that is the same weight as the project yarn and the backward loop method (see page 39), cast on an even number of stitches. One extra stitch is made between each one cast on, so you need half the number of stitches required for the piece, rounded up to the next whole number. (For example, if 61 stitches are needed, cast on 31; 30 more will be made.) With the project yarn and starting with a purl row, work four rows in stockinette stitch (see page 60).

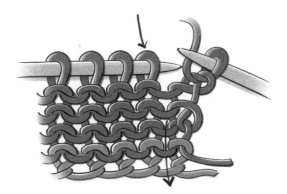

2. To make it easy to see how to work this step, the illustration indicates the stitches, but without showing them actually worked. The next row will be a wrong-side row. Purl the first stitch on the left-hand needle, then take the yarn between the needles to the back of the work. Insert the tip of the right-hand needle under the loop on the first row in the main color, in the direction indicated by the lower arrow, slip that loop onto the left-hand needle, and knit it as if knitting through the back loop of a stitch (see page 77). Then bring the yarn forward between the needles and purl the next stitch on the left-hand needle, the one indicated by the upper arrow.

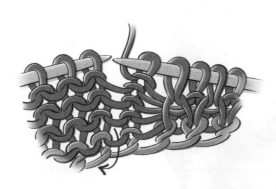

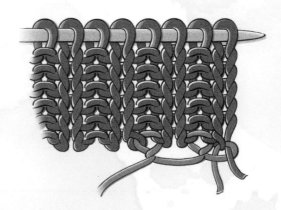

3. Continue in this way, knitting the loops of the first row and purling the stitches on the left-hand needle, until all the stitches and loops have been purled and knitted.

4. Work a few rows in single rib (see page 61), following the established pattern of knit and purl stitches. Then carefully unpick the waste yarn from the bottom of the ribbing.

PICOT CAST ON

Perfect for when you want to make the edgings of your project look a bit more special, a picot cast on adds decorative detail to a simple knit. You can have different numbers of stitches between the picot tails, and different numbers cast on to make longer or shorter tails. Be careful to keep track of the stitches cast on for the picot tails, and those needed for the cast-on edge.

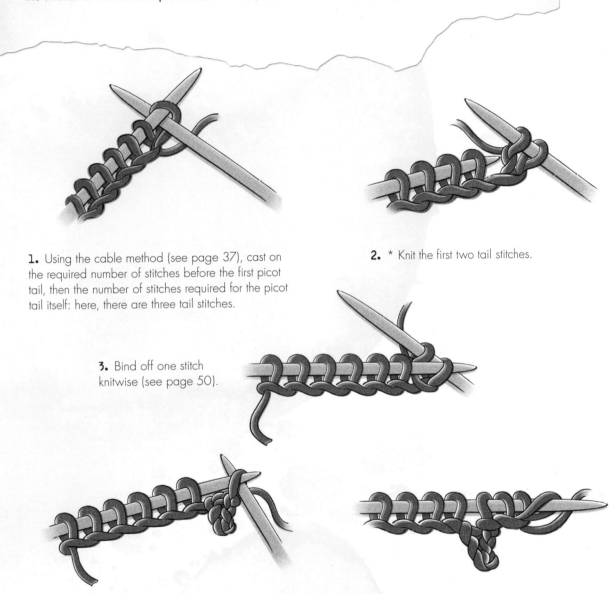

1. Using the cable method (see page 37), cast on the required number of stitches before the first picot tail, then the number of stitches required for the picot tail itself: here, there are three tail stitches.

2. * Knit the first two tail stitches.

3. Bind off one stitch knitwise (see page 50).

4. Then knit and bind off another stitch, then one more. You have bound off the three tail stitches and formed the first picot tail. The stitch remaining on the right hand needle is one of the stitches cast on for the edge, so slip that stitch knitwise (see page 77) back onto the left-hand needle.

5. Using the cable cast on method, cast on the required number of stitches before the next picot tail, plus the number of stitches needed for the tail itself. Repeat from * until the required number of stitches are cast on to the left-hand needle.

HEM PICOT CAST ON

This hem produces a scalloped edge that is formed by eyelets worked in a turned-up hem. So that you can clearly see the techniques needed to make an eyelet, the first two steps show the actions being worked on a row of plain knitting.

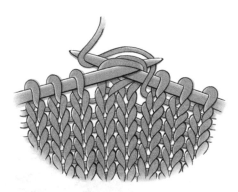 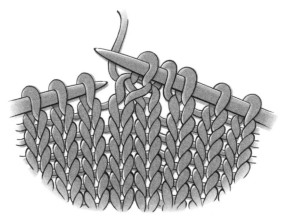

1. Using your preferred cast on method (see pages 36–39), cast on the required number of stitches. The picots require an odd number of stitches, plus any stitches needed for seams (see page 221). Work in stockinette stitch (see page 60) until the hem is the required depth, ending with a wrong-side row. On the next (right-side) row, knit any seam stitches, *then make a yarnover (see page 136), and knit the next two stitches together (see page 90).

2. One eyelet is completed. Repeat from * across the row—making a yarnover then knitting the next two stitches together—to the end of the row, or the seam stitches.

3. Purl the next row, purling into the loop of each yarnover as if it was a stitch. Complete the piece of knitting. The picot hem row has a series of evenly spaced holes.

4. Turn the hem up along the picot row and sew it (see page 243), or graft it (see page 245), using the knitting yarn. Or the hem can be knitted in (see page 244).

PROVISIONAL CAST ON

This method is particularly useful when you haven't decided what kind of border you want, or you want to use one that is more effective worked as a bound-off edge than as a cast-on one, or if you want to graft a hem (see page 245). A provisional cast on keeps the stitches "live" so that they can be picked up later. A crochet hook and waste yarn are needed.

1. Using waste yarn that is the same weight as the project yarn, make a slip knot (see page 34) onto the crochet hook. Catch the working yarn with the hook and pull it through the slip knot to make a chain stitch.

2. Continue making chain stitches in this way until you have one for every cast on stitch required, plus a couple of extra chains at the end. Secure the chain by taking the end of the yarn through the last loop and pulling it tight.

3. Tie the knitting yarn to the tail of the slip knot at the start of the chain. Insert a knitting needle into the first bump on the back of the crochet chain. Wrap the knitting yarn around the tip of the needle and pull a loop through. Continue in this way, pulling a loop through each bump on the chain until you have the required number of stitches on the needle. Start knitting…

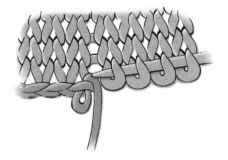

4. When the knitting is complete, carefully unpick the end loop of the crochet chain. Then pull gently on the tail to unravel the chain one stitch at a time, sliding a knitting needle into the knitted stitch loops as you go. Work the edge as required.

THE STITCHES

There are only two stitches to learn, knit stitch and purl stitch. But there are different ways of forming them, depending on how you hold the needles, and which is your dominant hand.

KNIT STITCH: US/UK

The knit stitch is the easiest to create and the one that beginners will learn first. It is worked from the cast-on row as shown here, and the yarn is always held at the back of the work. If you knit every row you create a fabric called garter stitch (see page 60).

1. Hold the needle with the stitches on in your left hand, with the working yarn at the back, controlled by your right hand (see page 30). *Insert the right-hand needle from left to right through the front of the first stitch on the left-hand needle.

2. Wrap the working yarn from left to right over the tip of the right-hand needle.

3. Keeping the yarn taut over the right-hand needle, begin to draw the needle back through the stitch on the left-hand needle.

4. Draw the right-hand needle, and the yarn wrapped over it, completely through the stitch, so forming a stitch on the right-hand needle.

5. Slip the original stitch off the left-hand needle, keeping the new stitch on the right-hand needle. You have knitted one stitch. Repeat from * until all the stitches have been knitted off the left-hand needle onto the right-hand needle: you have knitted one row. Swap the needle with the stitches on into your left hand to start the next row. If you are working garter stitch then the next row will be another knit row. If you are working stockinette stitch (see page 60), the next row will be a purl row (see opposite).

PURL STITCH: US/UK

The purl stitch is the next basic stitch to learn and is worked in the opposite way to the knit stitch. Some beginners may find it slightly more difficult to master than the knit stitch, but the principle is still the same. The yarn is always held at the front of the work.

1. Hold the needle with the stitches on in your left hand, with the working yarn at the front, controlled by your right hand (see page 30). *Insert the right-hand needle from right to left through the front of the first stitch on the left-hand needle.

2. Wrap the working yarn from right to left around the tip of the right-hand needle.

3. Keeping the yarn wrapped around the right-hand needle, begin to draw the needle backward through the stitch on the left-hand needle.

4. Bring the right-hand needle and the yarn wrapped around it completely through the stitch, so forming a stitch on the right-hand needle.

5. Slip the original stitch off the left-hand needle, keeping the new stitch on the right-hand needle. You have purled one stitch. Repeat from * until all the stitches have been purled off the left-hand needle onto the right-hand needle: you have purled one row. Swap the needle with the stitches on into your left hand to start the next row. If you are working stockinette stitch (see page 60), the next row will be a knit row (see opposite).

KNIT STITCH: CONTINENTAL

In this method the left hand holds the working yarn instead of the right. Once this technique is mastered it can be a quick way to knit, but can create a slightly uneven fabric. Knitters who use this method are sometimes called "pickers" because of the way the right-hand needle catches or "picks" the yarn.

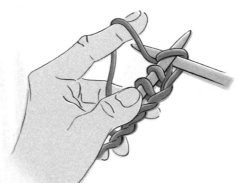

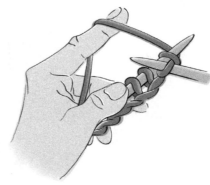

1. Hold the yarn and needles the Continental way (see page 33). *With the yarn at the back, from left to right put the tip of the right-hand needle into the first stitch on the left-hand needle.

2. Wrap the working yarn over the tip of the right-hand needle.

3. Lower your left-hand index finger slightly, and keeping the yarn taut over the right-hand needle, draw it, and the yarn wrapped around it, completely through the stitch on the left-hand needle, so forming a new stitch on the right-hand needle.

4. Slip the original stitch off the left-hand needle, keeping the new stitch on the right-hand needle. You have knitted one stitch. Repeat from * until all the stitches have been knitted off the left-hand needle onto the right-hand needle: you have knitted one row. Swap the needle with the stitches on into your left hand to start the next row. If you are working garter stitch (see page 60), then the next row will be another knit row. If you are working stockinette stitch (see page 60), the next row will be a purl row (see opposite).

PURL STITCH: CONTINENTAL

The purl stitch can be trickier to get to grips with using the Continental method as you are taking the yarn counterclockwise, which can be a bit fiddly. However when alternating knit and purl stitches—as for rib or seed stitch (see page 61)—the Continental method can be the quickest way to create the fabric.

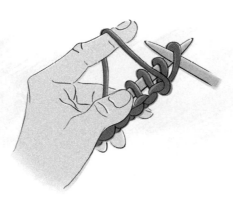

1. Hold the yarn and needles the Continental way (see page 33). *With the yarn in front, from right to left put the tip of the right-hand needle into the first stitch on the left-hand needle.

2. Wrap the working yarn over the tip of the right-hand needle, and press the yarn down with the index finger of your left hand to keep it taut.

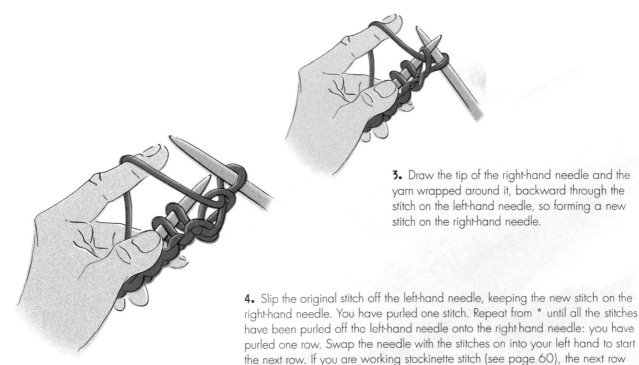

3. Draw the tip of the right-hand needle and the yarn wrapped around it, backward through the stitch on the left-hand needle, so forming a new stitch on the right-hand needle.

4. Slip the original stitch off the left-hand needle, keeping the new stitch on the right-hand needle. You have purled one stitch. Repeat from * until all the stitches have been purled off the left-hand needle onto the right-hand needle: you have purled one row. Swap the needle with the stitches on into your left hand to start the next row. If you are working stockinette stitch (see page 60), the next row will be a knit row (see opposite).

KNIT STITCH: LEFT-HANDED

Knitting is a two-handed skill however you do it, and many left-handers are happy working right-handed. Instructions are almost invariably written for US/UK or Continental styles, so for a beginner, I would advise trying a right-handed way first; as the Continental method involves using the left hand to manage the yarn, that may be a suitable method to start with. However, here is a left-handed style, and looking at instructions for right-handed techniques in a mirror can be useful.

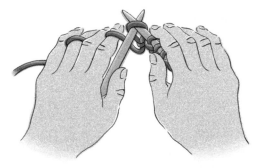

1. Hold the needle with the stitches on in your right hand and the working yarn in your left hand (see page 31). *With the yarn at the back, put the tip of the left-hand needle from front to back into the first stitch on the right-hand needle.

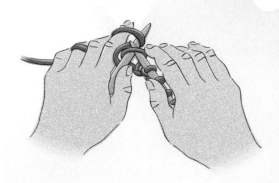

2. Wrap the working yarn under and then, from right to left, over the tip of the left-hand needle.

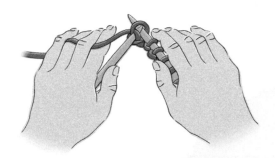

3. Draw the tip of the left-hand needle and the yarn wrapped around it, through the stitch on the right-hand needle, so forming a new stitch on the left-hand needle.

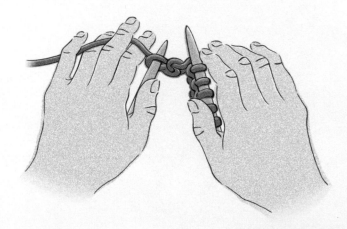

4. Slip the original stitch off the right-hand needle, keeping the new stitch on the left-hand needle. You have knitted one stitch. Repeat from * until all the stitches have been knitted off the right-hand needle onto the left-hand needle: you have knitted one row. Swap the needle with the stitches on into your right hand to start the next row. If you are working garter stitch (see page 60), then the next row will be another knit row. If you are working stockinette stitch (see page 60), the next row will be a purl row (see opposite).

PURL STITCH: LEFT-HANDED

These illustrations show the technique for working the purl stitch for left-handed knitters who have struggled with the right-handed methods of knitting.

1. Hold the needle with the stitches on in your right hand and the working yarn in your left hand (see page 31). *With the yarn at the front, from left to right put the tip of the left-hand needle into the first stitch on the right-hand needle.

2. Wrap the working yarn over and around the tip of the left-hand needle from left to right.

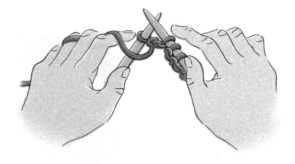

3. Draw the tip of the left-hand needle and the yarn wrapped around it, backward through the stitch on the right-hand needle, so forming a new stitch on the left-hand needle.

4. Slip the original stitch off the right-hand needle, keeping the new stitch on the left-hand needle. You have purled one stitch. Repeat from * until all the stitches have been purled off the right-hand needle onto the left-hand needle: you have purled one row. Swap the needle holding the stitches into your right hand to start the next row. If you are working stockinette stitch (see page 60), the next row will be a knit row (see opposite).

BINDING OFF

When you have completed a piece of knitting, you have to bind off the stitches to prevent them from unraveling. Different methods create different edges, some of which are decorative.

BINDING OFF KNITWISE

This is the most commonly used bind-off. On a stockinette stitch neckband, be careful not to bind off too tightly; consider a suspended bind-off (see page 52) instead.

1. Knit the first two stitches on the left-hand needle (see page 44).

2. *Slip the tip of the left-hand needle through the front of the first stitch on the right-hand needle.

3. Lift this stitch over the second stitch, then drop it off the needle. You have bound off one stitch.

4. Knit the next stitch and repeat from * until all stitches have been worked off the left-hand needle and only one stitch remains on the right-hand needle.

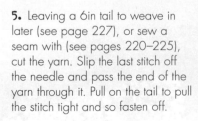 

5. Leaving a 6in tail to weave in later (see page 227), or sew a seam with (see pages 220–225), cut the yarn. Slip the last stitch off the needle and pass the end of the yarn through it. Pull on the tail to pull the stitch tight and so fasten off.

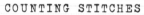

COUNTING STITCHES

If you bind off some stitches within a row (for example, for a buttonhole, see page 254), one stitch will be left on the right-hand needle and how you count that stitch can cause confusion. If there are nine stitches on the left needle and one on the right needle, some patterns say to knit ten stitches, even though you don't actually work the stitch on the right needle. Other patterns will tell you to knit nine stitches, which can be misleading if you do a stitch count. Very helpful patterns might say, "K10 ibos" or some such phrasing, with "ibos" being the abbreviation for "including bound-off stitch," referring to the stitch on the right-hand needle.

BINDING OFF PURLWISE

This is the same principle as knitwise, but on a purl row, and the bound-off edge will sit in a slightly different place. A purl bind off looks particularly good on garter stitch as it resembles another stitch ridge.

1. Purl two stitches. *Slip the tip of the left-hand needle through the back of the first stitch on the right-hand needle.

2. Lift this stitch over the second stitch, then drop it off the needle. You have bound off one stitch. Purl the next stitch and repeat from * to complete the bind off, fastening off as for a knitwise bind off (see opposite).

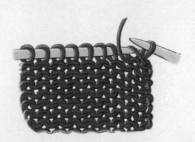

BINDING OFF IN PATTERN

This method is shown here on a rib stitch; by binding off in rib you produce a stretchier bound-off edge, which is particularly useful in neckbands to ensure they are not too tight. However, the principle applies to all stitch patterns.

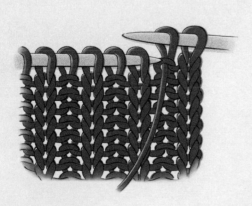

1. Knit one stitch then purl one stitch, following the rib pattern.

2. Take the yarn to the back, ready to work the next stitch, then use the tip of the left-hand needle to lift the first stitch over the second stitch. Complete the bind off in this way, knitting or purling the stitches following the stitch pattern, then fasten off as for a knitwise bind off (see opposite).

SUSPENDED BIND OFF

This bind off is a bit stretchier than the standard version, so it's good for edges that need flexibility, such as neckbands, or anywhere you need to have "give." It's also a good option if you generally tend to bind off very tightly. Work it on a knit row and it looks almost the same as a standard knitwise bind off (see page 50).

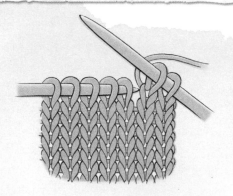

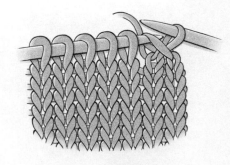

2. *Use the tip of the left-hand needle to lift the first knitted stitch over the second one and off the tip of the right-hand needle, but do not drop it off the left-hand needle.

1. Knit the first two stitches as for a standard knitwise bind off.

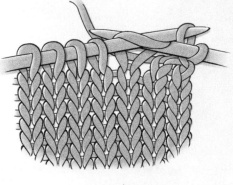

3. Put the right-hand needle knitwise into the next stitch on the left-hand needle and knit it.

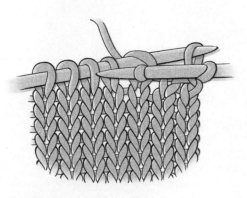

4. The two loops on the right-hand needle are from the second and third stitches knitted. Drop the loops of the first stitch knitted and the stitch you have just knitted into off the left-hand needle. Three stitches have been knitted into and one stitch has been bound off.

5. Repeat the process from *, until all the stitches have been knitted off the left-hand needle. Lift the first stitch on the right-hand needle over the other stitch and fasten off in the usual way (see page 50).

THREE–NEEDLE BIND OFF

This technique is used when binding off two pieces together, such as on shoulders where it is particularly useful to have a stable seam that is neat, and isn't bulky. The working yarn should be left on the piece of knitting that will be at the front, the piece that will have the right side facing away from you.

1. With the right sides of the work together, hold both needles in your left hand, the tips facing in the same direction. The needles are shown spaced apart here to make it easier to see what's happening, but you would hold them so they were touching.

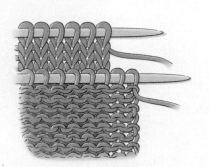

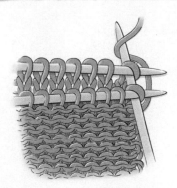

2. Hold a third needle in your right hand. Put the point of the right-hand needle into the first stitch on the front left-hand needle and then into the first stitch on the back left-hand needle, going into the stitches as shown.

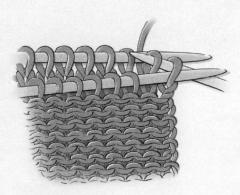

3. Using the working yarn from the front piece, wrap it over the point of the right-hand needle, then draw the loop through both stitches on the left-hand needles. Drop the stitches off the left-hand needles, keeping the single new stitch on the right-hand needle. Knit the next two stitches on the left-hand needles together in the same way so that there are two stitches on the right-hand needle.

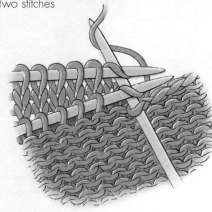

4. Using the tip of one of the left-hand needles, pass the first stitch on the right-hand needle over the second stitch and drop the stitch off the needle as if you were binding off knitwise (see page 50).

5. Knit the next two stitches on the left-hand needles together and repeat the process until all the stitches on the left-hand needles have been bound off. Fasten off as for a knitwise bind off.

SEWN BIND OFF

This creates a very flat edge that can be worked loosely to prevent the knitting pulling in. It's good for lace patterns as it doesn't create a hard edge, and on garter stitch it creates an edge that is similar to the long tail cast on (see page 38).

1. Measure out a length of the working yarn that is five times the width of the edge to be bound off. Cut the yarn and thread a blunt-tipped sewing needle with it. Take the sewing needle purlwise (see page 64) through the first two stitches to be bound off.

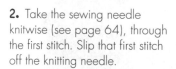

2. Take the sewing needle knitwise (see page 64), through the first stitch. Slip that first stitch off the knitting needle.

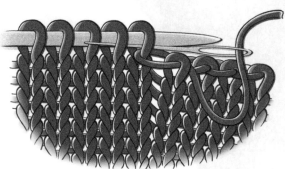

3. Continue across the row in this way: take the needle purlwise through two stitches.

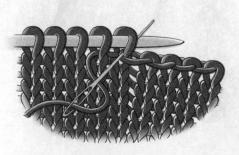

4. Then take it knitwise through the first of those two stitches, before dropping that first stitch off the knitting needle.

PICOT BIND OFF

The picot bind off takes a little longer than the standard version, but is worth the effort for the pretty edge it provides. Worked on a single rib, it makes a wavier finish for an even more decorative edge. Allow for more yarn than you would usually for a bind off, because you are casting on stitches as well as binding off.

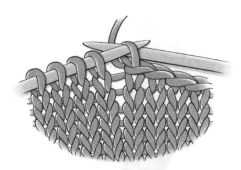

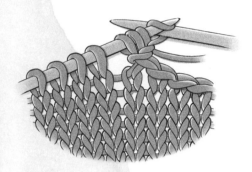

1. Bind off knitwise (see page 50) the required number of stitches before the first picot tail. *Slip the stitch on the right-hand needle knitwise onto the left-hand needle (see page 64).

2. Using the cable cast on method (see page 37), cast on the number of stitches needed for the picot tail.

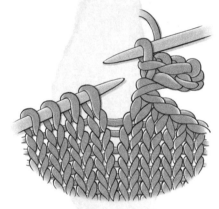

3. Knit and bind off all the tail stitches so one stitch remains on the right-hand needle.

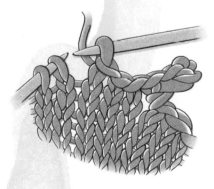

4. Bind off the required number of stitches from the left-hand needle before the next picot. Repeat from * until all the stitches are bound off.

I-CORD BIND OFF

A cord worked along the edge of a piece of knitting makes a firm, robust finishing detail with a clean rounded edge. This is an ideal bind off for edges that need to stay stable, such as the openings of bags or the top edges of blankets. You can cast on the extra stitches in a contrast color and use that to work the cord if you prefer.

1. Using the backward loop method (see page 39), cast on the required number of stitches for the i-cord: here, there are three cord stitches.

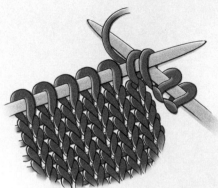

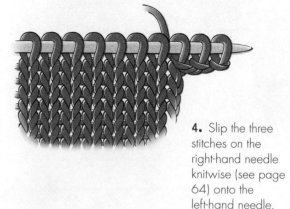

2. *Knit the first two cord stitches. (If you have cast on more than three stitches for the cord, knit them all except one.)

3. Knit the third (the final) cord stitch together (see page 90) with the first stitch of the main knitting, knitting through the back loops (see page 77). One stitch has been bound off.

4. Slip the three stitches on the right-hand needle knitwise (see page 64) onto the left-hand needle.

5. Repeat from * across the row. When all the stitches have been knitted off the left-hand needle, slip the three stitches on the right-hand needle onto the left-hand needle and knit them together through the back loops (see page 92), then fasten off in the usual way (see page 50).

SINGLE CROCHET BIND OFF

This produces a bind off similar to the knitwise method (see page 50). Use a hook of a similar size to the knitting needles that have been used, or use a larger crochet hook for a looser bind off, which can be useful where you don't want too tight an edge on a piece. Some knitters, particularly those who are crocheters, too, find this a quick and easy method.

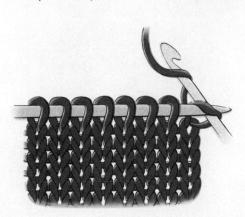

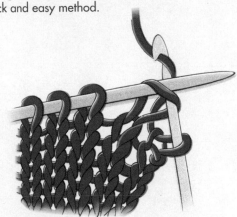

1. Put the hook knitwise (see page 64) into the first stitch. Draw a loop of yarn through the stitch, then drop the stitch off the left-hand needle.

2. *Work the next stitch in the same way so that there are two stitches on the crochet hook.

3. Wrap the yarn around the hook and pull the loop through both stitches on the hook. Repeat from * until all the stitches have been bound off. Fasten off as for a knitwise bind off (see page 50).

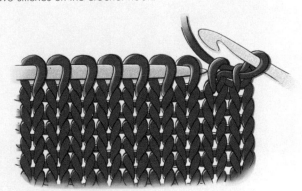

PROVISIONAL BIND OFF

There will be times when you need to leave some stitches "live" so that you can return to them later and place them back on the needle. For example, when working the first side of a neck the pattern may ask you to leave stitches not being worked on a spare needle, but it is much easier to slip them onto waste yarn.

1. Thread a blunt-tipped sewing needle with a length of waste yarn that's more than twice as long as the knitting is wide. Take the yarn through the stitches on the knitting needle, being careful not to split the yarn with the sewing needle. Drop the stitches off the knitting needle as you go. Tie the ends of the waste yarn together to keep the stitches secure until they are needed.

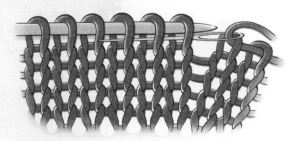

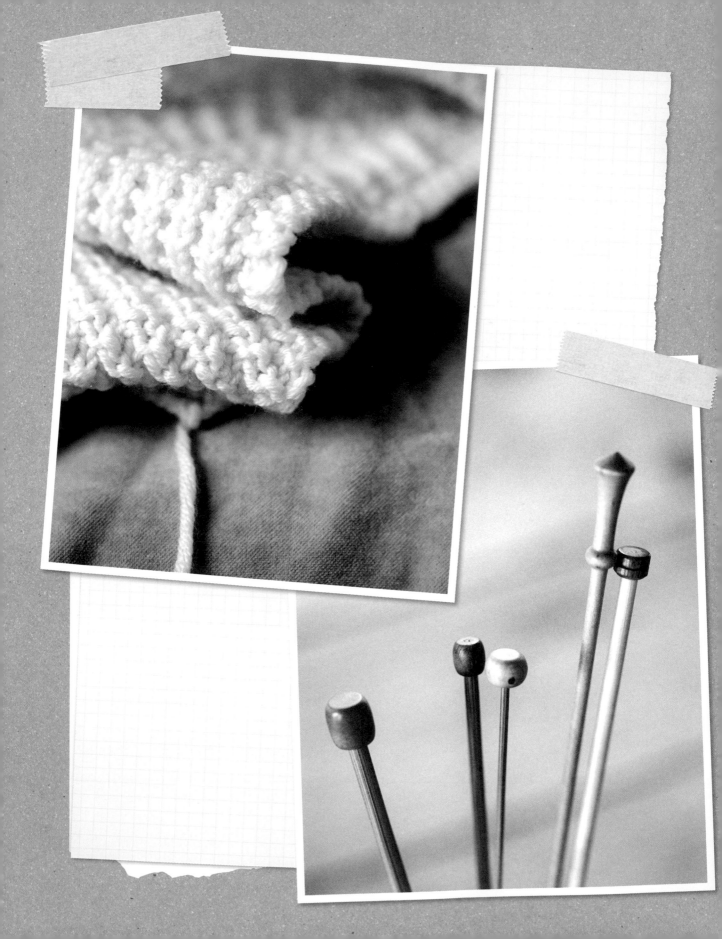

UNDERSTANDING
KNITTING

Now that you have learned how to make basic stitches on your knitting needles, it's time to explore some of the technical aspects of knitting. The language and terminology of written patterns can seem impenetrable at first, and charts can be confusing, and that's before you've even contemplated the mysteries of gauge and stitch counts. However, nothing is as tricky as it might seem, and this chapter takes you step-by-step through everything you'll need to understand in order to knit projects from patterns, plus a couple of extra techniques that are useful to master early on.

BASIC KNITTED FABRICS

The simplest combinations of knit and purl stitches can create beautiful knitted fabrics. The most commonly used fabric is stockinette stitch, which has knit on the right side and purl on the wrong side, while my particular favorite is seed stitch, which can also be used for a border as an alternative to rib. The simpler the stitch, the more important it is to choose a smooth, good-quality fiber that shows it well.

THE STRUCTURE OF KNITTED FABRIC

No matter which stitches you use or how complicated the pattern is, knitted fabric is just a series of linked loops of yarn. In patterns such as cables (see pages 120–128), or lace (see page 136–140), the links may be twisted or interrupted, but in the basic fabrics that make up most knitting projects, the links are simple: each loop is one stitch on one row, and each stitch is linked to the stitches on either side, and to the rows above and below.

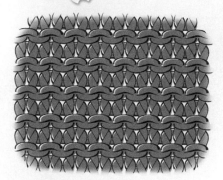

GARTER STITCH

This is the simplest stitch pattern; you just knit every stitch and every row. Garter stitch is usually what a beginner knitter chooses for their first project, but its neat texture and the stable, flat, reversible fabric it produces make it an essential stitch for master knitters, too.

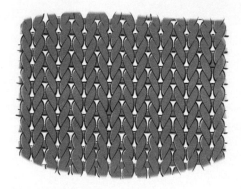

STOCKINETTE STITCH

Stockinette stitch is the most popular of all knitted fabrics and is made up of alternate rows of knit and purl stitches. The rows and columns of interlocking V shapes create a smooth surface that is a perfect background for areas of stitch texture, and that shows off the qualities of textural yarns.

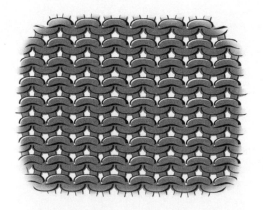

REVERSE STOCKINETTE STITCH

This is often dismissed as just the "wrong side" of stockinette stitch, but it's actually a valuable fabric in its own right. Made in the same way as stockinette stitch, the subtle texture is most often used as a background for cables (see page 120).

SINGLE RIB

This stitch has a natural elasticity and is most commonly used for welts and cuffs on garments such as sweaters and cardigans. It is made up of alternate knit and purl stitches across a row, and on subsequent rows the stitches that were purled on the previous row are knitted, and vice versa.

The exact pattern depends on whether the ribbing is being worked over an even or odd number of stitches (see page 62 for more on reading knitting patterns).

For an even number of stitches
Row 1: [K1, p1] to end.
Rep row 1 as required.
For an odd number of stitches
Row 1: [K1, p1] to last st, k1.
Row 2: [P1, k1] to last st, p1.
Rep rows 1–2 as required.

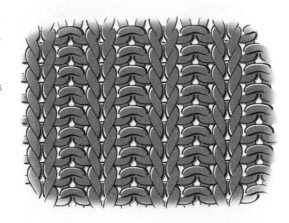

DOUBLE RIB

This is a popular, chunky variation of single rib and is worked over an even number of stitches divisible by four, or four plus two stitches. It can be used in the same way as single rib, though it is less stretchy.

Number of stitches divisible by four
Row 1: [K2, p2] to end.
Rep row 1 as required.
Number of stitches divisible by four plus two stitches
Row 1: [K2, p2] to last 2 sts, k2.
Row 2: [P2, k2] to last 2 sts, p2.
Rep rows 1–2 as required.

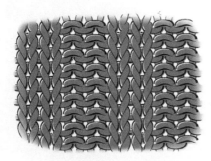

KNITTING RIBBING

As the yarn moves back and forth between the knit and purl stitches the rib fabric can become loose and floppy if the yarn isn't kept evenly tensioned. Working ribbing on needles that are one or two sizes smaller than those used for the main fabric of the garment will help keep ribbing relatively stretchy.

SEED STITCH

This is an ideal fabric for edgings and collars as it lies flat and has a lovely texture that adds simple detail to any project. As with single rib, seed stitch is worked by alternately knitting and purling stitches across a row, but on subsequent rows the stitches that were purled on the previous row are purled again, and vice versa.

The exact pattern depends on whether the seed stitch is being worked over an even or odd number of stitches.

For an even number of stitches
Row 1: [K1, p1] to end.
Row 2: [P1, k1] to end.
Rep rows 1–2 as required.
For an odd number of stitches
Row 1: [K1, p1] to last st, k1.
Rep row 1 as required.

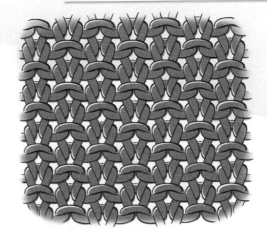

READING A KNITTING PATTERN

Some aspects of knitting patterns will vary depending on the style of the designer, manufacturer, or publisher, but there is a common language that runs through them all, and you can expect to find the same basic elements. I'm using the way I set out patterns as examples here, but always check abbreviations and terms in a pattern that's new to you in case details vary. As a novice knitter, decoding pattern language can take some time initially, but once you understand the terminology, you will be able to work from patterns with confidence.

BEFORE YOU START

Make sure that you have everything you are going to need to complete the pattern. There is little more annoying than not being able to complete a project because you didn't buy the specified amount of yarn, and now the dye lot (see page 19) is no longer available.

Do read the pattern through before you start, but don't worry if some of it is unclear; often instructions only make sense once you start knitting them. It's a good idea to mark sizes and measurements needed in the pattern before you start knitting it (see below). And when you pause in your knitting, always mark where you are in the pattern as it can be easy to get confused, especially if you stop for a while.

SIZES AND MEASUREMENTS

If a project can be made in different sizes, then the smallest size is printed first and the other sizes follow in brackets, a colon separating each size—for example, "size 8(10:12:14)." The same format is used to give instructions for each size—for example, "knit 4(6:8:10) sts." So, if you were knitting the size 12, you would knit 8 stitches for that instruction. It is a good idea to go through a sized pattern and mark the size/instruction you are going to knit in every instance, just so you don't make a mistake. It's even better if you photocopy the pattern and mark the copy; if you knit the garment again in another size you won't get confused.

A "0" means that for that particular size no stitches are worked. For example, "K0(2:4) sts, p to end of row." means that if you are making the smallest size, you just purl to the end of the row, but if you were making the second size you would knit two stitches before purling the rest of the row.

The pattern will give some measurements—such as chest and sleeve length—so you should measure yourself (see page 268) before deciding which size to knit. Remember that if you alter the given dimensions—maybe make the garment longer—this will alter the amount of yarn you will need.

If a pattern says "To fit chest...", then the actual garment measurements given are not the same as the measurements of the body size it is designed for. A deliberately baggy sweater might be several inches larger around the chest than the actual chest measurement it is designed to fit. You can get an idea of how loose a fit will be by measuring other garments you own before deciding which size to knit.

If a pattern gives both imperial and metric measurements, stick to one system throughout, and be careful not to mix the two systems up when working an instruction. Again, marking the measurements you are going to need before you start knitting is a good idea.

MATERIALS

The list of materials needed will include the amount of yarn, sizes of needles, and any notions such as buttons or zippers. The yarn amounts quoted are based on the gauge instruction (see page 68).

ABBREVIATIONS

Knitting instructions are usually given as abbreviations to save space. Often the most commonly used abbreviations are listed together elsewhere in the book, and additional abbreviations specific to a project are given on the project page. Note that not all knitting designers use exactly the same abbreviations, so do check that you understand everything written in a pattern before you start it.

Here are some of the most commonly used abbreviations.

A, B, C	yarn colors as listed in materials	LH	left hand	sk2	skip next two stitches
alt	alternate; alternatively	LL1	lifted increase left	skpo	slip one stitch, knit one stitch, pass slipped stitch over
approx	approximately	lp(s)	loop(s)		
BC	back cross	LR1	lifted increase right		
beg	begin(s)(ning)	LT	left twist	sk2po	slip one stitch, knit two stitches together, pass slipped stitch over
bet	between	m	meter(s)		
BO	bind off	M1	make one stitch		
C4B	cable four stitches (or number stated) back	M1L(F)	make one stitch left (front)	sl	slip
		M1R(B)	make one stitch right (back)	sllk	slip one stitch knitwise
C4F	cable four stitches (or number stated) front	mb	make bobble	sllp	slip one stitch purlwise
		MC	main color	sppo	slip one stitch, purl one stitch, pass slipped stitch over
CC	contrast color	mm	millimeter(s)		
cm	centimeter(s)	no	number		
CN	cable needle	oz	ounce(es)	ssk	slip one stitch, slip one stitch, knit slipped stitches together
CO	cast on	p	purl		
col	color	plb	purl stitch in row below		
cont	continue	p2tog	purl two stitches (or number stated) together	ssp	slip one stitch, slip one stitch, purl slipped stitches together
cr(oss)	cross two stitches				
2L(F)	(or number stated) left (front)	patt(s)	pattern(s)	st st	stockinette stitch
		pb	place bead	st(s)	stitch(es)
2R(B)	(or number stated) right (back)	pfb	purl into the front and back of a stitch	tbl	through back of loop
				tog	together
dbl	double	pm	place marker	WS	wrong side
dec(s)	decrease(s)(ing)	pnso	pass next stitch over	wyb	with yarn at the back
DK	double knit	prev	previous	wyf	with yarn at the front
dpn	double-pointed needle	psso	pass slipped stitch over	yb	yarn back
FC	front cross	ptbl	purl through back of loop	yf	yarn forward
foll(s)	follow(s)(ing)	pu	pick up (stitches)	yfrn	yarn forward and round needle
g(r)	gram	pwise	purlwise		
g st	garter stitch	RC	right cross	yfwd	yarn forward
in(s)	inch; inches	rem	remain(ing)	yo	yarn over needle
inc	increase(s)(ing)	rep	repeat	yo2	yarn over twice
incl	include	rev st st	reverse stockinette stitch	yon	yarn over needle
k	knit	RH	right hand	yrn	yarn round needle
klb	knit stitch in row below	rnds	rounds	[ ]	work instructions within brackets as many times as stated
k2tog	knit two stitches (or number stated) together	RS	right side		
		RT	right twist		
kfb	knit into the front and back of a stitch	s2kpo	slip two stitches together, knit one, pass slipped stitches over	*	work instructions following/between asterisks as many times as stated
ktbl	knit through back of loop	s2p3tog	slip two stitches, purl three stitches together		
kwise	knitwise				
LC	left cross	sk	skip		

TERMINOLOGY

For beginners, a knitting pattern can look like a foreign language. Not only are there abbreviations to understand (see page 63), but some of the terms used can be mystifying. Here are explanations of some often used phrases.

1st and 3rd sizes only You only work the next instruction if you are knitting the first or the third size in the project. For the other sizes, the instruction does not apply.

Above marker(s) Knitting worked above a row where stitch marker(s) (see page 73) have been placed.

Alt rows Alternate rows; you are being asked to work the instruction on every alternate row. This will usually, but not always, be a right-side row. Sometimes this instruction might read "every other row."

At front edge An edge that will be in the center of the finished piece.

At side edge An edge that will be at the side of the finished piece, and will usually, but not always, be sewn to another piece of knitting.

At the same time This is used when you are asked to do two things at the same time over a given number of rows. For example, you might be decreasing for a neck at one end of every alternate row, and decreasing for an armhole at the other end of every fourth row.

Beg (or end) with a k row The first (or last) row you work must be a knit row.

Beg (or end) with a p row The first (or last) row you work must be a purl row.

Cont in patt A color or stitch pattern will have been given separately, or established over previous rows, and you must keep to that pattern (sometimes while also working other instructions) until instructed otherwise.

Ending on a right side (RS) row The last row you knit must be on the right side of the work.

Ending on a wrong side (WS) row The last row you knit must be on the wrong side of the work.

From beg From the beginning, either of the whole piece of work, or a specified point, such as the armhole shaping. This is usually used when you have to work for a specified measured length. When you are measuring, do so with the work lying completely flat, but not stretched in any way.

Knitwise Put the needle into the stitch as if you were going to knit it (see page 44).

On 2nd and on every foll 6th row Work one row, then work the instruction on the second row, then work five rows, then repeat the instruction on the sixth row. Work another five rows and repeat the instruction on the sixth row, and continue in this way for the number of rows specified in the pattern.

Pick up and knit Pick up the stated number of stitches along the edge specified (see page 74) and knit them.

Purlwise Put the needle into the stitch as if you were going to purl it (see page 45).

Reversing shaping You must knit a piece that is a mirror image of one with full instructions. For example, the instructions for the left front of a jacket are given in full, and then the pattern says "Work right front as for left front, reversing shaping." If you are unsure about what to do, write out the left front pattern, reversing the instructions for each row to give yourself a full pattern for the right front.

Selvedge edge An edge that has been worked with an edging to make a selvedge (see pages 240–241).

Until 10 sts rem Sometimes in shaping instructions you are asked to repeat a decrease, or increase, row until a specified number of stitches are left on the needle.

With right (wrong) sides together (facing) Put the two pieces of knitting together with the right (wrong) sides of each piece touching one another.

With right side facing The right side of the work must be facing you.

With wrong side facing The wrong side of the work must be facing you.

Work sts from holder Stitches that have been placed on a stitch holder at some point in the pattern will need to be knitted again. Either slip the stitches from the holder onto a needle, or use the stitch holder as the left-hand needle and knit the stitches straight off it.

Work straight (even) Work without shaping for the specified number of rows or to a given measurement.

Work to last 2 sts Work across the row until you have two stitches on the left-hand needle.

[ ] and * These denote instructions that are to be repeated. Note that sometimes round brackets are used for repeated instructions, which can be confusing if they are also used for different size instructions. Some designers use [ ] for repeats, some use *, and some use both. So be sure you understand what you are being asked to do.

For example: "[K1, p1] to end of row." means that you knit one stitch, then purl one stitch until you get to the end of the row. "*K1, p1; rep from * to end of row." means exactly the same thing. "*K3, [p1, k1] six times, p1; rep from * to end of row." means that you knit three stitches, then work 12 stitches alternately purling and knitting them, then purl one stitch, then start the instructions after the asterisk again and repeat the whole sequence until you get to the end of the row.

Be aware as to how many times you are being asked to work a sequence. "[K3, p1] twice." involves working eight stitches, but "*K3, p1, rep from * twice more." involves working 12 stitches.

READING A CHARTED PATTERN

Color motifs or designs are often given as charts within a written pattern. Sometimes the instructons are written out as well, but usually the written instructions will tell you how to place the chart on the knitting, and then how much of the chart to knit, or how often you should repeat it. Charts have an advantage over words in that you can see what the pattern you are producing should look like, but texture charts can look very complicated and be a bit tricky to decipher.

READING A CHARTED PATTERN

Whether a chart is showing a color pattern or a texture pattern, a single block represents one stitch, so a horizontal line of blocks is one row. Colors will be shown either with colored blocks or symbols, and textures with symbols. The chart will have a key that tells you what each colored block or symbol represents.

The first row is the bottom one, and you will usually start a chart on a right-side row in the knitting, in which case the first stitch you knit from the chart will be the bottom right-hand one.

If you are knitting back and forth, then right-side rows are read from right to left, and wrong-side rows from left to right. However, if you are knitting in the round (see pages 108–109), then every chart row is read from right to left. For more on color knitting in the round, turn to page 166.

Usually a chart will be divided by heavier lines into blocks of ten rows and stitches, which makes it easier to count the squares and keep track of where you are in the design. It's a good idea to cross off rows on a chart as you work them, though you might want to photocopy the chart and mark that rather than marking the original pattern. Alternatively, use a sticky note and just move it up to cover one row at a time as you knit them.

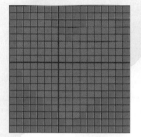
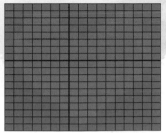

A knitted stitch is wider than it is tall, so a charted motif drawn on squared paper will not accurately show what the shape will look like when knitted up. The charts on the left depict exactly the same heart motif, but the one on the far left is drawn on squared paper, and the nearer one is drawn on proportional graph paper, which more accurately represents the shape of an actual knitted stitch, and so shows you what the knitted result will look like. The other charts on the following pages are all drawn on proportional graph paper. For more advice on using this paper, turn to page 282.

COLOR CHARTS

When these charts are drawn in color they are simple to understand, as the different colored blocks simply correlate to different colored yarns. The chart key will list the colors, usually referring to them by the color name of the yarn, or by the letter chosen to represent them and given in the materials list for the project.

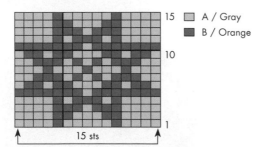

□ A / Gray
■ B / Orange

If a chart uses symbols instead of colors, then the same principles apply, and the key will tell you which symbol represents which color. One advantage of a symbol chart over a color chart is that it is easy to photocopy if you want to mark off rows, but not mark the original pattern. However, most photocopy outlets now offer a color photocopying service as well as a black and white one.

If this chart was written out as a pattern—with the gray color defined as color A and the orange as color B—it would read as follows:

Row 1 (RS): K4A, k1B, k5A, k1B, k4A.
Row 2: P4A, p2B, p3A, p2B, p4A.
Row 3: K4A, k3B, k1A, k3B, k4A.
Row 4: P4A, p1B, p1A, p3B, p1A, p1B, p4A.
Row 5: K7B, k1A, k7B.
Row 6: [P1A, p2B] twice, p3A, [p2B, p1A] twice.
Row 7: K2A, k3B, [k1A, k1B] 3 times, k2B, k2A.
Row 8: [P3A, p1B] 3 times, p3A.
Row 9: K2A, k3B, [k1A, k1B] 3 times, k2B, k2A.
Row 10: [P1A, p2B] twice, p3A, [p2B, p1A] twice.
Row 11: K7B, k1A, k7B.
Row 12: P4A, p1B, p1A, p3B, p1A, p1B, p4A.
Row 13: K4A, k3B, k1A, k3B, k4A.
Row 14: P4A, p2B, p3A, p2B, p4A.
Row 15: K4A, k1B, k5A, k1B, k4A.

You can see that the written pattern looks relatively complicated, and you have no idea what the finished result will look like. However, the charted pattern is both easy to follow, and you can quickly tell if you have made a mistake, as your knitting won't match the chart.

TEXTURE CHARTS

These charts use symbols to represent stitches or groups of stitches. A key thing to remember is that symbols are not universal; different designers and pattern companies use different symbols to represent the same stitch, so always check the key that comes with the pattern you are knitting from.

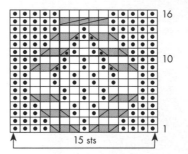

⊡ purl on RS, knit on WS

□ knit on RS, purl on WS

C3B: slip next stitch onto cable needle and hold at back, k2, k1 from cable needle

C3F: slip next 2 stitches onto cable needle and hold at front, k1, k2 from cable needle

C3L: slip next 2 stitches onto cable needle and hold at front, p1, k2 from cable needle

C3R: slip next stitch onto cable needle and hold at back, k2, p1 from cable needle

C5B: slip next 3 stitches onto cable needle and hold at back, k2, k3 from cable needle

Depending on the symbols used and how complicated the pattern is, texture charts can look very dense and complex. However, it is easy to see the shape of the design you are creating, and easy to establish a rhythm once you have established what the symbols mean. Some patterns will give the pattern both in writing and as a chart, so you can follow whichever suits you.
This chart shows a diamond-shaped cable, with reverse stockinette as the background on either side, and double seed stitch filling the middle of the diamond.
If this chart was written out as a pattern, it would read as follows:

Row 1 (RS): P4, C3B, p1, C3F, p4.
Row 2: K4, p3, k1, p3, k4.
Row 3: P3, C3B, p1, k1, p1, C3F, p3.
Row 4: K3, p3, [k1, p1] twice, p2, k3.
Row 5: P2, C3B, [p1, k1] twice, p1, C3F, p2.
Row 6: K2, p3, [k1, p1] 3 times, p2, k2.

Row 7: P2, k2, [p1, k1] 4 times, k1, p2.
Row 8: K2, p2, [k1, p1] 4 times, p1, k2.
Row 9: P2, C3L, [p1, k1] twice, p1, C3R, p2.
Row 10: K3, p2, [k1, p1] 3 times, p1, k3.
Row 11: P3, C3L, p1, k1, p1, C3R, p3.
Row 12: K4, p2, [k1, p1] twice, p1, k4.
Row 13: P4, C3L, p1, C3R, p4.
Row 14: K5, [p2, k1] twice, k4.
Row 15: P5, C5B, p5.
Row 16: K5, p5, k5.

PATTERN REPEATS

If a color, or a texture, pattern is repeated several times across a row, then often just the repeated section will be charted, plus any stitches needed to start and to finish off the design neatly at the ends of the row. Usually the very first and last stitches won't have any patterning, making it easier to sew up the knitting once it is completed (see pages 220–225).

Setting out a repeat pattern using a chart in this way is usually the most concise approach, and the easiest one to follow.

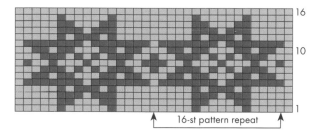

16-st pattern repeat

This chart shows the first edge stitch, then the pattern repeat of 16 stitches, then the fifteen stitches that are needed to finish the last motif in the pattern as a mirror image of the first motif, then the final edge stitch.

The pattern will tell you how many rows to work before you start working from the chart, then how many times to work the chart, then how to continue once you've completed all the charted knitting.

So if you were working across 97 stitches on the needle, you would knit the first edge stitch, then the 16-stitch pattern repeat five times, then the fifteen stitches needed to complete the pattern, then the final edge stitch.

The chart is 16 rows high, so if you were working it over 64 rows, you would repeat the whole chart four times.

If this chart was incorporated into a written pattern for the stitch and row counts given above, following four rows of plain knitting and with five rows of plain knitting after it—and with the gray color defined as color A and the orange as color B—it would read as follows:

Row 1 (RS): Knit in A.
Row 2: Purl in A.
Rep rows 1–2 once more.
Row 5: Place chart row 1; k1A, *k4A, k1B, k5A, k1B, k5A; rep from * five times more. This row sets the position of the chart.
Work the 16 rows of the chart four times.
Row 69: Knit in A.
Row 70: Purl in A.
Rep rows 69–70 once more, then row 69 once more.
Bind off.

This is both concise and easy to follow, plus it is simple for the knitter to keep track of where they are in the pattern, because the emerging knitted pattern will match the colored chart.

GAUGE

Many knitters are guilty of ignoring a pattern's gauge instruction in their eagerness to get started on the project, but when they complete all the (weeks of) knitting and sew up the garment, they discover that it is too big, or too small, even though they followed the pattern exactly. The answer will almost always be that they didn't knit to the correct gauge. It only takes a short time to knit a gauge square; certainly much, much less time than it does to re-knit an entire project...

In the instructions for a pattern there will be a gauge instruction; it will usually say something like, "22 sts and 28 rows to 4in over st st using US size 6 needles." What this means is that there must be 22 stitches in a horizontally measured 4in of your knitted fabric, and 28 rows when you measure it vertically. The point of knitting a gauge square is to make sure that you can get the right number of stitches and rows to the specified measurement.

The ball band of a yarn will have a gauge printed on it (see page 19), and this is the manufacturer's gauge. But the designer of the pattern you are going to knit may have worked to a different gauge, and it is the designer's gauge that you need to match.

KNITTING A GAUGE SWATCH

Using the needles, yarn, and stitch pattern specified in the gauge instruction, cast on at least 10 more stitches than you need to be able to measure; so if the instruction asks for 22 sts to 4in, then cast on at least 32 sts. Work 10 rows more than you need to measure and bind off loosely. Smooth out the swatch on a flat surface, but do not stretch it. If possible, leave the square to "relax" for a while.

You need two pins and a ruler to measure your gauge. Do not use a cloth tape measure as it may not lie completely flat on the swatch.

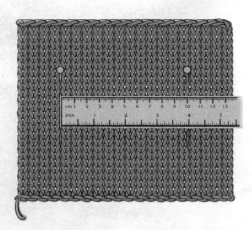

To check the stitch gauge, lay the ruler horizontally on the swatch, with the end a few stitches in from one edge. Put in a pin at the end of the ruler and another at the 4in mark. Count the number of stitches between the pins.

To check the row gauge, lay the ruler vertically on the swatch, with the end a few rows down from the bound-off edge. Put in a pin at the end of the ruler and another at the 4in mark. Count the number of rows between the pins.

Everyone has a "natural" gauge that they knit to. Some people knit very tightly, others loosely. The way in which you wind the yarn around your fingers (see page 30), the yarn you are using, and even the material your knitting needles are made from can affect your gauge. Many beginner knitters take a while to settle down to a natural gauge, and if you learn a better way to hold the yarn or needles, your gauge can change.

The gauge squares shown are all knitted in the same brand and weight of yarn, using the same size needles, with the same number of rows and stitches in each one. But they were knitted by different people, each of whom has a different natural gauge that they knit to. The differences in size are very obvious.

If you have knitted a gauge square and you do not have the right number of stitches and rows, then you need to try again. However, you must not try to just knit a bit tighter or looser than your natural gauge; you won't be able to maintain the false gauge, and at best your knitting will be uneven.

What you must do is change the size of the needles you are knitting with. The rule of thumb is that needles one size different will make a difference of one stitch in your gauge. So, if you were using US size 6 needles and needed 22 stitches but had 23, then your gauge is too tight and you need to try again using US size 7 needles. If you only had 19 stitches to 4in, then your gauge is too loose and you should try US size 5 needles.

If you have managed to get the right stitch gauge, but your row gauge is still out by one row, then you can simply work fewer rows. So if the gauge was supposed to be 28 but you had 29, then you can work 27 rows for every 28 given in the pattern, although this can quickly become complicated if stitch patterns, color knitting, or a lot of shaping are involved. However, many simpler garment patterns will tell you to knit pieces to a specified measurement rather than a row count, so if your row gauge is off by one row, it shouldn't make any difference to the look of the finished project.

If the gauge instruction says 22 sts to 4in and you have 23 sts, then you may well be tempted to think that just one stitch difference won't matter... But when you cast on 110 sts for the brim of a beret, knit the piece and expect it to measure 20in across, yours will measure only a tiny amount over 19in. Likewise, if you only have 21 sts to 4in, your 110 stitches will measure 21in. If the beret is supposed to fit snugly, the difference of an inch would make it either uncomfortably tight, or loose enough to slip down over your eyes.

If the piece you were knitting was the back of a fitted sweater and you had a similar discrepancy in the front piece, then the whole sweater would be 2in too small, or 2in too large. And that is the result of just a single stitch difference from the stated pattern gauge.

The other reason for obtaining accurate gauge is that it will affect how much yarn you use. If you are knitting your project too big, then you will use more yarn than the designer did.

Some projects, such as bags or toys, might say that a specific gauge is not needed for this project. However, it's still a good idea to knit a swatch, just to see how the yarn looks when knitted to your natural gauge (see below). If, for example, you knit very loosely and you're knitting a bear, then his stuffing might show through the stitches when he's finished.

SUBSTITUTING YARN

Knitting patterns will always quote the name, brand, and number of balls of a yarn used in the project. However, if wearing the recommended fiber causes you discomfort, or the pattern is a vintage one and the specified yarn is no longer available, you can substitute the yarn quoted in a pattern with a different one, although there are some basic rules that you must follow to avoid disappointment.

The first point to make is that you shouldn't make the decision to change yarns lightly. The pattern designer chose the yarn they used for good reasons, and a different yarn might not produce the same effect. Stitch detail that showed perfectly in a crisp cotton yarn can almost entirely vanish in a fuzzy wool yarn, and a shawl that draped elegantly in a silk/alpaca mix yarn might be stiff and uncomfortable in a man-made fiber.

And, unless you know what you are doing when it comes to altering knitting patterns, you must choose a substitute yarn that is the same weight as the pattern yarn. If you knit a pattern designed for DK yarn in a 4-ply yarn, the finished result will be very small indeed unless you make a lot of alterations to the pattern.

However, if the yarn the designer has specified doesn't come in your favorite shade of green, and another yarn in the same fiber and weight does, then you can substitute one for the other. But before buying all the yarn needed, buy just one ball and knit a gauge square (see page 68) to ensure that you can meet the designer's gauge with the substitute yarn: not all yarns made of the same fiber and of the same weight will knit up to the same gauge. The ball band of the substitute yarn will have the manufacturer's gauge printed on it (see page 19), and as long as that isn't more than one stitch from the designer's gauge, you should be able to get the right gauge by changing needle size (see page 69).

And you can't just buy the number of balls of yarn asked for in the pattern, as the yarn quantity is calculated by yardage, and your substitute yarn may well not have the same number of yards per ball as the pattern yarn. Having said all that, only simple math is needed to work out how much substitute yarn to buy.

The math is in two parts. Firstly you need to work out the number of yards of yarn in one ball of pattern yarn, multiplied by the number of balls needed, to give you the total number of yards of yarn needed.

Then you divide the total number of yards needed by the number of yards of yarn in one ball of the substitute yarn to give you the number of balls of substitute yarn you need to buy.

For example

There are 117 yards per ball of the pattern yarn, and 16 balls are needed.
117 x 16 = 1872 yards of yarn needed.

There are 103 yards per ball of the substitute yarn.
1872 ÷ 103 = 18.17.

So you will need to buy 19 balls of the substitute yarn. If the sum works out at even a tiny amount over a whole number, you must always round up to the next whole number. And it's a good idea to buy an extra ball, just in case.

JOINING IN A NEW BALL OF YARN

It is important to join in at an edge and not in the middle of a row. Joining in will always show when it is done within the knitted fabric and will spoil the look of the project. At the edge you can sew in the ends of the yarn along the seam. However, if sewing an edge to a piece, as for some front bands, make sure the ends are on the sides that are being sewn together so you still have a clean edge on the center fronts.

The technique is the same whether you are joining in a different color yarn, rejoining yarn to stitches left on a stitch holder, or joining in a new ball of the same color. If the latter, then as you get toward the end of a ball, calculate how many rows you can work before you need to join in the new ball.

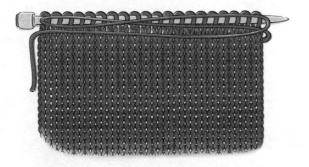

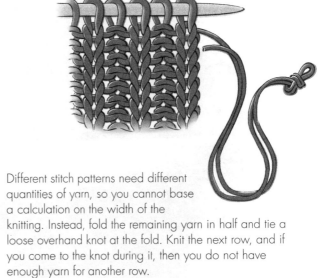

If you are working stockinette, reverse stockinette, or garter stitch, then spread the knitting out flat on one needle. Loop the remaining yarn loosely back and forth across the knitting; you need three times the width to work one row.

If the knitting is too wide to be spread flat, then measure the width of the knitting and the length of the remaining yarn.

Different stitch patterns need different quantities of yarn, so you cannot base a calculation on the width of the knitting. Instead, fold the remaining yarn in half and tie a loose overhand knot at the fold. Knit the next row, and if you come to the knot during it, then you do not have enough yarn for another row.

1. To join in the new yarn, tie the free end around the tail of the old yarn in a single knot.

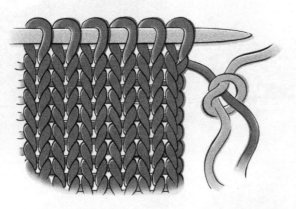

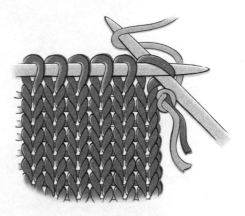

2. Slip the knot up the tail of the old yarn until it is tight against the knitting, then start the row using the new yarn. When you have completed the knitting, you can unpick the knot (if need be) and sew the ends in (see page 229).

COUNTING STITCHES AND ROWS

When checking the stitches and rows in your gauge square before you start a project, you will count them over 4in, which you can do within the square. But at some point you will need to count stitches and rows from the cast-on edge of your project, particularly if you have lost your place in a pattern. Some patterns are easier to count than others; for example, seed stitch or garter stitch can be trickier than stockinette stitch.

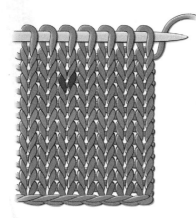

STOCKINETTE STITCH

One of the most common mistakes is to count the cast-on row as a knitted row, giving you one more row than you thought you had. However, you do include the row of stitches that is on the needle. In this illustration the cast-on row is colored lilac, so starting with the first knitted row, the one above the cast-on row, 12 rows have been knitted. There are seven visible stitches in a single row, colored pale pink. And a single stitch has been colored purple.

If you are working reverse stockinette stitch (see page 60), it is usually easier to count the rows on the wrong side, the stockinette side.

GARTER STITCH

As with stockinette stitch, you do not count the cast-on row, colored lilac in this illustration. Each ridge, colored pale pink, is made by two rows, so you can count in pairs; eight rows have been knitted. Every row is knitted and here, a single stitch on each side has been colored purple so you can see how they are formed.

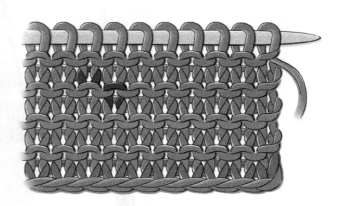

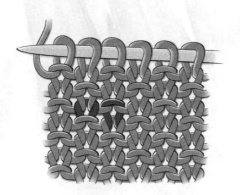

STITCH PATTERNS

For complicated stitch patterns it's best to put in markers at regular intervals as you knit and count from those (see opposite). In simpler patterns, such as the seed stitch shown here, it's a question of picking out identifiable points you can count. Each pale pink bump is the top of one stitch, so by zigzagging up you can count all the rows knitted, missing off the cast-on row, as always. Eight rows are visible here; seven bumps and the stitches on the needle. Seed stitch is alternate knit and purl stitches, one each of which is colored purple here.

MARKING ROUNDS, ROWS, AND REPEATS

Using markers lets you keep track of shaping, position pattern panels, and locate seam points. They can also be invaluable when working a lace or Aran pattern, as it can be difficult to count the intricately knitted rows. If a marker has to be placed around a stitch, loosely tie a loop of contrast yarn around the stitch so you can easily remove it later.

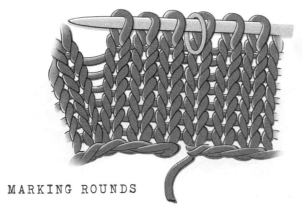

MARKING ROUNDS

When you are knitting in the round it is a good idea to place a marker to denote the start of the round. There are different types of these (see page 23); the one illustrated is a plain metal ring that you just slip from one needle to another when you come to it.

MARKING ROWS AND REPEATS

It can be very difficult to accurately count stitches and rows in complicated stitch patterns, and the answer is to use stitch markers. Again, there are various types of these (see page 23); the ones illustrated are plastic rings that loop onto a leg of a stitch. Put one into a stitch on the first row of every pattern repeat, as shown, or on every tenth or twentieth row if you find that easier to keep track of.

PUTTING IN LIFELINES

There are two reasons for putting in a lifeline: either you've made a mistake and need to unravel, or the pattern is very complicated and you think you might make a mistake…

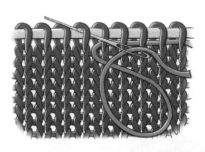

If you realize you have made a mistake in your knitting and you need to unravel several rows (see page 300), you can put in a lifeline before you pull the rows out to help you pick up the stitches again easily. Thread a blunt-tipped sewing needle with a length of waste yarn that's longer than the knitting is wide. Pass the needle through the right-hand leg of each stitch in the row you need to unravel to, being careful not to split the yarn with the needle. Then unravel the rows; the lifeline will prevent you unraveling beyond it. Follow the path of the lifeline to put the stitches back on the needle.

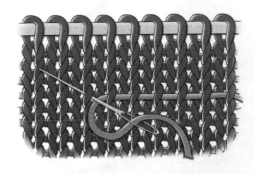

If you are about to start on a more complicated part of a pattern, then you can put in a lifeline on the current row, just in case. Thread a blunt-tipped sewing needle with a length of waste yarn that's longer than the knitting is wide, and just slide it through the stitches on the needle. Regular lifelines can be a good idea on complicated lace patterns, which are very difficult to accurately pick up stitches in if you have to unravel.

PICKING UP STITCHES

When adding to a piece of knitting—such as when creating neckbands, jacket front borders, or working sleeves that are knitted from the shoulders down to the cuffs—you will need to pick up stitches from the main piece. Stitches will be picked up from the right side of the work and worked from left to right.

PICKING UP WITH A KNITTING NEEDLE

1. This technique is shown here along a bound-off edge, but the principle is the same on any edge (see also page 76). With the right side of the work facing you, insert the point of a knitting needle from front to back into the knitted fabric at the point you want to start picking up from. Loop the yarn around the point of the needle.

2. Draw the loop through to the front to form a new stitch on the needle. If you start picking up on the right-hand end of an edge, then the first row will be a wrong-side row.

3. Continue in this way along the edge to pick up as many stitches as are needed, pulling each stitch taut as you go.

PICKING UP STITCHES WITH A HOOK

If you find it tricky to maneuver a knitting needle through the fabric, then use a crochet hook instead.

The principle is the same for picking up with a knitting needle; you just pull the loop through with the hook then slip each stitch in turn from the hook onto the needle. If you start picking up on the left-hand end of an edge, then the first row will be a right-side row.

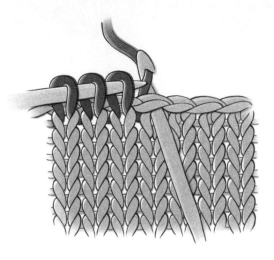

If you are picking up from a row rather than from an edge, it is easier with a crochet hook. On the right side, put the hook under the upper loop of the first stitch to be picked up from. Catch the yarn with the hook, pull a loop through, and slip the stitch onto a knitting needle. Pull the yarn gently to make sure the stitch sits snugly around the needle. Continue in this way, picking up one stitch from each knitted stitch as needed. Take the loose starting end through to the back and sew it in (see page 227).

PICKING UP STITCHES ALONG A CAST-ON OR BOUND-OFF EDGE

The principle is the same for either edge, though it is shown here on a bound-off edge.

Put the needle, or hook, into the stitch immediately below the bound-off edge and pull a loop through. In this way the new stitches will grow smoothly out of the old ones. When picking up along a cast-on edge, put the needle into the stitches of the cast-on row.

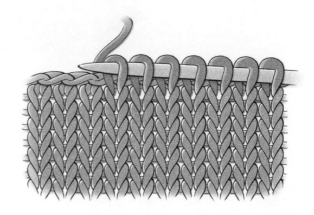

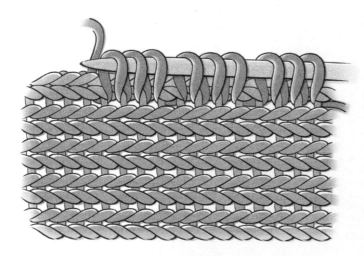

PICKING UP STITCHES EVENLY ALONG A ROW EDGE

You need to take into account the fact that a knitted stitch is wider than it is tall when picking up along the row edge of a piece of knitting.

Put the needle, or hook, into the space between the edge stitch and the next stitch. Wrap the yarn around the needle and pull a loop through. As the stitches you are picking up are wider than the rows you are picking them up from, after every third picked-up stitch, skip one row.

PICKING UP STITCHES EVENLY AROUND A CURVED EDGE

This technique will usually be used when you are picking up stitches from a neckline to make a neckband or collar.

Insert the needle, or hook, into the stitches one row below the bound-off edge and not between the stitches, because this may form a hole. Wrap the yarn around the needle and pull a loop through. When you reach the part of the neck where you will knit stitches left on a stitch holder at the front or back, avoid a hole by lining up the first row worked on the side neck and the stitches on the holder. Work across to the first stitch on the holder.

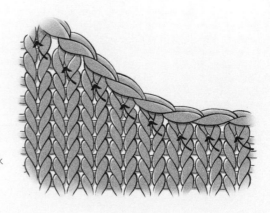

SLIPPING STITCHES

Slipping stitches is simply passing them from one needle to another without working them. They can be slipped knitwise or purlwise, but unless stated otherwise in a pattern, slip them purlwise. Slipped stitches are commonly used in shaping (see pages 78–105), bead knitting (see page 98), and in slip stitch colorwork patterns (see pages 174–175).

KNITWISE

To slip a stitch knitwise on a knit row, from left to right, insert the right-hand needle into the next stitch on the left-hand needle and slip it over onto the right-hand needle without knitting it.

A stitch can also be slipped knitwise on a purl row (see page 174).

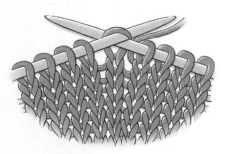

PURLWISE

To slip a stitch purlwise on a purl row, from right to left, insert the right-hand needle into the next stitch on the left-hand needle and slip it over onto the right-hand needle without purling it.

A stitch can also be slipped purlwise on a knit row (see page 174).

THROUGH THE BACK LOOP

Knitting into the back of the loop twists the stitch, which can give a more decorative look to a stitch pattern. When decreasing (see pages 90–97), working through the back of the loops makes the stitches slant to the left on a knit side.

KNITWISE

Knitting through the back of a stitch, rather than through the front, is very simple on a knit stitch.

From right to left, insert the right-hand needle into the back loop of the next stitch on the left-hand needle. Wrap the yarn around the needle and pull the new stitch through in the usual way. You can see that the stitch two rows below the one being knitted is twisted, as it was also knitted through the back loop.

PURLWISE

You need to twist the right-hand needle to put the tip into the back of the stitch.

Twist the right-hand needle so that you can insert it from the left into the back loop of the next stitch. Wrap the yarn around the needle and pull the new stitch through in the usual way. You can see that the stitch two rows below the one being purled is twisted, as it was also purled through the back loop.

SHAPING

Most shaping techniques in knitting involve adding or subtracting stitches to make the piece wider or narrower. The methods you can use range from the very simple to the slightly trickier, and the results vary from visible and decorative, to almost indiscernible; the choice is yours and depends on the effect you want to achieve.

You can also create domed or dished shapes, such as the heel of a sock, using a technique called short-row shaping. This way of shaping is one of those knitting mysteries that worries people, but is actually very simple and effective to work.

INCREASES

INCREASE ON A KNIT ROW

This increase is usually abbreviated as "inc." It slopes to the left on stockinette stitch and there will be a visible bar of yarn across the bottom of the increased stitch. As it also tends to leave a slight hole, it is better used on edges that will be taken into a seam. However, the bar can be useful in counting rows and is less visible on garter stitch. This increase is also known as a "bar increase."

1. Knit into the front of the next stitch on the left-hand needle in the usual way (see page 44), but do not slip the original stitch off the left-hand needle.

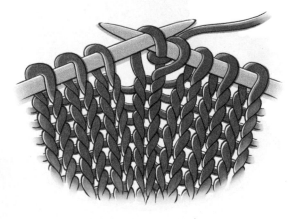

2. Move the right-hand needle behind the left-hand needle and insert it into the same stitch again, but through the back loop (see page 77).

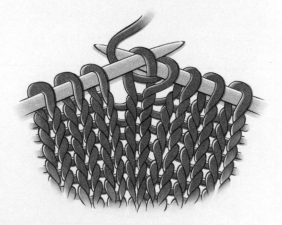

3. Knit the stitch through the back loop.

4. Slip the original stitch off the left-hand needle. You have increased by one stitch.

INCREASE ON A PURL ROW

This increase is also usually abbreviated as "inc" when working a purl row, or "inc pws." It slopes to the right on stockinette stitch (the left on reverse stockinette). As with inc on knit row, there will be a visible bar of yarn across the bottom of the increased stitch, so it is better used on an edge that will be taken into a seam when sewing up.

1. Purl into the front of the next stitch on the left-hand needle in the usual way (see page 45), but do not slip the original stitch off the left-hand needle.

2. Twist the right-hand needle backward to make it easier to insert it into the same stitch again, but through the back loop (see page 77).

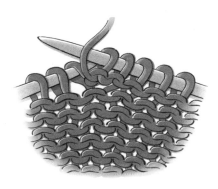

3. Purl the stitch through the back loop.

4. Slip the original stitch off the left-hand needle. You have increased by one stitch.

MAKE ONE LEFT ON A KNIT ROW

This method is one of the neatest and creates a virtually invisible increase, so it can be used in the middle of a row. The slight hole it can create is closed by knitting into the back of the raised strand, thus twisting it. It is usually abbreviated as "m1" or "m1l": if a pattern just says "m1," this is the increase it refers to. The increase slopes to the left on stockinette stitch. This increase is also known as a "raised increase."

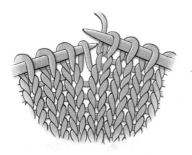

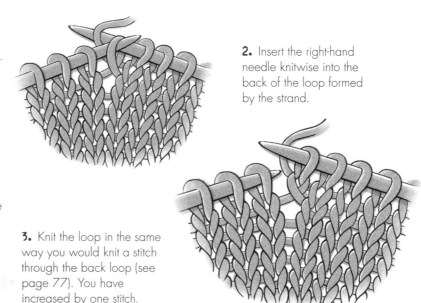

2. Insert the right-hand needle knitwise into the back of the loop formed by the strand.

1. From the front, slip the tip of the left-hand needle under the horizontal strand of yarn lying between the last stitch on the right-hand needle and the first stitch on the left-hand needle.

3. Knit the loop in the same way you would knit a stitch through the back loop (see page 77). You have increased by one stitch.

MAKE ONE RIGHT ON A KNIT ROW

In a pattern this increase will usually be abbreviated as "m1r" and it will slope to the right on stockinette stitch. As with m1l, you can purl into the raised strand—rather than knit into it—if that suits the stitch pattern better.

1. From the back, slip the tip of the left-hand needle under the horizontal strand of yarn lying between the last stitch on the right-hand needle and the first stitch on the left-hand needle.

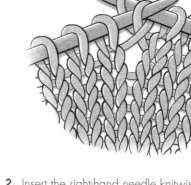

2. Insert the right-hand needle knitwise into the front of the loop formed by the strand, and knit it in the same way you would knit a stitch (see page 44). You have increased by one stitch.

MAKE ONE LEFT ON A PURL ROW

You can also work make one increases on a purl row, so there is every option you need for increasing using this technique. You will usually see this version abbreviated as "m1lp" in a knitting pattern, and it slopes to the left on stockinette stitch (the right on reverse stockinette). In order to avoid making a small hole, purl into the back of the raised strand.

1. From the front, slip the tip of the left-hand needle under the horizontal strand of yarn lying between the last stitch on the right-hand needle and the first stitch on the left-hand needle.

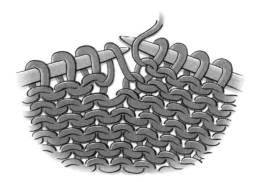

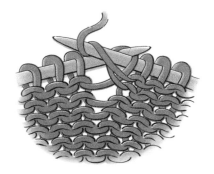

2. Insert the right-hand needle purlwise into the back of the loop formed by the strand.

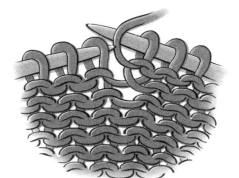

3. Purl the loop in the same way you would purl a stitch through the back loop (see page 77). You have increased by one stitch.

MAKE ONE RIGHT ON A PURL ROW

This increase slopes to the right on stockinette stitch (the left on reverse stockinette), and is usually abbreviated as "m1rp." Both purlwise make one increases can be knitted into—rather than purled into—if that suits the stitch pattern.

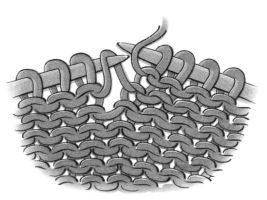

1. From the back, slip the tip of the left-hand needle under the horizontal strand of yarn lying between the last stitch on the right-hand needle and the first stitch on the left-hand needle.

2. Insert the right-hand needle purlwise into the front of the loop formed by the strand, and purl it in the same way you would purl a stitch (see page 45). You have increased by one stitch.

LEFT LIFTED INCREASE ON A KNIT ROW

The lifted increase methods are also virtually invisible, but because they are worked from the row below, to prevent puckering it is better to use them when there are three or more rows between increases. They are sometimes called "raised increases." This version of the increase slants to the left on stockinette stitch and is usually abbreviated as "lli."

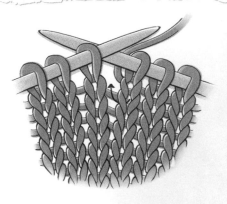

1. From the right, insert the left-hand needle into the stitch two rows below the last stitch on the right-hand needle, as indicated by the arrow.

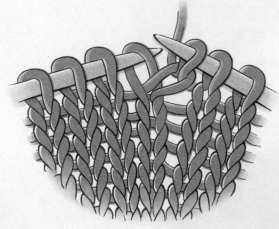

2. Lift this loop onto the left-hand needle.

3. Knit into this loop in the same way you would knit a stitch (see page 44).

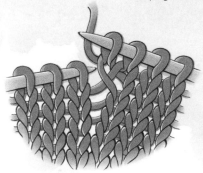

4. Drop the loop off the left-hand needle. You have increased by one stitch.

RIGHT LIFTED INCREASE ON A KNIT ROW

This version of the lifted increase slants to the right on stockinette stitch. In a knitting pattern it is usually abbreviated as "rli." It is worked in a different way to the left-slanting lifted increase (see opposite), but the result is equally invisible.

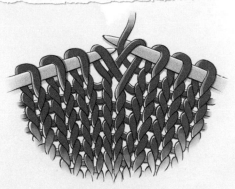

1. From the front, insert the right-hand needle into the top of the stitch directly below the next stitch on the left-hand needle.

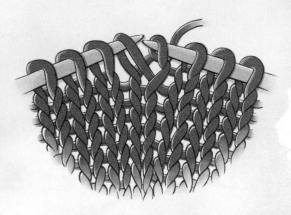

2. Insert the left-hand needle into this loop and knit it in the same way you would knit a stitch (see page 44).

3. Insert the right-hand needle knitwise into the next stitch on the left-hand needle.

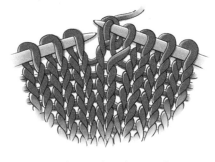

4. Knit this stitch in the usual way. You have increased by one stitch.

LEFT LIFTED INCREASE ON A PURL ROW

There are purlwise versions of both the left and right lifted increases, providing a full range of increases using this technique. This version slants to the left on stockinette stitch (the right on reverse stockinette), and is usually abbreviated in knitting patterns as "llip."

2. Insert the left-hand needle into this loop and purl it in the same way you would purl a stitch (see page 45). Then purl the next stitch on the left-hand needle in the usual way. You have increased by one stitch.

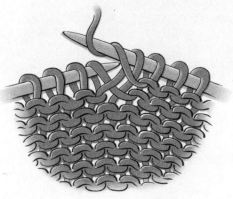

1. From the back, insert the right-hand needle into the top of the stitch directly below the next stitch on the left-hand needle.

RIGHT LIFTED INCREASE ON A PURL ROW

As with the knitwise lifted increases, the purlwise versions are worked differently from one another, though the results are both very discreet. The right lifted increase is usually abbreviated in knitting patterns as "rlip," and slants to the right on stockinette stitch (the left on reverse stockinette).

1. From the front, insert the left-hand needle into the top of the stitch two rows below the last stitch on the right-hand needle.

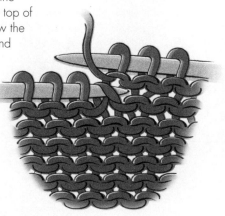

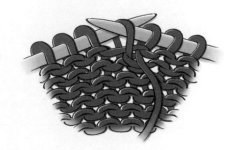

2. Purl into this loop in the same way you would purl a stitch (see page 45). You have increased by one stitch.

DOUBLE LIFTED INCREASE

This final increase in the library of lifted increases allows you to increase by two stitches at a time, or to increase only on knit rows but add as many stitches as if you were increasing on every row. Any of the increase techniques shown here can be worked either side of a knitted stitch (mirroring left and right-slanting versions for a neat symmetrical effect), but the method shown here is worked into one stitch.

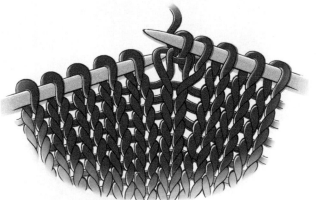

1. From the front, lift the stitch from the row below the next stitch on the left-hand needle and knit into it, as for a right lifted increase (see page 85). Knit the next stitch on the left-hand needle. Then from the back, lift the stitch previously knitted into onto the left-hand needle, as shown here, and knit it once again. You have increased by two stitches.

YARNOVER INCREASE

This increase produces a strand over the needle that is then worked into as for a normal stitch on the next row. Because it leaves a hole in the fabric, this increase is usually used in lace patterns to form an eyelet (see page 252). In the US all yarnovers are called "yo," though they have different names in the UK (see pages 136–139).

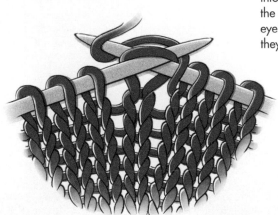

1. Bring the yarn forward between the tips of the needles, then insert the right-hand needle into the next stitch on the left-hand needle in the usual way. Take the yarn back over the top of the right-hand needle and around the tip.

2. Knit the stitch, then complete the row.

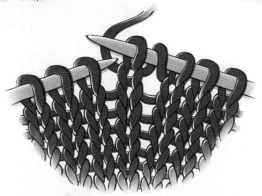

3. On the next row (here, a purl row), work into the yarnover loop on the needle as if it were a stitch. You have increased by one stitch.

CAST ON INCREASES

This method is used for when you need to cast on more than one stitch at the beginning or end of a row. There are two methods, the backward loop increase (see also page 39), and the cable cast on increase (see also page 37). For sheer speed I tend to use the former, but if you need firmness rather than elasticity, the cable cast on will give you more stability.

BACKWARD LOOP INCREASE

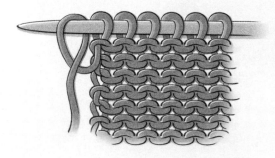

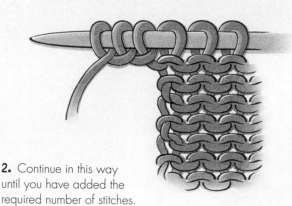

1. Hold the needle with the knitting on in your right hand. Wrap the working yarn in a loop around your left thumb from front to back, slip the needle under the loop, then slide your thumb out and pull the new stitch tight on the needle.

2. Continue in this way until you have added the required number of stitches.

CABLE CAST ON INCREASE

1. Hold the needle with the knitting on in your left hand. Insert the right-hand needle into the first stitch on the left-hand needle as if to knit it and draw a loop through, then place the loop onto the left-hand needle.

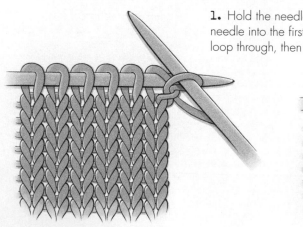

2. Cast on subsequent stitches by inserting the right-hand needle between the last two stitches to draw a loop through, as for a cable cast on (see page 37).

INCREASE TWO ON A KNIT ROW

This method allows you to increase by two stitches at a time, but there will be a visible bar across the bottom of the first increased stitch, and a small hole below the group of three stitches. In knitting patterns this increase is usually abbreviated to "inc2." For a less visible double increase, work the double lifted increase (see page 87).

1. Knit into the front and back of the stitch as for inc on a knit row (see page 80). Do not drop the original stitch off the left-hand needle.

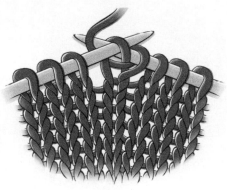

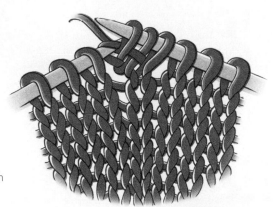

2. Move the right-hand needle in front of the left-hand needle and knit into the front of the stitch again. Slip the original stitch off the left-hand needle. You have increased by two stitches.

INCREASE TWO ON A PURL ROW

This is the purlwise version of this double increase. As with the knitwise version, there is a visible bar and a small hole below the increase. It is usually abbreviated to "inc2" if working on a purl row, or "inc2 pws."

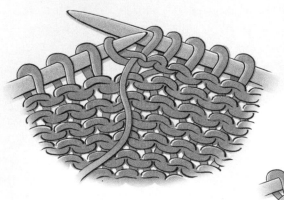

1. Purl into the front and back of the stitch as for inc on a purl row (see page 81). Do not drop the original stitch off the left-hand needle.

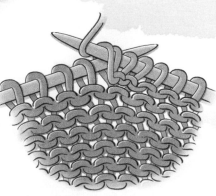

2. Move the right-hand needle in front of the left-hand needle and purl into the front of the stitch again. Slip the original stitch off the left-hand needle. You have increased by two stitches.

DECREASES

Decreases involve reducing the number of stitches on your needle. The general rule of thumb is that the decreases should slant in the same direction as the edge of the fabric (see page 97).

KNIT TWO TOGETHER

This is the easiest decrease to work as it simply involves knitting two stitches together as one. This decrease slants to the right on stockinette stitch and so is usually used when working the left side of an edge shaping—such as a neck—to slant in the same direction as the fabric. It is usually abbreviated to "k2tog."

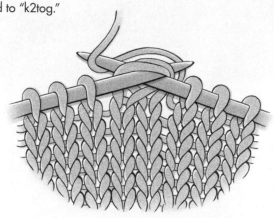

1. Insert the right-hand needle knitwise through the next two stitches on the left-hand needle instead of through one.

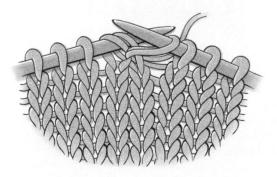

2. Wind the yarn around the tip of the right-hand needle and draw a loop through both stitches.

KNIT THREE TOGETHER

To decrease by two stitches at the same time, insert the right-hand needle knitwise through the next three stitches on the left-hand needle instead of through two, then knit all three together as one. You have decreased by two stitches.

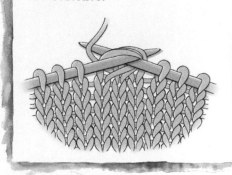

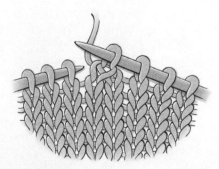

3. Drop both stitches together off the left-hand needle. You have decreased by one stitch.

PURL TWO TOGETHER

This is also an easy decrease to work as it is simply purling two stitches together to make one stitch. This decrease slants to the right on stockinette stitch (the left on reverse stockinette), so is usually used on the wrong side when working the left side of a shaping such as a neck. It is usually abbreviated to "p2tog" in a knitting pattern.

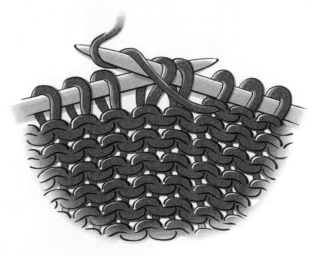

1. Insert the right-hand needle purlwise through the next two stitches on the left-hand needle instead of through one.

2. Wind the yarn around the tip of the right-hand needle and draw a loop through both stitches.

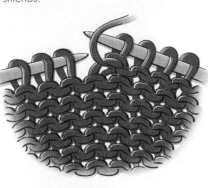

3. Drop both stitches together off the left-hand needle. You have decreased by one stitch.

PURL THREE TOGETHER

To decrease by two stitches at a time, insert the right-hand needle purlwise through the next three stitches on the left-hand needle instead of through two, then purl all three together as one. You have decreased by two stitches.

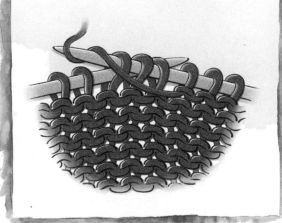

KNIT TWO TOGETHER THROUGH BACK LOOPS

This decrease slants to the left on stockinette stitch, with a rather pronounced sloping strand. It is worked in a similar way to k2tog, but knitting through the backs of the loops makes the decrease slope in the opposite direction and twists the stitches. It usually abbreviated to "k2togtbl."

1. From right to left, insert the right-hand needle through the backs of the next two stitches on the left-hand needle and knit them together as one, as for k2tog (see page 90). You have decreased by one stitch.

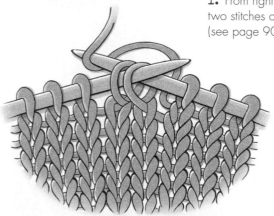

PURL TWO TOGETHER THROUGH BACK LOOPS

This is the purlwise version of this decrease, usually abbreviated to "p2togtbl." This decrease slants to the left on stockinette stitch (the right on reverse stockinette).

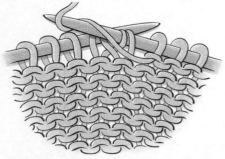

1. From left to right, insert the right-hand needle into the next two stitches on the left-hand needle, as shown. This can be tricky if your gauge is tight: try inserting the needle through the stitches purlwise first, and gently stretching them.

2. Purl the two stitches together as one, as for p2tog (see page 91). You have decreased by one stitch.

SLIP ONE, KNIT ONE, PASS SLIPPED STITCH OVER

This decrease slants to the left on stockinette stitch. It is similar in appearance to k2tog (see page 90), and so is good paired with that decrease when working symmetrical shaping. It does not produce such a pronounced sloping strand as k2togtbl (see opposite), and is abbreviated in knitting patterns as "skpo" or "skp."

1. Insert the right-hand needle knitwise into the next stitch on the left-hand needle and slip it onto the needle (see page 77).

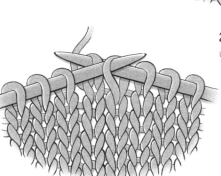

2. Knit the next stitch in the usual way.

3. Use the left-hand needle to lift the slipped stitch on the right-hand needle over the stitch just knitted, then drop it off both needles. You have decreased by one stitch.

SLIP ONE, PURL ONE, PASS SLIPPED STITCH OVER

This method is exactly the same as skpo, but is worked purlwise on the purl side. It produces a decrease that slants to the right on stockinette stitch (the left on reverse stockinette). This method is usually abbreviated in knitting patterns to "sppo" or "spp."

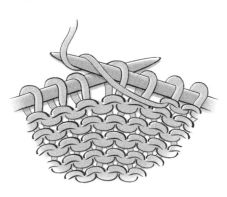

1. Insert the right-hand needle purlwise into the next stitch on the left-hand needle and slip it onto the needle (see page 77).

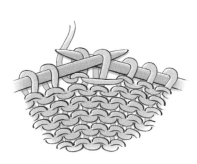

2. Purl the next stitch in the usual way. Take the yarn to the back, then use the left-hand needle to lift the slipped stitch on the right-hand needle over the stitch just purled, then drop it off both needles. You have decreased by one stitch.

SLIP, SLIP, KNIT

This method of decreasing slants to the left on stockinette stitch. It is very similar to skpo (see page 93), but many knitters prefer it as it lies slightly flatter. In knitting patterns it is abbreviated to "ssk."

1. Insert the right-hand needle knitwise into the next stitch on the left-hand needle and slip it onto the right-hand needle (see page 77). Do the same again with the next stitch, so two stitches have been slipped.

2. Insert the left-hand needle through both slipped stitches, going in front of the right-hand needle, and knit them together as one, as for k2tog (see page 90). You have decreased by one stitch.

SLIP, SLIP, PURL

This decrease is similar to sppo but as in the knit stitch version, it lies slightly flatter. It slants to the left on the right side of stockinette stitch. It is usually abbreviated in knitting patterns to "ssp."

1. Insert the right-hand needle knitwise into the next stitch on the left-hand needle and slip it onto the right-hand needle (see page 77). Do the same with the next stitch, so two stitches have been slipped.

2. From right to left, insert the left-hand needle through both slipped stitches and slip them back onto that needle, so they have swapped positions.

3. Insert the right-hand needle through both slipped stitches, going in front of the left-hand needle, and purl them together as one, as for p2tog (see page 91). You have decreased by one stitch.

SLIP ONE, KNIT TWO TOGETHER, PASS SLIPPED STITCH OVER

Sometimes it is necessary to decrease more than one stitch at the same time; this is referred to as double decreasing. The decreased stitches slant in either side of a central stitch, lying either on top of or underneath it depending on the method used. In this version they lie on top. This decrease is usually abbreviated to "sk2po" or "sk2togpo."

1. Insert the right-hand needle knitwise into the next stitch on the left-hand needle and slip it onto the right-hand needle (see page 77).

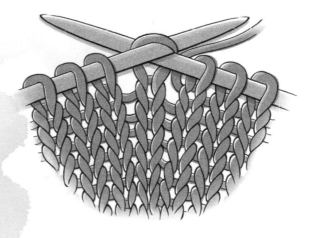

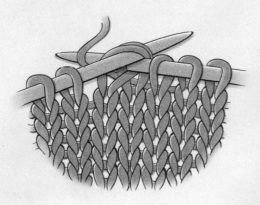

2. Insert the right-hand needle knitwise through the next two stitches on the left-hand needle instead of through one. Knit these two stitches together as one (see page 90).

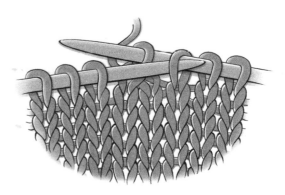

3. Use the left-hand needle to lift the slipped stitch on the right-hand needle over the stitch just knitted, then drop it off both needles. You have decreased by two stitches.

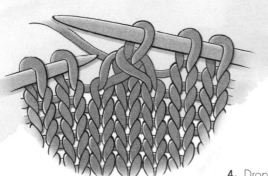

4. Drop the slipped stitch off both needles. You have decreased by two stitches.

SLIP TWO TOGETHER, KNIT ONE, PASS SLIPPED STITCHES OVER

This is another double decrease and in knitting patterns it is usually abbreviated to "s2togkpo," or sometimes to the longer "sl2tog, k1, p2sso." The two decreased stitches slant in from either side to lie under the central stitch.

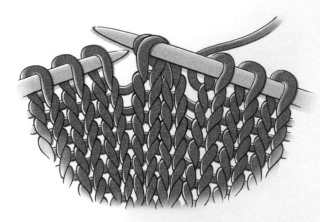

1. Insert the right-hand needle knitwise into the second stitch and then into the first stitch on the left-hand needle and slip them onto the right-hand needle.

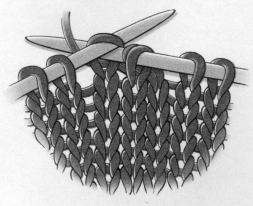

2. Knit the next stitch in the usual way (see page 44).

3. Use the left-hand needle to lift the slipped stitches on the right-hand needle over the stitch just knitted.

4. Drop the slipped stitches off both needles. You have decreased by two stitches.

SLIP TWO STITCHES, PURL THREE TOGETHER

This double decrease is worked on a purl row. On the stockinette stitch side of the fabric, the two decreased stitches slant in from either side to lie under the central stitch.

1. Insert the right-hand needle knitwise into the next stitch on the left-hand needle and slip it onto the right-hand needle (see page 77). Do the same with the next stitch, so two stitches have been slipped.

2. From right to left, insert the left-hand needle through both slipped stitches and slip them back onto that needle, so they have swapped positions.

3. Going in front of the left-hand needle, insert the right-hand needle through both slipped stitches and through the next stitch on the left-hand needle, and purl all three together as one, as for p3tog (see page 90) You have decreased by two stitches.

FULLY FASHIONED SHAPING

With this technique, the increases and decreases are worked two or three stitches in from the edge of the knitting, so they are a visible feature. This creates decorative detailing that can give interest to a plain stockinette garment, or when working raglans. As they are designed to be seen, you need to pair increases and decreases to slope the right way.

PAIRED INCREASES

At the start of a right-side row in stockinette stitch, use "m1r" (see page 82), paired with "m1l" (see page 82) at the end of the row. Or use "rli" (see page 85) at the start of the row, and "lli" (see page 84) at the end of the row.

At the start of a wrong-side row in stockinette stitch, use "m1rp" (see page 83), paired with "m1lp" (see page 83) at the end of the row. Or use "rlip" (see page 86) at the start of the row, and "llip" (see page 86) at the end of the row.

If reverse stockinette is the right side, then swap the positions of the increases.

PAIRED DECREASES

At the start of a right-side row in stockinette stitch, use "k2togtbl" (see page 92), or "skpo" (see page 93), or "ssk" (see page 94), paired with "k2tog" (see page 90) at the end of the row.

At the start of a wrong-side row in stockinette stitch, use "p2togtbl" (see page 92), paired with "p2tog" (see page 91) at the end of the row. Or use "ssp" (see page 94), paired with "sppo" (see page 93) at the end of the row.

If reverse stockinette is the right side, then swap the positions of the increases.

SHORT-ROW SHAPING

This technique involves turning the work before the row is completed, hence the term "short rows." The result is that part of the work has more rows than the rest, creating shaping for elements such as heels or collars.

WRAP AND TURN ON A KNIT ROW

If short rows are just turned, a hole will appear between the stitches worked and not worked. This can be eliminated by "wrapping" a slipped stitch at the point where the work is turned. This wrap can then be hidden later (see page 100).

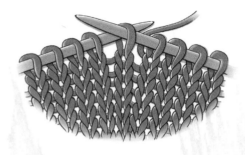

1. Knit to the position of the turn. Slip the next stitch purlwise (see page 77) from the left-hand needle to the right-hand needle.

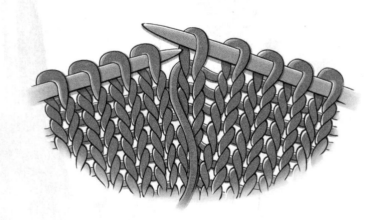

2. Bring the yarn forward between the tips of the needles.

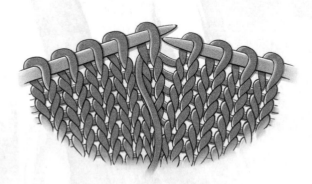

3. Slip the stitch back onto the left-hand needle.

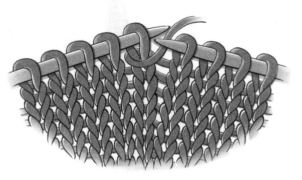

4. Take the yarn to the back, ready to purl the next row, and turn the work.

WRAP AND TURN ON A PURL ROW

The basic technique is the same as on a knit row, but when wrapping the slipped stitch the yarn is taken to the back rather than to the front. When you work back across the wrapped stitch on the next or a subsequent row, the wrap is picked up and hidden (see page 100).

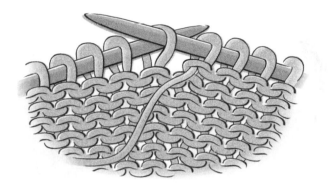

1. Purl to the position of the turn. Slip the next stitch purlwise (see page 77) from the left-hand needle to the right-hand needle.

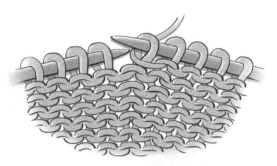

2. Take the yarn back between the tips of the needles.

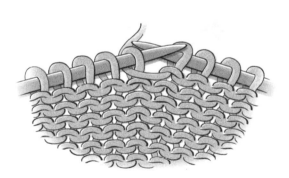

3. Slip the stitch back onto the left-hand needle.

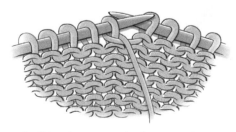

4. Bring the yarn to the front, ready to knit the next row, and turn the work.

PICK UP THE WRAP ON A KNIT ROW

When all the short rows are complete you work across the whole row of stitches, and this technique is used to eliminate the wraps around the slipped stitches, so that each hole is still closed but the wrap has disappeared, leaving a neat, even fabric. Bear in mind that depending on how many short rows the pattern has asked you to make, there may be several wraps to eliminate in one row.

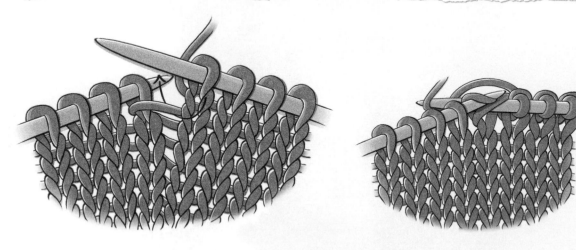

1. Knit to the wrapped stitch. Insert the right-hand needle up through the front of the wrap, as indicated by the arrow.

2. Keeping the wrap on the right-hand needle, insert the needle into the stitch and knit the wrap and the stitch together as one.

PICK UP THE WRAP ON A PURL ROW

This is the technique used on purled return rows to eliminate the wrap around the slipped stitch. It uses the same principle as on the knit row, but the wrap and the stitch are worked together purlwise.

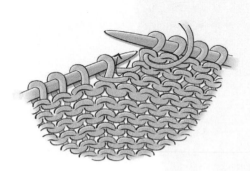

1. Purl to the wrapped stitch. Insert the right-hand needle up through the back of the wrap, as shown by the arrow.

2. Keeping the wrap on the right-hand needle, insert the needle into the stitch and purl the wrap and the stitch together as one.

SHORT ROW VARIATION

The wrap and turn method shown on pages 98–99 is the most commonly used method of preventing a hole forming at the point where the work is turned on a short row, but there are other techniques that are also effective. The method shown below is quick and easy to work.

1. On a knit row, knit to the position of the turn. From the front, insert the right-hand needle into the stitch directly below the next stitch on the left-hand needle, as shown by the arrow.

2. Wrap the working yarn around the tip of the right-hand needle and pull a loop through.

3. Slip the loop onto the left-hand needle. Turn the work.

4. When all the short rows are complete, work across the whole row, eliminating all the double stitches. On a knit row, knit to the first double stitch, then knit the two stitches together as one.

5. The same principle of doubling up the stitch at the position of the turn applies on purl rows. From the back, insert the right-hand needle under the top of the stitch directly below the next stitch on the left-hand needle and pull a loop through. Put the loop on the left-hand needle to make the doubled stitch. To eliminate doubled stitches on a row, purl them together as one.

SHORT-ROW SHOULDERS

The usual method of shaping shoulders involves binding off stitches on alternate rows (usually on each right-side row), which produces a stepped edge. By using short row shaping rather than binding off, the steps are eliminated and you have a smooth shoulder line. This makes it much easier to seam the shoulders and gives a neat, flat finish.

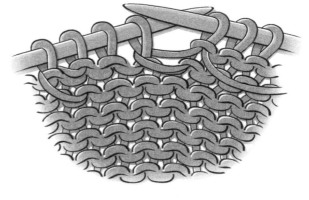

1. If the shoulder shaping read: "Bind off 4 sts at beg of every RS row" then you could knit the first right-side row and on the next row, the wrong-side row, work to four stitches from the end, then wrap and turn.

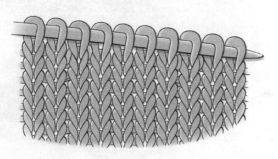

2. Repeat, wrapping and turning eight stitches from the end on the next wrong-side row and so on, until you have worked the last group of four stitches.

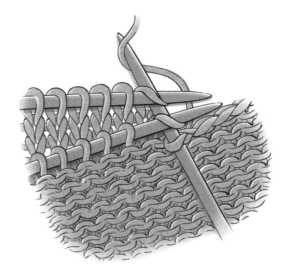

3. You can either bind off each shoulder and then sew them together (see page 223), or bind both shoulders off together (see pages 53 and 233).

USING SHAPING

Increases and decreases can be arranged and/or combined to create all sorts of shapes, from gently curving edges to tight corners, full gathers, or bias fabric.

TURNING CORNERS

Increase or decrease knitted fabric so that it will turn neatly around a corner and lie flat rather than curling up. A pattern will tell you how many stitches to work before the shaping, but the principles are always the same. For an inner corner you need to decrease the amount of fabric, and for an outer corner you need to increase it.

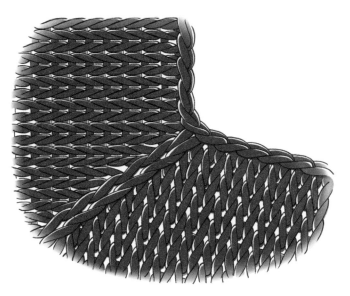

INNER CORNER

1. Mark the center stitch of the corner by threading a round marker onto the needle immediately before the stitch (see page 73). On a right-side row, knit to two stitches before the marker then work skpo (see page 93) or ssk (see page 94). Slip the marker, then knit the center stitch, and then work k2tog (see page 90). Continue to decrease in this way on either every row or every alternate row, depending on how sharp the angle of the corner needs to be. If you are decreasing on purl rows, then pair up the decreases to keep the corner symmetrical (see page 97).

OUTER CORNER

2. Mark the center stitch of the corner in the same way as for an inner corner, though if you find a dangling round marker fiddly to deal with, you can fix a stitch marker into the center stitch instead. On a right-side row, knit to the marker then work m1r (see page 82). Slip the marker, then knit the center stitch, and then work m1l (see page 82). Continue to increase in this way on either every row or every alternate row, depending on how sharp the angle of the corner needs to be. An elastic bind off, such as the suspended bind off (see page 52) can help keep the corner lying flat.

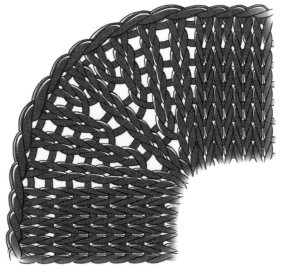

GATHERS AND FLARES

Shaping techniques can be used to create gathers and flares in a knitted fabric, so you can add details such as ruffles or peplums to a project without binding off and sewing on a separate knitted piece. It's worth experimenting with different methods of increasing and decreasing, and varying the frequency of the shaping, to make fuller or more subtle gathers. The choice of yarn will also have a big effect; a thin, silky yarn will create fluid, draping gathers, whereas a stiffer or thicker yarn will give more volume.

INCREASE GATHER

Here, increases have been made on two rows, with more on the second row than the first row. Mirrored make one increases on knit rows (see page 82) have been used. You can also cast on more stitches and then work decreases to create gathers, depending on whether you are knitting from the bottom up or top down.

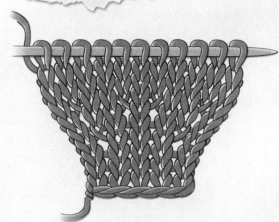

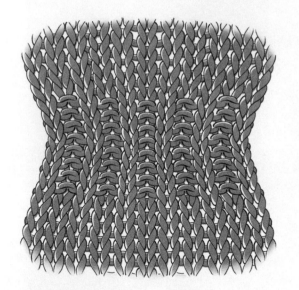

RIB GATHER

Another way of creating gathering is to change stitch pattern and needle size. Work in stockinette, and then change to needles one size smaller and work a section in knit one, purl one rib. The rib naturally pulls in more than the stockinette, and the smaller needle size increases the effect. The gathering will be soft rather than full. Here, a narrow section is worked in rib and then the larger needle size is used to knit more stockinette.

FLARE USING NEEDLE SIZE

You can create effective flares simply by changing needle size. Every few rows, change to needles one size larger and, although the changes in stitch size will be almost invisible (depending to some degree on the yarn used), the fabric will gradually get wider. Obviously it will also become looser and more open at the same time.

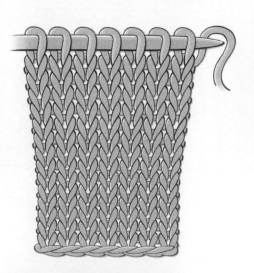

SHAPED KNITTED PIECES

You can create bias- and chevron-shaped pieces of knitted fabric by increasing and decreasing. Bias-knit fabrics are not more stretchy than straight-knit fabrics in the way that bias-cut woven fabrics are more stretchy than straight-grain fabrics, so the effect is primarily visual and can look really interesting if mixed with stripe patterns (see page 170).

BIAS

Bias knitting can slant to either the right, as shown, or the left, and the angle of the slant can be altered by changing the number of straight rows worked between shaping rows. To make the bias slope to the right, increase at the beginning and decrease at the end of every shaping row. For a bias slope to the left, decrease at the beginning and increase at the end of every shaping row. Using mirrored increases and decreases (see page 97) will create tidy edges.

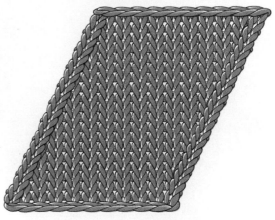

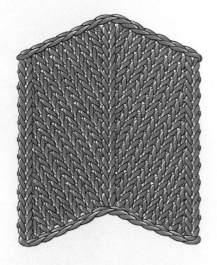

CHEVRON

Chevrons can point either upward, as shown, or downward, and—as with bias shapes—the angle can be altered by changing the number of straight rows worked between shaping rows. Start by casting on an odd number of stitches and marking the center stitch. To make the chevron point upward, decrease at each end of the row and increase either side of the center stitch; mirrored make one increases (see page 82) work well. To make the chevron to point downward, increase at each end of the row and work mirrored decreases (see page 97) either side of the center stitch. Alternatively, work a double decrease (see pages 95–97) at the center stitch.

DIAMOND

Diamond shapes can be knitted as individual pieces, or can be worked into a piece of straight knitting to form a gusset, as shown. These gussets are traditionally used to create underarm shaping on fisherman sweaters to allow for maximum freedom of movement in a heavy yarn garment.

Place a round marker either side of a center stitch. Knit to and then slip the first marker, make a stitch left (see page 82), knit the center stitch, make a stitch right, slip the second marker, and knit to the end. Purl the next row. Repeat these two rows until the triangle is the desired width.

To decrease the diamond, knit to and slip the first marker, work skpo (see page 93) or ssk (see page 94), knit to two stitches before the second marker, work k2tog (see page 90). Purl the next row. Repeat these two rows to complete the diamond gusset.

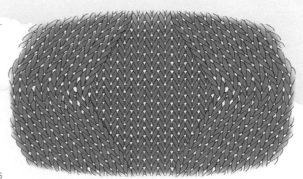

KNITTING IN THE ROUND

Until the beginning of the 20th century nearly all knitting was worked in the round. But as the craft became more generally popular, and more fashionable designs were created that called for extra shaping, knitters started to use two needles. The beauty of circular knitting (as this method is also called), is that you can work up to the armholes in the round and so there are no side seams to sew up. As you are always working in knit stitch, circular knitting is perfect for those knitters who tend to work a purl row tighter or looser than the knit row, which can result in an uneven fabric (see page 306).

METHODS FOR KNITTING IN THE ROUND

Small items such as socks or gloves tend to be worked on double-pointed needles, whereas circular needles are ideal for larger projects. Circular needles are also good for heavier projects, as the weight of the fabric rests on the cable.

CIRCULAR NEEDLE

This is two short needles connected by a flexible cable. It is important to have the right length needle for the number of stitches; too short and the stitches will fall off or be bunched, too long and the stitches will be stretched.

1. Using the cast-on method you prefer (see pages 34–39), cast on to one of the points of the needle the number of stitches needed; just ignore the cable connecting the two points and cast on the stitches as if you were using two separate needles. Spread out the cast-on stitches along the length of the cable; they should fill it between the two points without being stretched.

STRAIGHT CAST-ON EDGE

It is vital to check that the cast-on edge is not twisted before you join the stitches into the round, because if it is twisted then the whole piece of knitting will be permanently twisted. (It might be that this is your intention; Mobius strip scarves are quick and easy to knit in the round, just make sure there is one twist in the cast-on stitches before joining the round.)

2. The first stitch in the first round is the beginning of the round, and all subsequent rounds start in the same position unless the pattern instructs otherwise. To keep track of the rounds, place a round marker on the needle (see page 73) at the start of the first round, before knitting the first stitch.

If the cast-on edge is going to be visible, you can use a specific technique to avoid having a "jog" in the edge (see page 112).

3. Simply knit the stitches from the right-hand point of the needle to the left-hand point, sliding them around the cable as you work. When you get back to the marker, you have completed one round. Slip the marker onto the right-hand point of the needle and knit the next round.

DOUBLE-POINTED NEEDLES

Double-pointed needles come in sets of four or five. Four is the usual number, with three for holding the stitches and the fourth one to work with; five can be used for larger projects. They are not as difficult to use as they look, although they can be a bit fiddly when you first start working with them.

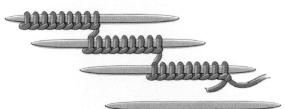

1. Divide evenly into three (if using a set of four needles), or into four (if using a set of five needles), the number of stitches you need to cast on. Here, a set of four needles is used. Using the cast-on method you prefer (see pages 34–39), cast on to one needle one-third of the number of stitches needed, plus one extra stitch. Slip the extra stitch onto the second needle to start casting on onto that needle.

2. Repeat the process, not forgetting to count the extra stitch, until the right number of stitches is cast on to each of the needles.

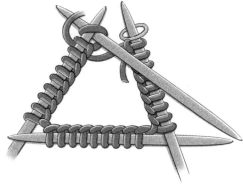

3. Arrange the needles in a triangle with the tips overlapping as shown right. As when knitting with a circular needle (see opposite), make sure that the cast-on edge is not twisted before you join it into the round. Place a round marker (see page 73) on the last needle, after the last stitch that was cast on. Pull the working tail of yarn across from the last stitch and using the free needle, knit the first stitch off the first needle, knitting it firmly and pulling the yarn tight.

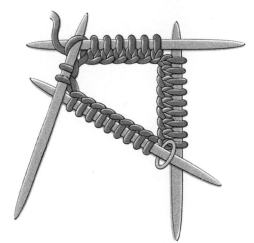

4. When all the stitches have been knitted off the first needle, that needle becomes the free one, ready to knit the stitches off the second needle. Knit the stitches off each needle in turn and when you get back to the marker, you have completed one round. Slip the marker onto the next needle and knit the next round.

AVOIDING BAGGY COLUMNS

You need to be careful to avoid baggy columns or ladders forming at the changeover points between needles, so either knit the first stitch on each needle very tightly, or occasionally move the changeover points by knitting one or two stitches from the next needle and slipping them onto the end of the previous needle before continuing the round.

MAGIC LOOP

This method enables you to knit using a circular needle that is rather too long for the number of stitches you are casting on. It works for smaller projects instead of double-pointed needles if you find multiple needles awkward. It also saves you having to have circular needles of varying lengths if you find the join on interchangeable needles annoying. Magic loop is particularly useful if the knitting is going to increase in size rapidly, as you don't have to change from double-pointed needles to circular.

1. Using the cast-on method you prefer (see pages 34–39), cast on to one of the points of the circular needle the number of stitches needed (see page 108). Slide all the stitches onto the cable part of the needle, then halfway along the cast-on row, fold the cable and pull it through between the stitches, so that you have a loop of cable with half of the stitches on either side of it.

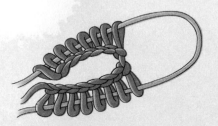

2. Slide the stitches down to the points of the needle, so that half the cast-on row is on each point.

3. *Arrange the needles so that the point with the working tail of yarn hanging from it is in your right hand and the other point is in your left hand. Then pull the right-hand point through the stitches so that they sit on the cable, but keep the stitches on the point in your left hand.

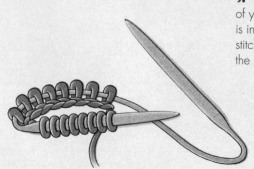

4. Pull the working yarn across tightly and, using the right-hand point, knit all the stitches on the left-hand point.

5. Slide both lots of stitches onto the points again, and then repeat the process from *.

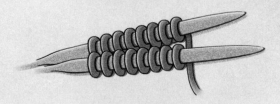

STARTING & FINISHING

The nature of knitting in the round means there are some common problems, such as a jog or jump when casting on or binding off, or when working in stripes. What follows will help eliminate the problems and make your knitting look as perfect as possible.

JOINING IN YARN

Because circular knitting produces a tube there isn't the usual side seam where you can sew in the ends of new or completed balls of yarn. You can sew ends in afterward on the back (see page 227), but they can be difficult to disguise. An alternative is to use either of these two methods.

SPLICING METHOD

Use this method to join in a new ball of the same color. It works best on yarns with two or more plies (see page 15).

1. Thread the new end into a blunt-tipped sewing needle (see page 26). Carefully slide the needle through the plies of the old yarn for about ¾in, starting a short distance from the end and separating the plies. Ease the new yarn through the old one then slide the needle off it, leaving the tail hanging loose. Knit a few stitches past the join, then trim off the loose tails of yarn.

KNITTING METHOD

Use this method to join in a ball of a different color.

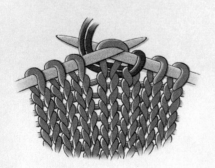

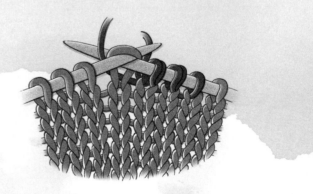

1. To join in a different colored yarn, or one that isn't suitable for the previous method, start by knitting a stitch in the new color, leaving a tail of about 6in.

2. Using the working yarn and the tail held together, knit another two stitches, then drop the tail. Knit the rest of the round using a single strand of yarn as usual. Then knit the doubled stitches, knitting the two loops together as one. Trim off the loose tail.

AVOIDING A CAST-ON JOG

As circular knitting essentially spirals rather than runs in rows, there will be a jog in the cast-on row where it begins and ends. There are various ways of avoiding this, but this is the one I think is simple and works best. It can be used with all circular techniques.

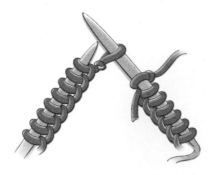

1. Cast on the stitches onto a circular needle (as here) or double-pointed needles in the usual way (see pages 108–109). Slip the first cast-on stitch from the left point onto the right point.

2. Then slip the last cast-on stitch over the one just slipped and onto the left point. You can loosen the stitch to make this easier, then pull it tight again once it is in position. Place a marker (see page 108), and start knitting.

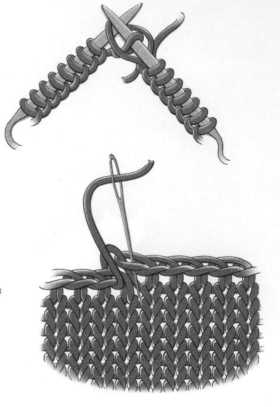

AVOIDING A BIND-OFF JOG

There will be a jog at the finish as well as the start of your knitting. This is a simple way to make a neat and flat bound-off edge.

1. Bind off in the usual way (see page 50), leaving a 4in tail of yarn when you fasten off the last stitch. Thread the tail into a blunt-tipped sewing needle (see page 26), and take it under both strands of the first bound-off stitch, then back down into the last bound-off stitch, as shown. Ease the tail gently taut so that the edge is flat, then secure the tail on the back.

AVOIDING A STRIPE JOG

If you are knitting stripes in the round, there will be a jog in each new color at the start of the round. There are various ways of fixing these jogs, but I have found that this is an easy and very effective method of dealing with them.

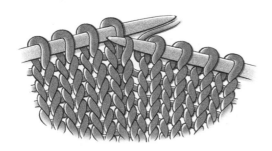

1. Knit the round in the new color. You can join in the new yarn using the splicing method (see page 111), but the knitting method can make the first stitch lumpy. Here, a tail of the new yarn has been left at the back to be sewn in later (see page 227). When you get back to the starting point, slip the right-hand needle purlwise into the stitch below the first stitch in the new color.

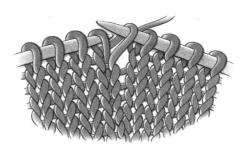

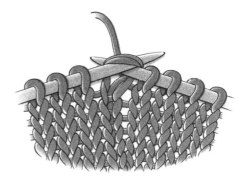

2. Lift the stitch and slip it purlwise onto the left-hand needle.

3. Knit the lifted stitch and the first stitch in the new color together.

CIRCULAR KNITS

Circular knitting can produce all manner of wonderful things, from socks, to medallions that can be sewn together to make afghans or baby blankets, to i-cords that can be practical and can add decorative detail.

KNITTED MEDALLIONS

These can be round, square, or multi-sided and are knitted in one piece using four or five double-pointed needles. Sew them together to make patchwork blankets, or use them on their own for homewares such as coasters or table mats. Bind off loosely to prevent the medallion curling at the outer edges.

1. Cast on the required number of stitches on to one double-pointed needle. Then divide the stitches equally between four needles and arrange them with the points overlapping as shown. Place a round marker (see page 109) on the last needle, after the last stitch that was cast on.

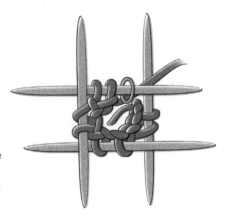

2. Using the fifth needle, knit the first round: this will often be a plain knit round. As there are so few stitches on the needles, the needles are more likely to slip out, so slide the stitches to the middle of each needle after knitting them. The following round will often require you to increase in every stitch, and this first increase round can be a bit tricky to work.

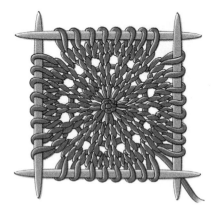

3. The increases in the pattern will make the work lie flat rather than form into a tube. As medallions grow quite quickly, you may need to transfer the stitches to longer double-pointed needles as you work. Alternatively, transfer the stitches to a circular needle.

MEDALLION PATTERN
This is a basic pattern for a medallion worked using 5 double-pointed needles. Cast on 8 sts and place 2 sts on each of 4 needles. Knit using the 5th needle.

Round 1: Knit tbl.
Round 2: Inc in every st. *(16 sts, 4 on each needle)*
Round 3: Knit.
Round 4: [Inc, k1] to end. *(24 sts, 6 on each needle)*
Rep rounds 3–4 until medallion is desired size.
Bind off.

I-CORDS

I-cords can be used to decorate your knits, or to use in place of a ribbon when threaded through eyelets. You work on two double-pointed needles, and the number of stitches is variable. It is best to have a firm gauge and to take care with the first stitch in each row, as they have a tendency to be baggy and reveal the join.

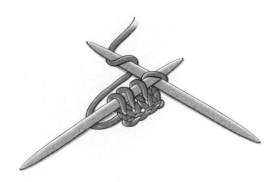

1. Using the cast-on method you prefer (see pages 34–39), cast on the required number of stitches: here there are four. *Slide the stitches along the double-pointed needle until they are at the right-hand end, and the working yarn is on the left of the cast-on row. Pull the yarn across the back of the stitches and knit the first stitch firmly. Pull the working yarn tight and knit the remaining stitches.

2. Repeat from * until the i-cord is the required length. After the first couple of rows, it will become easier to pull the yarn neatly across the back of the stitches. Finish the cord by either binding off in the usual way (see page 50), or by knitting stitches together (see page 90) until one stitch remains, then fastening that off as for binding off.

EMBELLISHED I-CORDS

Cords can be worked in texture stitch patterns, such as seed stitch or rib. Cables are also effective; just work a twist (see pages 122 and 123) every few rows.

Working increases (see page 80), knitting a few rows, then working decreases (see page 90) will create a bobbled i-cord. Or you can work a longer cord than is needed and simply tie knots in it.

An i-cord can be beaded using the knitted-in technique (see page 201) to add beads to as many stitches as required.

SOCKS

Hand-knitted socks are hugely popular, and are not as hard to knit as they look. The part that most people worry about is turning the heel, so here is a generic pattern to illustrate the technique. The actual pattern you use will give precise instructions for the whole sock, but if you are a beginner then you can try this out first to avoid confusion when knitting the real thing.

1. Cast on 42 stitches and arrange them evenly with 14 stitches on each of three double-pointed needles. Work single rib for the top edge of the sock, making it as deep as required. Change to stockinette stitch (so knit every round), until the leg is the required length from the cast-on edge to the top of the heel. Cut the yarn, leaving a 4in tail to sew in later (see page 227).

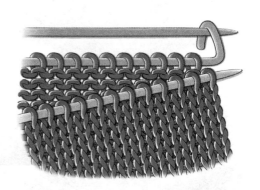

2. Slip the heel stitches onto one needle; in this example these are the first 11 and the last 11 stitches of the last round worked. Slip the remaining 20 stitches onto a stitch holder to be picked up again later.

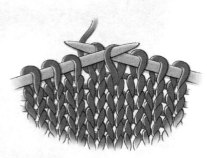

3. With the right side facing, join the yarn (see page 71) to the right-hand side of the heel stitches. Knit the 22 stitches, then turn the work and purl them. Continue working back and forth in stockinette stitch until the piece is long enough to reach from the top of the heel to about two-thirds of the way down it (usually about 3in), ending with a wrong-side row. On the next row, start to decrease, and to shape the heel using short row shaping (see pages 98–101). In this example, knit 14 stitches then skpo (see page 93). Wrap the next stitch (see page 100) and turn the work. There are 6 stitches on the right-hand needle and 15 stitches on the left-hand needle.

4. Purl 7 stitches then p2tog (see page 91). Wrap the next stitch (see page 101), then turn the work. There are 6 stitches on the right-hand needle and 14 stitches on the left-hand needle.

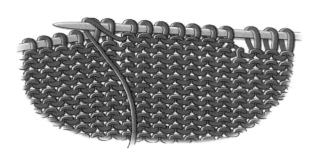

5. On the next row, knit 7 stitches, skpo, wrap and turn. On the next row, purl 7 stitches, p2tog, wrap and turn. Repeat the last two rows until only 8 stitches in total remain on the needle, omitting wrapping a stitch at the end of the last two rows, and ending with a purl row. Turn the work.

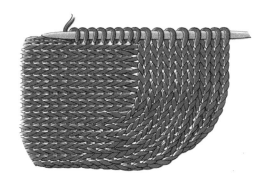

6. Now go back to working in rounds on double-pointed needles. Knit the 8 heel stitches, then pick up and knit (see page 76) stitches along the row ends up the side of the heel, picking up enough to reach the stitches that were left on the stitch holder; here 10 stitches are picked up. Using a second needle, knit the 20 stitches that are on the stitch holder.

7. Using a third needle, pick up and knit stitches along the row ends on the other side of the heel, picking up enough to match the first side, so here that is 10 stitches. Finally, knit half the stitches from the first needle, so 4 stitches in this example. Place a marker at this point to mark the start of the round. There will be a total of 48 stitches on the three needles: 14 stitches on the first needle, 20 on the second needle, and 14 on the third needle.

8. Knit 1 round. On the next round, knit to the last three stitches on the first needle, then k2tog (see page 90), and knit the last stitch.

9. Knit the 20 stitches on the second needle. Knit 1 stitch from the third needle, then skpo, and knit to the end of the round.

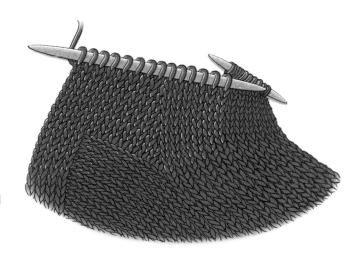

10. Repeat this decrease round as instructed in the pattern until the heel shaping is complete. Then work the foot of the sock, knitting in rounds. When it is the required length, decrease to shape the toe. Finally, transfer the stitches so that you have an equal number on each of two needles and bind them off together (see page 53).

KNITTING TEXTURE

One of the things that inspires me most about hand knitting is the way in which you can build up wonderful landscapes of texture. Three-dimensional cables add depth to the surface of Aran styles, while eyelets in lace allow light in to produce airy, delicate knits. There are ways to bind stitches together, and to create bobbles, loops, and tails that stand out from the surface. There are also techniques that manipulate the fabric, such as pleats, tucks, and entrelac.

CABLES, CROSSES, & TWISTS

All cables involve moving stitches across the fabric. This can be done in groups of stitches, such as when they are crossed behind or in front of each other, or using single stitches, such as when they are "traveled" across the fabric. Cables are the basic component of Aran knitting, developed on the Aran Islands to knit fishermen's sweaters.

FABRICS FOR CABLES

Cables are usually worked on a background of reverse stockinette to define them clearly, though other texture stitches can be used, or the cables can be purled on a stockinette background. Traditionally cables were knitted in wool or wool-blend yarns, which give elasticity to what can be a rather solid fabric. Cotton or cotton-blend yarns create crisp cables, but can produce a slight gap at the edges of the twist (see page 305).

REVERSE STOCKINETTE STITCH

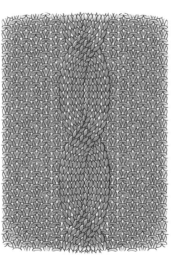

This is what is often referred to as the "wrong" side of stockinette stitch, but it is also a perfectly valid fabric in its own right. Usually abbreviated to rev st st, this fabric makes a good contrast with a stockinette cable. The only common problem is long, unsightly strands on the left of the cable between the last knit stitch of the cable and the first purl stitch of the background, but this can be reduced or eliminated (see page 305).

SEED STITCH

This fabric is most often used to fill open sections of cables, such as the center of a diamond. But it can be used as an overall background, and is more visually textural than reverse stockinette stitch. Using seed stitch as the background also eliminates the stretched strands that can occur on the left of a cable with a reverse stockinette stitch background.

RIB STITCH

Cables are usually worked as part of a larger pattern involving other cable stitches, columns of rib, and bobbles (see pages 129–135). If the knit stitch columns in a rib pattern are more than two stitches wide, then the left-hand stitch in the column can be looser than the others, but the problem can be fixed (see page 305).

CASTING ON FOR CABLES

If your cast on is going straight into cables, rather than into a border such as rib first, the crosses of the cabling can make the hem flare. The method shown here will help eliminate that flare. Be careful not to use too tight a cast on, particularly when using a cotton yarn, so that the fabric doesn't bell out above the hem.

1. Using the cast-on method you prefer (see pages 34–39), cast on all the stitches needed for the background, but only half the number of stitches needed for each cable. So for a six-stitch cable with ten stitches of reverse stockinette on either side, cast on 23 stitches. Work the background to the position of the first cable.

2. Increase (see page 89) into each stitch cast on for the cable to create the right number of stitches, then complete the row. Work the rest of the cable pattern in the usual way.

BINDING OFF FOR CABLES

When binding off across a cable pattern—for example, at a shoulder—the seam can look wavy over the cables, so it is much neater to reduce the number of cable stitches before binding off. The example here shows k2tog (see page 90) on a back cross; for extra neatness you can work skpo (see page 93) over a front cross.

1. Bind off the background stitches to the first cable. Knit the first two stitches of the cable together (see page 90).

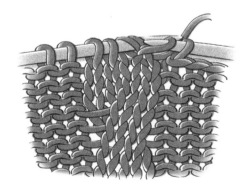

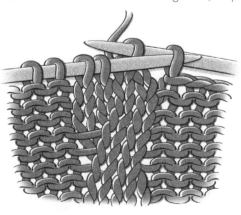

2. Lift the last bound-off background stitch over the knitted-together cable stitch, then bind off the next two cable stitches together. Bind off in this way across the row, working k2tog across all the cable stitches.

CABLE BACK

This cable has stitches held at the back of the work on a cable needle while the next stitches on the left-hand needle are worked, followed by those on the cable needle; the cable twists to the right. The example shown is over four stitches and would be abbreviated as "C4B" in a knitting pattern. Fewer stitches can be used—such as in C2B, which creates a delicate rope cable—or more, but with a bulkier yarn using too many stitches should be avoided.

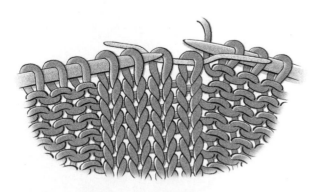

1. Work to the position of the cable. Slip the next two stitches from the left-hand needle onto the cable needle.

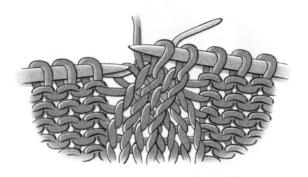

2. Move the cable needle and the stitches on it to the back of the work, then knit the next two stitches from the left-hand needle.

CABLE NEEDLES

Using a cranked or hooked cable needle, rather than a straight cable needle (see page 24), can be easier if you are new to cabling, as it's almost impossible for the stitches to fall off while you are working the cable.

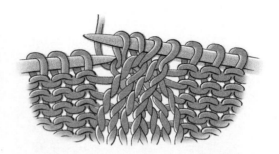

3. Then knit the two stitches from the cable needle to complete the cable.

CABLE FRONT

This cable has stitches held at the front of the work on a cable needle while the next stitches on the left-hand needle are worked, followed by those on the cable needle; the cable twists to the left. The example shown here is over four stitches and would be abbreviated to "C4F" in a knitting pattern, but fewer or more stitches can be used. This technique produces a cable that looks like a rope, if you use a cable front followed by a cable back, a "snake" will be formed.

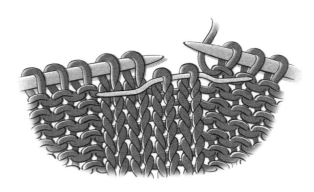

1. Work to the position of the cable. Slip the next two stitches from the left-hand needle onto the cable needle.

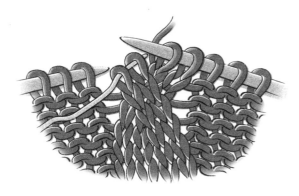

2. Bring the cable needle and the stitches on it to the front of the work, then knit the next two stitches from the left-hand needle.

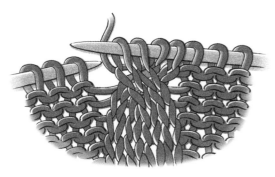

3. Then knit the two stitches from the cable needle to complete the cable.

TRAVELING CABLE RIGHT

This style of cable is also sometimes referred to as a "wandering cable" and is usually abbreviated as "Cr3R." Rather than crossing over itself, the cable consists of stitches in stockinette that travel diagonally on a reverse stockinette stitch background. Here, there are two stockinette stitches, but there can be more.

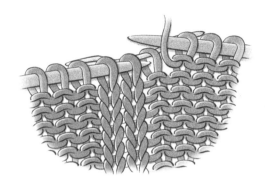

1. Work to one stitch before the cable stitches. Slip the next stitch from the left-hand needle onto the cable needle.

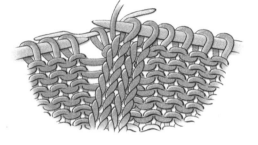

2. Move the cable needle and the stitch on it to the back of the work, then knit the two cable stitches from the left-hand needle.

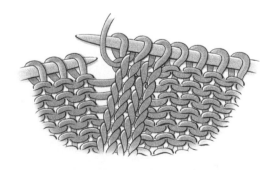

3. Then purl the stitch from the cable needle to complete the traveling cable.

TRAVELING CABLE LEFT

This cable is usually abbreviated as "Cr3L." It is worked as for the version that travels to the right (see opposite), but the stitches are held on a cable needle at the front of the work.

1. Work to the cable stitches and slip them both from the left-hand needle onto the cable needle.

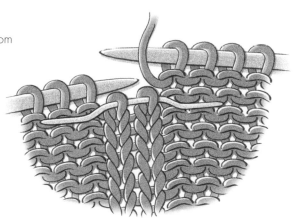

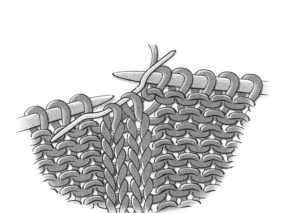

2. Bring the cable needle and the stitches on it to the front of the work, then purl the next stitch from the left-hand needle.

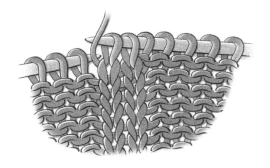

3. Then knit the two stitches from the cable needle to complete the traveling cable.

BACK CROSS ON A KNIT ROW

There isn't universal agreement in knitting patterns as what to call a single stitch that moves across the fabric. In this book, a cross stitch is a single knit stitch on a stockinette background. The back cross is often abbreviated as "Cr2B," and it moves a single stitch to the right. A twist stitch (see page 128) is a single knit stitch on a reverse stockinette background.

1. Work to one stitch before the stitch that will move. Put the right-hand needle knitwise into the second stitch on the left-hand needle (the stitch that will move) and knit it, but do not drop the original stitch off the left-hand needle.

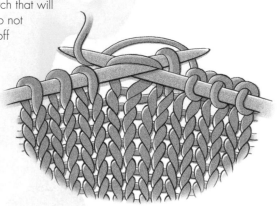

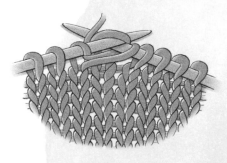

2. Put the right-hand needle knitwise into the first stitch on the left-hand needle and knit it. Then drop both original stitches off the left-hand needle to complete the cross.

FRONT CROSS ON A KNIT ROW

There also isn't universal agreement on how to abbreviate cross and twist stitches, so always check abbreviations in a pattern you are following. This front cross is often abbreviated as "Cr2F."

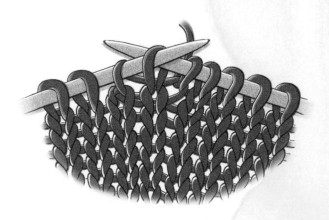

1. Work to the stitch that will move. Put the right-hand needle into the back of the second stitch on the left-hand needle and knit it through the back loop, but do not drop the original stitch off the left-hand needle.

2. Put the right-hand needle knitwise into the first stitch on the left-hand needle and knit it. Then drop both original stitches off the left-hand needle to complete the cross.

BACK CROSS ON A PURL ROW

A back cross can also be worked on a purl row of stockinette, and then it is often abbreviated as "Cr2Bp." The cross shown here moves a single stitch to the right on the right side of stockinette fabric.

1. Work to one stitch before the stitch that will move. Put the right-hand needle purlwise into the second stitch on the left-hand needle (the stitch that will move) and purl it, but do not drop the original stitch off the left-hand needle.

2. Put the right-hand needle purlwise into the first stitch on the left-hand needle and purl it. Then drop both original stitches off the left-hand needle to complete the cross.

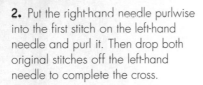

FRONT CROSS ON A PURL ROW

A front cross worked on a purl row of stockinette is often abbreviated as "Cr2Fp." It moves a single stitch to the left on the right side of stockinette fabric.

1. Work to the stitch that will move. Put the right-hand needle into the back of the second stitch on the left-hand needle and purl it through the back loop; it can be easier to have the right needle above the left needle, as shown, when doing this. Do not drop the original stitch off the left-hand needle.

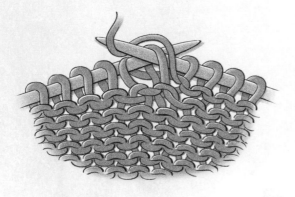

2. Put the right-hand needle purlwise into the first stitch on the left-hand needle and purl it. Then drop both original stitches off the left-hand needle to complete the cross.

BACK TWIST

In this book, a twist stitch is a single knit stitch on a reverse stockinette stitch background. This twist is sometimes abbreviated as "T2B" and moves a single knit stitch to the right. A cross stitch (see page 126) is a single knit stitch on a stockinette stitch background.

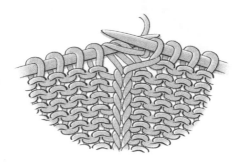

1. Work to one stitch before the knit stitch, the stitch that will move. Take the yarn to the back, put the right-hand needle knitwise into the second stitch on the left-hand needle (the knit stitch that will move) and knit it, but do not drop the original stitch off the left-hand needle.

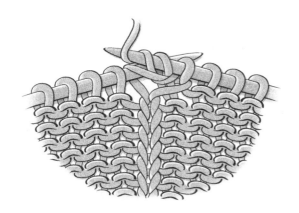

2. Bring the yarn to the front, put the right-hand needle purlwise into the first stitch on the left-hand needle and purl it. Then drop both original stitches off the left-hand needle to complete the twist.

FRONT TWIST

This twist is sometimes abbreviated as "T2F." Here, the twist moves a single knit stitch to the left on a reverse stockinette stitch background.

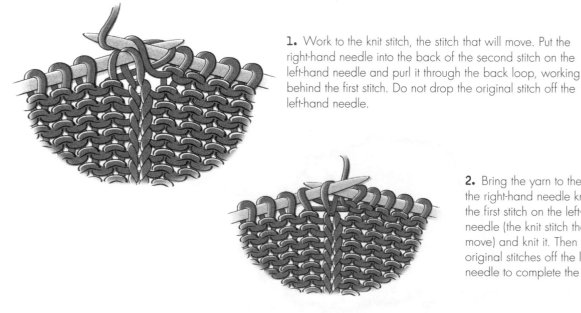

1. Work to the knit stitch, the stitch that will move. Put the right-hand needle into the back of the second stitch on the left-hand needle and purl it through the back loop, working behind the first stitch. Do not drop the original stitch off the left-hand needle.

2. Bring the yarn to the front, put the right-hand needle knitwise into the first stitch on the left-hand needle (the knit stitch that will move) and knit it. Then drop both original stitches off the left-hand needle to complete the twist.

BOBBLES

Bobbles can add beautiful surface detail to your knitting. They can be used with cables to produce designs based on traditional Aran knits, or added between ribs on a border, or used to edge a collar. There are many ways to make a bobble (you can have fun inventing your own), but here are some popular and useful methods.

POPCORN BOBBLE

This is a small bobble, sometimes called a knot. Because of its size it can be a good bobble to use with chunkier yarns. It is shown here on reverse stockinette fabric, but it can be worked on other backgrounds, too.

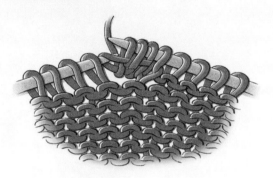

1. Work to the position of the bobble. Take the yarn to the back and, using the same principle as for increasing knitwise (see page 80), knit into the front, then the back, then the front again, and then the back again of the next stitch, and then drop the original stitch off the left-hand needle.

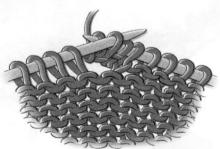

2. Using the tip of the left-hand needle, lift the second stitch on the right-hand needle over the first stitch.

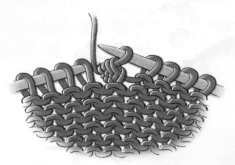

3. In turn, lift the third then the fourth stitches over the first one to complete the popcorn bobble.

LARGE BOBBLE

There are a lot of variations on the way a bobble can be knitted, and by working more or fewer rows or stitches, you can change the size. The method shown here is a stockinette stitch bobble on a reverse stockinette stitch background. If you knit the first row of the bobble rather than purl it, you can create a reverse stockinette stitch bobble.

1. Work to the position of the bobble. Knit, then purl, then knit, then purl into the next stitch, taking the yarn to the back and front as needed to make the stitches. Then drop the original stitch off the left-hand needle.

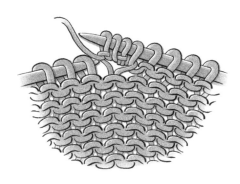

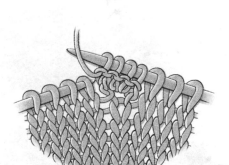

2. Turn the work and purl the four bobble stitches.

3. Turn the work again and knit the four bobble stitches. Then turn the work and purl the stitches again; three rows of stockinette stitch have been worked on the bobble stitches.

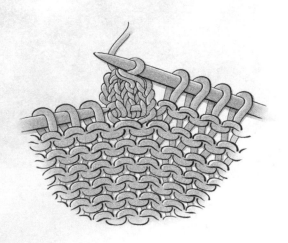

4. Turn the work so that the right side is facing. Slip the first two stitches knitwise (see page 77) onto the right-hand needle. Knit the next two stitches together (see page 90), then, one at a time, lift the two slipped stitches over the knitted stitch to complete the large bobble.

YARNOVER BOBBLE

Another way of making a bobble is to use yarnovers (see pages 136–137). This creates a less pronounced and flatter bobble than the large bobble (see opposite). The example shown here is a stockinette stitch bobble on a reverse stockinette stitch background.

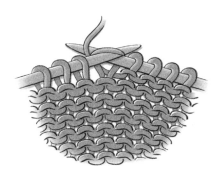

1. Work to the position of the bobble. Take the yarn to the back and knit into the next stitch, but do not slip it off the needle.

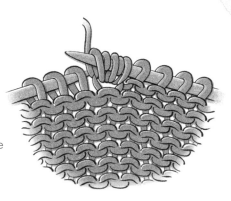

2. Make a yarnover (see page 136), then knit into the stitch again, make another yarnover and knit into the stitch for a third time. Then drop the original stitch off the left-hand needle.

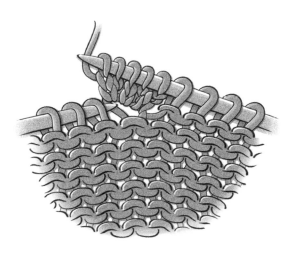

3. Turn the work and purl the five bobble stitches, then turn the work again and knit the stitches. Turn and purl two stitches together (see page 91), purl one stitch, then purl the last two stitches together; there are three stitches remaining.

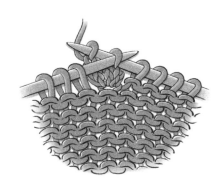

4. Turn the work so that the right side is facing. Slip one stitch knitwise, knit the next two stitches together then lift the slipped stitch over the knitted stitch (see page 95), to complete the yarnover bobble.

I-CORD BOBBLE

This is a combination of a bobble and an i-cord. Because you don't have to turn the work, this can be a good bobble to use on a heavier or large project such as a blanket. It's shown here as a stockinette stitch bobble on a reverse stockinette stitch background, but it can be used on other backgrounds.

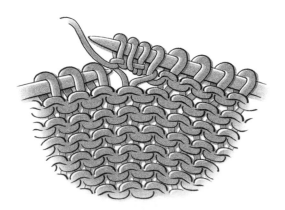

1. Work to the position of the bobble. Knit, then purl, then knit, then purl into the next stitch, taking the yarn to the back and front as needed to make the stitches. Then drop the original stitch off the left-hand needle.

2. Take the yarn to the back. *Slip the four bobble stitches knitwise back onto the left-hand needle. Pull the working yarn across the back of the stitches and then knit them, as for an i-cord. Pulling the yarn very tightly will make the bobble more tubular, while keeping it a little bit looser will make the bobble rounder.

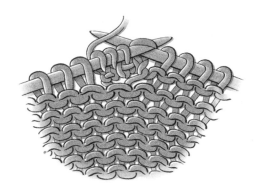

3. Repeat from * twice more. Slip the first two stitches knitwise (see page 77) onto the left-hand needle. Knit these two stitches together (see page 90), then, one at a time, lift the first two stitches on the needle over the knitted stitch to complete the i-cord bobble.

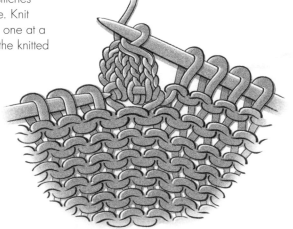

CROCHET HOOK BOBBLE

This is a quick and easy bobble to make, but it doesn't have the firmness of a knitted bobble so it usually works best on chunkier weight yarns. Use a crochet hook that is a similar thickness to the knitting needles that the background fabric is worked on. The technique is shown here on stockinette stitch, but can be worked on any stitch pattern.

1. Work to the position of the bobble. Slip the hook knitwise into the next stitch on the left-hand needle and slip that stitch off the needle. Wind the working yarn around the hook.

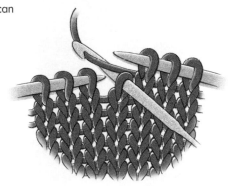

2. *Draw a loop through the stitch, then wind the yarn around the hook again.

3. Put the hook into the stitch, then repeat from * three more times. There will be four loops and four winds on the hook.

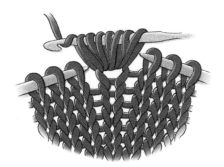

4. Carefully draw the last wind on the hook through all the other loops and winds; one loop is on the hook. Then wind the working yarn around the hook again.

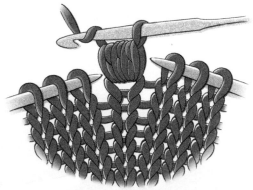

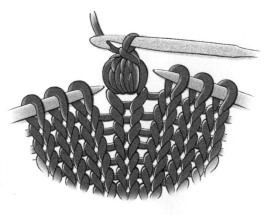

5. Draw the last wind on the hook through the loop on it to complete the crochet hook bobble. Slip the bobble stitch onto the right-hand needle.

CONTRAST TEXTURE BOBBLE

Knitted bobbles can be the same texture as or a different texture to the background fabric. You can change those featured in this chapter by simply swapping the knit and purl instructions on the turning rows. Bobbles that are worked in a contrasting texture to the background will show up better than those worked in the same texture.

If bobbles are being worked with cables (see pages 120–128) as part of an Aran pattern, then they will often be worked in stockinette stitch on a background of reverse stockinette. The bobbles shown on pages 129–132 are all being worked in this way. The result is a smooth, prominent bobble that stands out well on the lightly textured background.

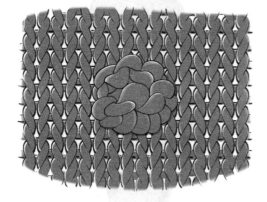

Swapping the textures is also effective; work a bobble in reverse stockinette on a background of stockinette stitch. The bobble will be round and textural on the flat background fabric.

A subtler effect is achieved by working a bobble in the same stitch as the background; here, both are stockinette stitch, but could equally well be worked in reverse stockinette. The bobbles will show, but not boldly, so it is worth experimenting with swatches to ensure that you are happy with the result before you start a project.

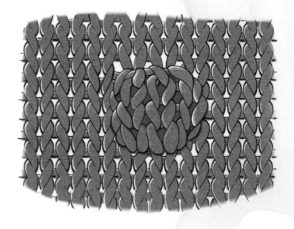

CONTRAST COLOR BOBBLE

As color provides a strong contrast to the background, these bobbles can be worked in the same stitch as the background and will still show up well. About 10in of yarn will usually be enough for one large bobble. There can be a tendency for the background shade to work itself into the bobble, but the method shown here will help prevent that.

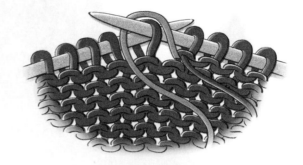

1. To prevent the background color intruding into the bobble, you need to work a foundation stitch in the bobble color. On the row before the one on which you want to place the bobble, work to the position of the bobble. Using the contrast color yarn, work the next stitch on the left-hand needle. Complete the row in the background color.

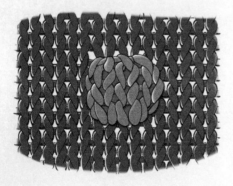

2. Work to the colored foundation stitch. Making sure that one end of the contrast yarn is left hanging with a tail long enough to sew in later, make a bobble with the other end. The bobble shown here is a large bobble (see page 130). Complete the row in the background color.

3. When the work is complete, pull gently on the tails of contrast color yarn to neaten and tighten the bobble, then using a blunt-tipped sewing needle, sew the tails into the back of the work, taking them through stitch loops in the same color (see page 227). If you are working a series of bobbles at short intervals across a row, it may be preferable to weave in the contrasting yarn (see page 187).

KNITTED LACE

Beautiful lace patterns range from simple to very intricate, but all of them are based on making yarnovers to create increases, and then working decreases to maintain the stitch count. There are different methods of making yarnovers depending on the stitches on either side. All yarnovers are abbreviated to "yo" in the US, but in the UK they have different names.

YARNOVER BETWEEN KNIT STITCHES

In the UK this method is called "yarn forward" and is abbreviated to "yfwd" or "yf." Be aware that "yf" can also be used to indicate that the yarn should be brought forward between the tips of the needles, as it sometimes is when slipping stitches (see pages 174–175).

1. Work to the position of the yarnover. Bring the yarn to the front, between the tips of the needles.

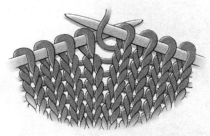

2. Take the yarn over the right-hand needle to the back and knit the next stitch on the left-hand needle. The loop of yarn made over the right-hand needle is the yarnover.

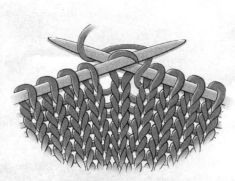

YARNOVER BETWEEN PURL STITCHES

In the UK this version of a yarnover is called "yarn round needle" and is abbreviated to "yrn." The yarn is wrapped right around the right-hand needle, so you need to tension it firmly to prevent the yarnover being baggy once the next stitch has been purled.

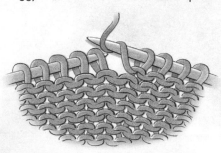

1. Work to the position of the yarnover. Wrap the yarn over and right around the right-hand needle.

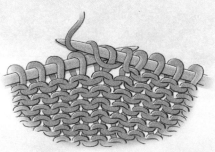

2. Purl the next stitch on the left-hand needle. The loop of yarn made over the right-hand needle is the yarnover.

YARNOVER BETWEEN KNIT AND PURL STITCHES

In the UK this yarnover is called "yarn forward round needle" and is abbreviated to "yfrn." The yarn is wrapped right around the right-hand needle, so you need to tension it firmly to prevent the yarnover being baggy once the next stitch has been purled.

1. Work to the position of the yarnover. Bring the yarn to the front, between the tips of the needles, and wrap it over and right around the right-hand needle.

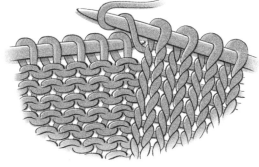

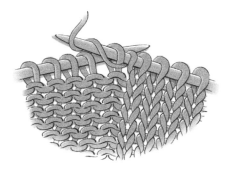

2. Purl the next stitch on the left-hand needle. The loop of yarn made over the right-hand needle is the yarnover.

YARNOVER BETWEEN PURL AND KNIT STITCHES

In the UK this version of a yarnover is called "yarn over needle" or "yarnover" and abbreviated to "yon" or "yo." However, be aware that if you are following a US pattern and the instruction is "yo," it only means this particular yarnover if there is a purl stitch before it and a knit stitch after it.

1. Work to the position of the yarnover. Leaving the yarn at the front of the work, insert the needle knitwise into the next stitch on the left-hand needle.

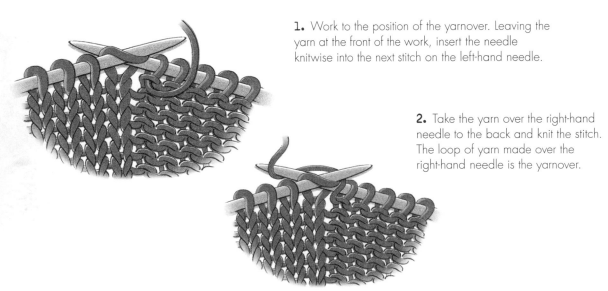

2. Take the yarn over the right-hand needle to the back and knit the stitch. The loop of yarn made over the right-hand needle is the yarnover.

YARNOVER AT START OF A KNIT ROW

This is the method for making a yarnover before knitting the first stitch at the beginning of a row. It is a very simple maneuver, but take care at the end of the next row not to drop the yarnover or miss working it.

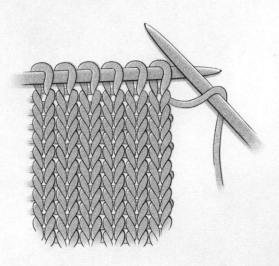

1. With the right-hand needle in front of the left-hand needle, drape the working yarn over the right-hand needle.

2. Insert the right-hand needle knitwise into the first stitch on the left-hand needle, then take the yarn around to the back and knit the stitch. The loop of yarn made over the right-hand needle is the yarnover.

YARNOVER AT START OF A PURL ROW

This is the method for making a yarnover before purling the first stitch at the beginning of a row. Watch out for the yarnover at the end of the next row and be careful not to drop it or miss working it.

1. With the yarn at the back, insert the right-hand needle purlwise into the first stitch on the left-hand needle.

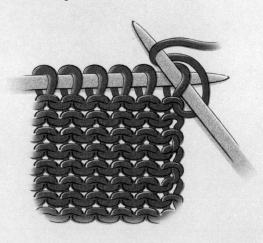

2. Bring the yarn around and under the right-hand needle. Purl the stitch, being careful to draw the yarn through the stitch only, not through the yarnover as well. The loop of yarn made over the right-hand needle is the yarnover.

MULTIPLE YARNOVERS

If you want to make larger holes—particularly in finer yarns—or to increase by two stitches in a row, you will need to make more than one yarnover. The method shown here uses yarn forward (see page 136), but the principle is the same for all yarnovers.

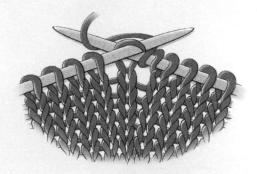

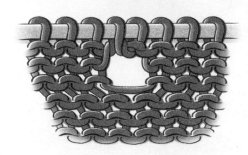

1. Work to the position of the yarnover. Make whatever yarnover is appropriate for the stitches either side, but wrap the yarn twice around the needle instead of once. For a larger hole, when you work back across the row, work into one of the yarnover loops and drop the other one off the needle.

2. If you want to increase the stitch count by two as well as making a hole, work into both loops of the yarnover when you work back across the row. On a purl row, purl the first loop and knit the second loop; on a knit row, knit the first loop and purl the second loop.

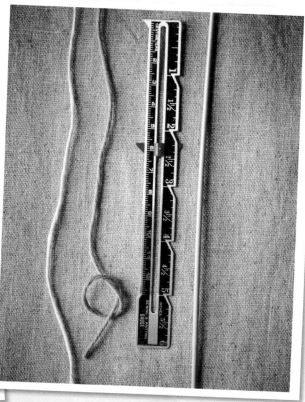

WORKING LACE REPEATS AND SHAPING

Lace designs are often shown as charts, but usually the chart only shows the lace repeat—not the whole piece to be knitted—and if the piece involves shaping, the written pattern may only give general instructions as to how to work the increases or decreases into the lace design. This can be confusing, so it's worth spending time working out exactly what you are being asked to do. This generic pattern explains the principles.

This chart shows an eight-stitch lace repeat over 12 rows, plus the extra stitches that need to be worked for the seams and to complete the pattern.

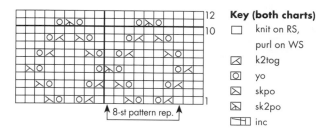

Key (both charts)

☐	knit on RS, purl on WS
◺	k2tog
◌	yo
◸	skpo
◿	sk2po
⊞	inc

If the chart was to be repeated over 27 cast-on stitches for 24 rows, the pattern instruction might read:
Cast on 27 sts.
Row 1: Chart row 1: k2, [k1, k2tog, yo, k1, yo, skpo, k2] to last st, k1. This row sets the chart.
Work the 12 rows of the chart twice.
Bind off.

If the pattern included shaping, with the edge stitches increased into on every right-side row of the first repeat starting with row 3, the pattern instruction might read:
Cast on 27 sts.
Row 1: Chart row 1: k2, [k1, k2tog, yo, k1, yo, skpo, k2] to last st, k1. This row sets the position of the chart.
Work rows 1–12 of chart as set, **and at the same time** inc in first and last st on every RS row beg with row 3.
Work lace patt as set without incs for 12 more rows, working lace patt into inc sts in half-patt rep.
Bind off.

So, with an edge stitch at either end of the row, you should establish the lace pattern repeat three times across the 27 cast-on stitches. Work the 12 rows of the lace pattern repeat once, increasing into the edge stitch on every right-side row starting with row 3; the increased stitches are worked in stockinette stitch. Then work the 12 rows as set again, without increasing, but working half the pattern repeat into the increased stitches. Remember that you must always keep a plain edge stitch.

Place a round marker one stitch in from the each end of the row before starting the increases. Increase before the marker at the beginning of the row and after it at the end of the row, then you can easily see how many stitches have been increased.

If this sample pattern was written out in full, with stitch counts on the increase rows, it would read as follows:
Cast on 26 sts.
Row 1: K1, [k2, k2tog, yo, k1, yo, skpo, k1] 3 times, k1.
Row 2 and every alt row: Purl.
Row 3: Inc, [k1, k2tog, yo, k3, yo, skpo] 3 times, inc. (*28 sts*)
Row 5: Inc, k1, k2tog, yo, k5, yo, [sk2po, yo, k5, yo] 3 times, skpo, inc. (*30 sts*)
Row 7: Inc, k2, [k1, yo, skpo, k3, k2tog, yo] 3 times, k2, inc. (*32 sts*)
Row 9: Inc, k2, [k3, yo, skpo, k1, k2tog, yo] 3 times, k4, inc. (*34 sts*)
Row 11: Inc, k4, [k3, yo, sk2po, yo, k2] 3 times, k4, inc. (*36 sts*)
Row 13: K2, [k1, yo, skpo, k3, k2tog, yo] 4 times, k2.
Row 15: K2, [k2, yo, skpo, k1, k2tog, yo, k1] 4 times, k2.
Row 17: K2, [k3, yo, sk2po, yo, k2] 4 times, k2.
Row 19: K2, [k2, k2tog, yo, k1, yo, skpo, k1] 4 times, k2.
Row 21: K2, [k1, k2tog, yo, k3, yo, skpo] 4 times, k2.
Row 23: K2, k2tog, yo, [k5, yo, sk2po, yo] 3 times, k5, yo, skpo, k1.
Row 24: Purl.
Bind off.

And a full chart with the half pattern repeats incorporated into the increased stitches would look like this.

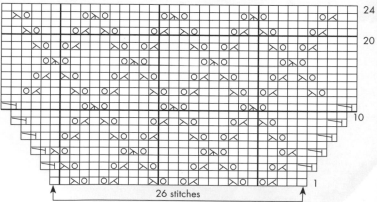

TEXTURAL STITCHES

There are many ways of creating texture in knitted fabric, and the work should be carefully blocked (see page 218) to make the most of the technique, as the more elastic the yarn, the more it tends to bounce and affect the result.

ELONGATED STOCKINETTE STITCH

Different versions of this decorative stitch are shown here on stockinette stitch and on garter stitch, but either method can be used on either fabric. With both methods you can wind the yarn around more times to create an even deeper band. Bear in mind that these bands will add to the overall length of the fabric.

1. Insert the right-hand needle knitwise into the stitch in the usual way, but wind the yarn twice around the right-hand needle and draw both loops through the stitch.

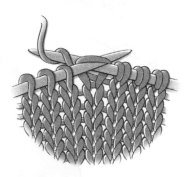

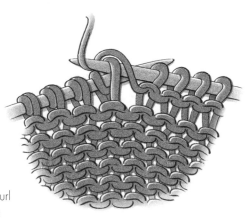

2. When you work back across the row, purl into the first of each pair of loops and drop the extra loop off the needle.

ELONGATED GARTER STITCH

This method is easier if you want to make deeper bands of elongated stitches, but be aware that very elongated stitches will snag easily.

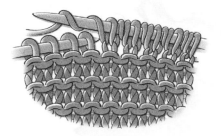

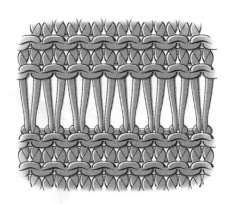

1. Knit the stitches in the usual way, but between each stitch, wind the yarn twice around the right-hand needle.

2. When you work back across the row, drop the extra loops and just knit the stitches.

DIP STITCH

These are pulled-up loops that can be made singly, slanting in different directions, of different lengths, or grouped to make flower-like shapes. You can use the working yarn, or a second yarn that is woven in across the back (see page 187) until it's needed.

1. Work to the position of the top of the dip stitch loop. Insert the right-hand needle into a stitch a few rows down; this can be directly below the next stitch on the left needle or to one side of it, and here the dip stitch loop will slant up and to the left.

2. Wrap the working yarn around the tip of the needle and draw through a loop of yarn that is just long enough to reach the working stitches. Slip the loop onto the left-hand needle.

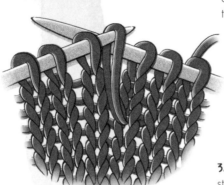

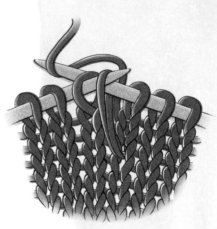

3. Knit the loop and stitch together through the back loops.

LOOP LENGTH

Adjust the length of the dip stitch loops carefully: if they are too short they will pucker the fabric and affect the gauge. If the loops are too long they can easily snag or get caught on fingers.

4. To create a flower-like shape, make one dip stitch from a few rows below the second stitch on the left-hand needle and knit the loop together with the first stitch. Then make dip stitches coming out of the same stitch and knit them together with the next two stitches on the left-hand needle.

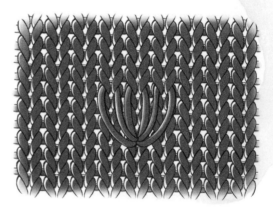

CREATING LADDERS

Dropped stitches are usually unintentional, but they can be used to create a ladder through which ribbon or yarn in a contrast color can be threaded. This is an option if you want fine vertical stripes, as working just one stitch in a contrast shade using intarsia (see pages 176–179) can be fiddly, and the stitch can sink into the fabric and not show up well, while duplicate stitch (see pages 192–193) can look too chunky. Alternatively, the ladder can be left to form a narrow gap in the fabric.

1. Work to the position of the bottom of the ladder. Make a stitch (see pages 82–83). You need to keep track of this stitch, so if you are worried about losing it, place a marker (see page 73).

2. Work to the depth you want the ladder to be.

3. On the next row—here a knit row, but it can be a purl row—drop the stitch that was made and unravel it to create the ladder. It will run down as far as the original made stitch, but not further.

4. You can weave a single ribbon or thread through the ladder, or you can darn it in matching or contrasting yarn. Simply secure the yarn on the back, then weave it in and out of the rungs of the ladder until it is as tightly darned as you want, then fasten off on the back.

BOUND STITCHES

This method of grouping stitches is very easy and quick to work, but the results are quite subtle, so try it with a crisp cotton yarn or a heavier weight yarn. You can work groups of bound stitches at regular intervals to create a texture, but if you are planning on adding bound stitches to an existing plain pattern, do work a gauge swatch first to check how the gauge is affected.

1. Work to the first of the stitches to be bound together. Slip the first stitch purlwise onto the right-hand needle (see page 77), keeping the yarn at the back of the work.

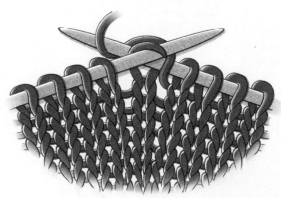

2. Knit the next stitch on the left-hand needle, then make a yarnover (see page 136) and knit the next stitch.

3. Put the tip of the left-hand needle into the slipped stitch and lift it over the first knitted stitch, the yarnover, and the second knitted stitch, binding the three together. On the next row, purl into each stitch and the yarnover in the usual way.

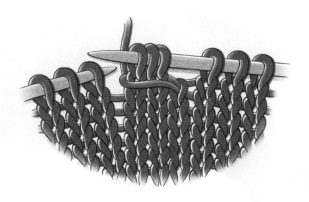

CLUSTERED STITCHES

This is a bolder way to group stitches and you will need a cable needle to work the technique. More stitches can be clustered together for a more pronounced textural surface, though the gauge of the fabric will be affected, so if you are planning on adding clustered stitches to an existing plain pattern, do work a gauge swatch first to check how the gauge is affected.

1. Work to the stitches to be clustered together and knit them; here three stitches are being clustered.

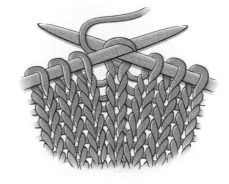

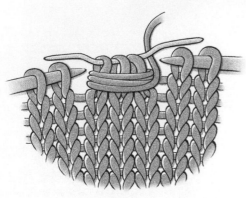

2. Slip the stitches to be clustered onto a cable needle. Bring the working yarn to the front and wrap it counterclockwise around the stitches on the cable needle.

3. You can vary the number of wraps; here, there are three. Finish the wrapping with the yarn at the back, and adjust the wraps to lie neatly and to pull the stitches together as closely as required.

4. Slip the stitches back onto the right-hand needle. Knit the next stitch to hold the wraps in place, then complete the row.

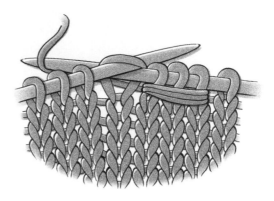

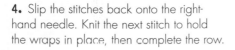

CLUSTER RIB SMOCKING

This technique is worked using the same principle as clustered stitches (see page 145), but the clusters are worked across a rib pattern, which give the appearance of smocking. This stitch can look lovely worked on the yoke of a child's dress.

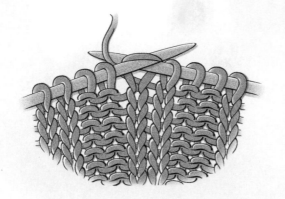

1. Work fabric in a rib pattern; here, it's a k2, p2 double rib, but you can use a different pattern. Try k1, p3 rib for a delicate look (see opposite), or k2, p3 for a chunky smocked effect.

2. Work the group of stitches to be clustered together, then follow Steps 2–4 of Clustered Stitches (see page 145). Here the stitches have been wrapped twice, and the next stitch after the cluster will be a purl stitch, so the wrapping yarn will need to be brought to the front to work it. Continue in the rib pattern.

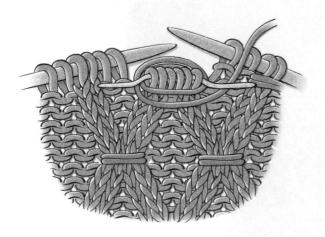

WORKING OUT A PATTERN

Clustering stitches for smocking will affect the gauge of the fabric, so if you are planning to smock an existing plain pattern, you will need to resize the pieces. Work swatches to decide on the rib and cluster pattern you prefer, and to establish a gauge over pattern.

3. Wrap the stitches in the rib pattern so that alternate columns of knit stitches are clustered to produce a classic diamond smocking pattern, as shown. The spacing between cluster rows can be varied to create longer or shorter diamonds.

SEWN SMOCKING

Traditionally smocking was worked on woven fabric, but it can be used on knitting, too. The beauty of sewn smocking is that you can use a contrast color to embroider the stitches. Shown here is a simple and plain smocking stitch, but there are fancier ones that you can explore. Experiment on swatches before you embroider a project.

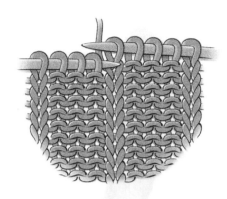

1. Work fabric in a rib pattern; here, it's a k1, p3 rib, but you can use a different pattern. Try a k2, p2 double rib (see opposite) for a bolder look.

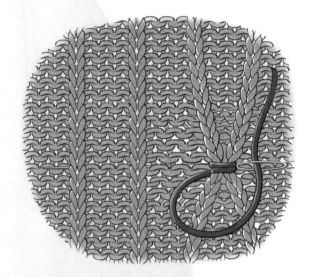

2. When the knitting is complete, start embroidering the smocking. Use a yarn with the same laundering requirements as the knitting yarn, and the effect will be neater if the yarns are also similar weights. Thread a blunt-tipped sewing needle with a long length of yarn. Bring it through to the front next to a column of knit stitches, where you want the smocking to start. Make a straight embroidered stitch across to an adjacent column of knit stitches and draw the two columns together, as shown. Don't pull too tight; the columns should sit beside one another but not be crushed together. Make as many straight stitches as you want; here, there are three. After the third stitch, take the needle across at the back of the fabric to the position of the next embroidered stitch. Do not pull the float at the back too tight.

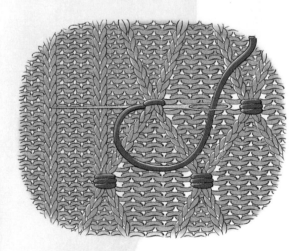

3. Embroider the stitches in the rib pattern so that alternate columns of knit stitches are drawn together to produce a classic diamond smocking pattern, as shown.

SMOCKING FABRIC

As with cluster rib smocking (see opposite), sewn smocking will affect the gauge of the fabric, so if you are planning to smock an existing plain pattern, you will need to resize the pieces. Work swatches to decide on the smocking pattern you prefer, and to establish a gauge over pattern.

SINGLE LOOPS

Loops on the right side of the work can be worked to make an all-over texture, or used to create a fake fur-style collar and cuffs on a jacket. They can also be cut to create fringes or a long-pile fur fabric. Loops should be avoided for any garment to be worn by a baby or small child, as little fingers can get caught in them.

1. On a knit row, work to the position of the loop. Knit the next stitch, but do not drop the stitch off the left-hand needle.

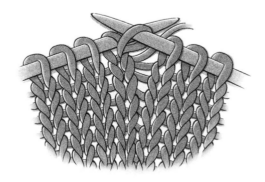

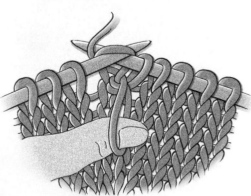

2. Bring the yarn to the front between the needles and wind it under your left thumb.

3. Take the yarn to the back again between the needles and knit into the same stitch on the left-hand needle. Slip the original stitch off the left-hand needle.

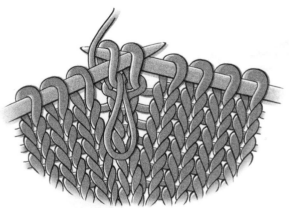

4. Slip both stitches back onto the left-hand needle and knit them together through the back of loops (see page 77) to complete the loop stitch.

CLUSTERED LOOPS

These make a much denser looped fabric than single loops (see opposite), but as all the loops in a cluster are made from the same strand of yarn, they can't be cut (most of the cut strands would simply work loose and fall out). The loops are made on a wrong-side row, but appear on the right side of the fabric.

1. On a wrong-side row, work to the position of the loop. Take the yarn to the back (the right side) of the work and insert the right-hand needle knitwise into the next stitch. Put two fingers of your left hand behind the right-hand needle (or three fingers for very long loops). Wind the yarn over the point of the right-hand needle, then over and around your fingers three times, finishing with the yarn going over the needle. (So the yarn goes over the needle four times, but around your fingers three times.)

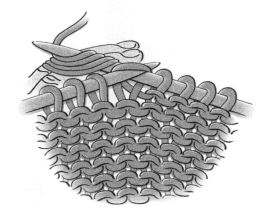

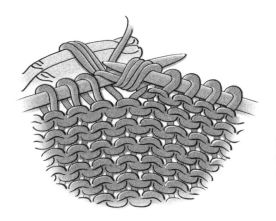

2. Draw the loops on the right-hand needle though the stitch, without allowing the original stitch to drop off the left-hand needle.

3. Slide your fingers out of the loops, and slip the loops from the right-hand needle onto the left-hand needle. Holding on to the loops, knit all of them together with the original stitch as one, knitting through the back of the loops and stitch (see page 77). Use your left hand to pull the loops firmly down on the right side.

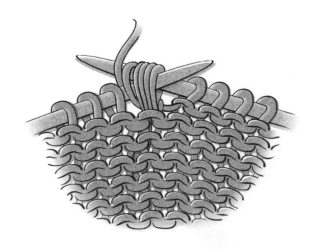

MANIPULATED KNITTED FABRICS

These are techniques that create three-dimensional knitted fabrics. Some of them can be quite fiddly to work, but they are worth trying for the effects they give. Go slowly and your patience will be rewarded.

PLEATS

These are best worked in stockinette stitch. I particularly like to work a pleat at the back of a baby's or small child's jacket to give it an A-line shape and to fit over diapers.

THE STRUCTURE OF A SINGLE PLEAT

A pleat has a face (the part you can see from the front), a fold-back (the part that folds back behind the face), and a return (the part at the back, which runs in the same direction as the face). All three parts are the same size and need the same number of stitches. For this example we are going to have each part five stitches wide, so the pleat will use 15 stitches in total. (For calculations for multiple and box pleats, see opposite.)

LEFT-FACING PLEAT

The opening of this pleat will face to the left as you look at it, or to the right when worn if it is part of a garment.

1. Work to the position of the start of the first pleat. Slip the five face stitches onto a double-pointed needle.

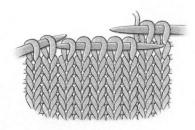

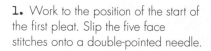

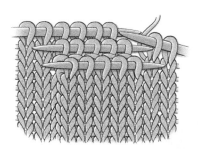

2. Slip the next five stitches, the fold-back stitches, onto another double-pointed needle and fold the knitting so that the wrong sides of the face and the fold-back are together and the double-pointed needles are next to one another. The five stitches for the return remain on the left-hand needle. Fold the knitting again so that the return stitches are right-sides together with the fold-back stitches.

3. *Insert the right-hand needle knitwise through the first stitch of the face, then the fold-back, then the return stitches. Wrap the working yarn around the tip of the right-hand needle as if to knit.

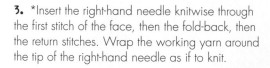

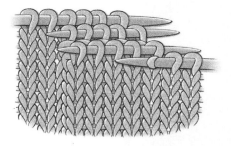

4. Draw a loop through all three stitches, then drop those stitches off their respective needles. Do this carefully, to avoid dropping any other stitches. Then pull the working yarn firmly to tighten up the stitch just made. Repeat from * until all five stitches for each part of the pleat have been knitted, then complete the row.

RIGHT-FACING PLEAT

The opening of this pleat will face to the right as you look at it, or to the left when worn if it is part of a garment. It is worked using the same principles as a left-facing pleat, but in reverse.

1. Work to the position of the start of the first pleat. Slip the five return stitches onto a double-pointed needle. Slip the next five stitches, the fold-back stitches, onto another double-pointed needle and fold the knitting so that the right sides of the return and the fold-back are together and the double-pointed needles are next to one another. The five stitches for the face remain on the left-hand needle. Fold the knitting again so that the face stitches are wrong-sides together with the fold-back stitches.

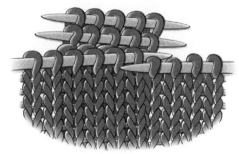

Pull the stitches on the right-hand needle forward, level with the left-hand needle, so that you can knit the stitches together following Steps 3–4 of Left-Facing Pleat (see opposite).

CRISP PLEATS

Using just stockinette will produce soft, full pleats. To make pleats that fold crisply, the last stitch of the face stitches will be slipped, and the last stitch of the fold-back will be purled. On wrong-side rows, all the stitches will be purled.

So for a crisp left-facing pleat you work the knitting below where the pleat is formed as follows.

Row 1 and every RS row: K4, sl1, k4, p1, k5.
Row 2 and every WS row: Purl.

Slip stitches onto the needles as for a left-facing pleat (see opposite), with the slipped stitch as the last face stitch and the purled stitch as the last fold-back stitch.

For a crisp right-facing pleat you work the knitting below where the pleat is formed as follows.

Row 1 and every RS row: K5, p1, k4, sl1, k4.
Row 2 and every WS row: Purl.

Slip stitches onto the needles as for a right-facing pleat (see above), with the purled stitch as the last fold-back stitch and the slipped stitch as the last face stitch.

MULTIPLE PLEATS

To knit a piece of pleated fabric, first decide how many pleats you want and how many stitches wide they will be. You need to multiply the number of stitches for the pleat width by three (the face, fold-under and return all need the same number of stitches).

For example, if you want eight pleats, each one five stitches wide, you need to do the following sum.

5 (the width of the pleat in stitches) x 3 (the face, fold-back, and return) = 15 stitches per pleat.

15 x 8 (the number of pleats wanted) = 120 stitches to cast on for the pleated section.

Work the fabric to the required depth, then work one pleat immediately after another.

BOX PLEATS

A box pleat is a left-facing pleat immediately followed by a right-facing pleat, so staying with the five-stitch pleat width, you would need fifteen stitches for each separate pleat, so 30 stitches for the whole box pleat. Box pleats usually look more effective with crisp folds (see left).

TUCKS

Tucks can be used to add a bit of drama and fun to your knitting. I often use the technique on baby bootees to define the sole. You can work tucks all along the row, or in small bursts, or add flashes of color by working a stripe from the pick-up row upward. Tucks are best worked in stockinette stitch.

1. Work for twice the required depth of the tuck, finishing with a wrong-side row. With the wrong side facing, from above slide a spare knitting needle under the top loops of the stitches in the row from which you are going to pick up the tuck. Make sure that the point of the spare needle is facing in the same direction as the needle holding the live stitches.

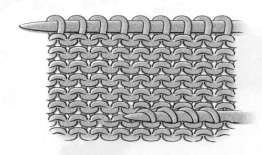

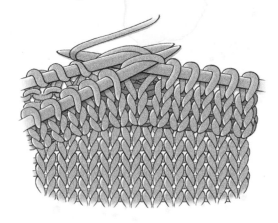

2. Fold the tuck so that the left-hand needle (with the live stitches on) and the spare needle are together. Knit the live stitches and pick-up stitches together; do this in a similar way to the three-needle bind off technique (see page 53), but not actually bind the stitches off, just knit them all.

CRISP TUCK

For a tuck that lies flatter, with a crisper edge, work a knit row on the wrong side at the depth of the tuck, so that when the tuck is folded, the knit row makes a ridge along the fold.

RUCHES

You can use the same principle to make ruches in a knitted fabric, rather than tucks that run right across a row. Pick up just a few stitches on the wrong side where you want the ruche to be. You might find it easier to use a double-pointed needle, or even a cable needle, to do this. Then knit them together with the live stitches in the same column as you work across the row.

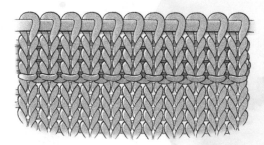

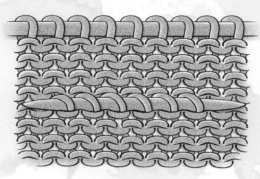

PICOTS

Picots can not only be used for pretty edgings on every side of your knitting (see pages 41, 55, and 241), but also to add decorative detail to the surface of a piece. They form little tails or spikes and can be worked to any length.

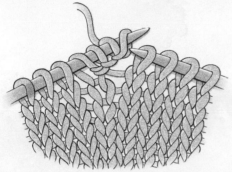

1. Knit to the position of the picot. Using the cable increase method (see page 88), cast on to the left-hand needle as many stitches as required for the picot: here, three have been cast on.

2. Knit two of the cast on stitches onto the right-hand needle.

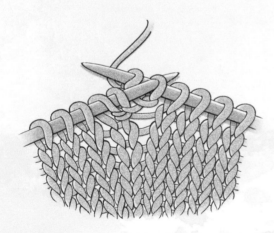

3. Use the tip of the left-hand needle to lift the first knitted stitch over the second one, binding off one stitch (see page 50). Bind off the rest of the picot stitches (three in this example) in this way.

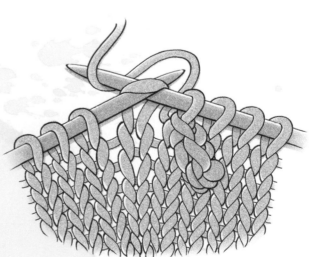

4. With the picot on the right side, complete the row.

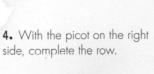

ENTRELAC

Entrelac looks so much more difficult to work than it actually is, and this is partly because the technique is difficult to illustrate. In these drawings, you need to imagine that all the open stitch loops are on the needles. The basic pattern given here will help you grasp the method, and will also show you how versatile it is. The triangles and rectangles can be worked in contrasting colors, or texture such as cables.

Cast on 40 sts very loosely.
Work base triangles as follows:
First base triangle
Rows 1–2: K2, turn, p2, turn.
Rows 3–4: K3, turn, p3, turn.
Rows 5–6: K4, turn, p4, turn.
Rows 7–8: K5, turn, p5, turn.
Rows 9–10: K6, turn, p6, turn.
Rows 11–12: K7, turn, p7, turn.
Rows 13–14: K8, turn, p8, turn.
Rows 15–16: K9, turn, p9, turn.
Row 17: K10, do not turn.
Leave these sts on right-hand needle.
Second, third, and fourth base triangles
Work as given for first base triangle. Turn.

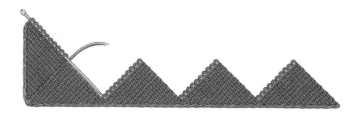

**Left-hand side edge triangle
Rows 1–2: P2, turn, sl 1, k1, turn.
Rows 3–4: Inc pwise into first st, p2tog, turn, sl 1, k2, turn.
Rows 5–6: Inc pwise into first st, p1, p2tog, turn, sl 1, k3, turn.
Rows 7–8: Inc pwise into first st, p2, p2tog, turn, sl 1, k4, turn.
Rows 9–10: Inc pwise into first st, p3, p2tog, turn, sl 1, k5, turn.
Rows 11–12: Inc pwise into first st, p4, p2tog, turn, sl 1, k6, turn.
Rows 13–14: Inc pwise into first st, p5, p2tog, turn, sl 1, k7, turn.
Rows 15–16: Inc pwise into first st, p6, p2tog, turn, sl 1, k8, turn.
Row 17: Inc pwise into first st, p7, p2tog, do not turn (all sts of fourth base triangle have been worked off).
Leave these sts on right-hand needle.

First rectangle
With right-hand needle and wrong side of work facing, pick up and p10 sts along other edge of fourth base triangle, turn.
Rows 1–2: Sl 1, k9, turn, p9, p2tog, turn.
Rep rows 1–2, 8 times more.
Next 2 rows: Sl 1, k9, turn, p9, p2tog, do not turn (all sts of third base triangle have been worked off).
Leave these sts on right-hand needle.

Second and third rectangles

Work as given for first rectangle, noting that the sts will be picked up from third and second base triangles and worked off from second and first base triangles.

Right-hand side edge triangle

With right-hand needle and wrong side of work facing, pick up and p10 sts along other side of first base triangle, turn.

Rows 1–2: K10, turn, p8, p2tog, turn.
Rows 3–4: K9, turn, p7, p2tog, turn.
Rows 5–6: K8, turn, p6, p2tog, turn.
Rows 7–8: K7, turn, p5, p2tog, turn.
Rows 9–10: K6, turn, p4, p2tog, turn.
Rows 11–12: K5, turn, p3, p2tog, turn.
Rows 13–14: K4, turn, p2, p2tog, turn.
Rows 15–16: K3, turn, p1, p2tog, turn.
Rows 17–18: K2, turn, p2tog.
Leave rem st on right-hand needle. Turn. **

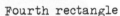
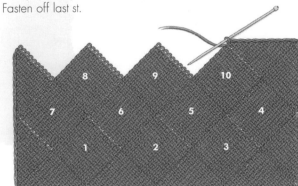

Fourth rectangle

With right-hand needle and right side of work facing, slip first st, then pick up and k9 sts along inside edge of right-hand side edge triangle, turn. *10 sts*
Rows 1–2: Sl 1, p9, turn, k9, skpo, turn.
Rep last 2 rows 8 times more.
Next 2 rows: Sl 1, p9, turn, k9, skpo, do not turn (all sts of third rectangle have been worked off).
Leave these sts on right-hand needle.

Fifth rectangle

With right-hand needle and right side of work facing, pick up and k10 sts along other side of third rectangle, then work as given for fourth rectangle (all sts of second rectangle have been worked off).

Sixth and seventh rectangles

Work as given for fifth rectangle, noting that sts will be picked up from second and first rectangles and worked off from first rectangle and left-hand side edge triangle.

Left-hand side edge triangle, and eighth, ninth, and tenth rectangles

Noting that the sts will be worked off and picked up from seventh, sixth, fifth, and fourth rectangles instead of base triangles, rep from ** to ** once more.
Work top edge triangles as follows:

First top triangle

With right-hand needle and right side of work facing, slip first st, then pick up and k9 sts along inside edge of right-hand side edge triangle, turn. *10 sts*
Rows 1–2: Sl 1, p9, turn, k9, skpo, turn.
Rows 3–4: Sl 1, p7, p2tog, turn, k8, skpo, turn.
Rows 5–6: Sl 1, p6, p2tog, turn, k7, skpo, turn.
Rows 7–8: Sl 1, p5, p2tog, turn, k6, skpo, turn.
Rows 9–10: Sl 1, p4, p2tog, turn, k5, skpo, turn.

Rows 11–12: Sl 1, p3, p2tog, turn, k4, skpo, turn.
Rows 13–14: Sl 1, p2, p2tog, turn, k3, skpo, turn.
Rows 15–16: Sl 1, p1, p2tog, turn, k2, skpo, turn.
Rows 17–18: Sl 1, p2tog, turn, k1, skpo, turn.
Rows 19–20: P2tog, turn, skpo, do not turn.
Leave rem st on right-hand needle.

Second, third, and fourth top triangles

With right-hand needle and right side of work facing, pick up and k9 sts more along tenth, ninth, and eighth rectangle edges, turn. *10 sts*
Complete as given for first top triangle.
Fasten off last st.

COLOR KNITTING

Knitting with color can be an exciting journey. Some of the techniques may be a little tricky to master, but the effort needed is well worth it because with such a huge range of shades available now in so many different fiber palettes, there has never been a better time to be able to create beautiful color patterns. There are also stunning variegated and self-striping yarns that create random patterns and stripes without having to use more than one ball of yarn.

UNDERSTANDING COLOR

Color is all around us, but we are often unaware of how important a part it plays in our lives. Our response to color is of course very personal, so all that follows are suggestions and guidelines, not rules.

CHOOSING COLORS

We may not be aware of the psychology of color, but those who wish to influence what we buy, or want to alter our mood, know just what shade to use for the best chance of getting the hoped-for result.

We all have favorite colors, and it can be very easy to fall into a color rut and just work in those shades that you love. If I did that then all my collections would feature a disproportionately large number of duck-egg blue garments…

It is good to explore and experiment with color, because sometimes colors we really like no longer suit our skin tones or hair color as well as we get older, and sometimes we just haven't looked at alternatives clearly enough, and a little exploration can produce new favorites.

For most knitters, their selection of yarn colors is limited to the ranges produced by manufacturers and designers (those knitters who dye their own yarns obviously have almost limitless options). Fortunately there are many producers—from tiny independents to huge companies—and the total range of yarns and colors available is vast. And now that the Internet makes ordering from far away sources possible (although sometimes expensive), it will usually be possible to find a color you love in the yarn type you need.

However, although most knitters are happy to choose a single color to work with, many approach selecting a palette of colors—for example, for a Fair Isle design—with trepidation. Picking the right balance, with the necessary contrasts and complements to make the design work successfully, can involve many stressful hours of thought. And if the balance you choose isn't quite right, often that only becomes obvious after quite a lot of knitting has been done, which is very disheartening.

But there are some basic principles that when understood can make the selection process much quicker, and the chance of getting it wrong much less. So the first few pages of this chapter will look at some of this color science, but only to the degree that is needed to help make more informed color choices.

WHAT IS COLOR?

Essentially color is a product of light; the colors of the rainbow are the colors of light. There is a wider range of colors of light than those we can perceive with our relatively simple human eyes, and the science of how we actually see color and how our brains process that information is complex. But for the purposes of discussing yarn palettes, the type of color we want to look at is what is usually referred to as pigment color. These are the colors of man-made products, including yarns.

The intensity of a color—how bright or dull it is—is referred to as its "saturation." A primary color is the most saturated version of that color or hue (those words mean the same thing for our purposes). And in simple terms, adding white makes a pastel or tint, adding gray makes a tone, and adding black makes a shade.

COLOR GROUPINGS

We are going to look at the color wheel and how that works (see below), and three basic ways of grouping colors: color families (see page 160), cool and warm colors (see page 161), and complementary and analogous colors (see page 162). These groupings work together in different ways and will help you to choose very different sorts of color palettes, depending on the effect you want to achieve. In addition, we'll have a brief look at color values (see page 163), as these are as important as the hues you choose in getting your color palette to work harmoniously.

THE COLOR WHEEL

This way of arranging colors will be familiar to many of us, and you may well have seen it presented in different ways for different purposes, but the basics will always be the same. The colors are arranged in a circle so that they can be compared and divided in specific ways.

A simple color wheel is made up of 12 standard colors. There are the three primary (first) colors—which are red, yellow, and blue. There are the secondary (second) colors—which are orange, green, and purple, and which are made by mixing primaries together. Finally there are the tertiary (third) colors—which are red-violet, red-orange, yellow-orange, yellow-green, and blue-green, and blue-violet, which are made by mixing the primary colors with their secondaries.

For example, primary blue and primary yellow mix to make secondary green. Then secondary green mixes with primary blue to make blue-green and with primary yellow to make yellow-green. The full range of colors is: blue, blue-violet, purple, red-violet, red, red-orange, orange, yellow-orange, yellow, yellow-green, green, and blue-green.

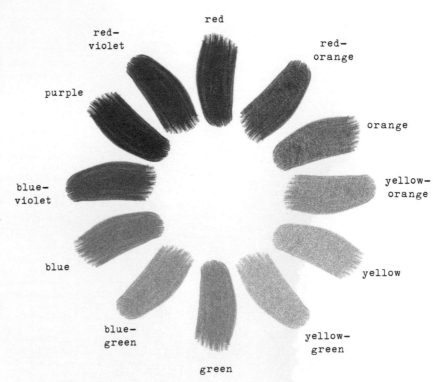

COLOR FAMILIES

A family of colors consists of all the tints, tones, and shades of a single hue, so a single family can be huge. However, like some human families, they don't all get on too well. Scarlet, maroon, carmine, ruby, and crimson are all members of the red color family, but putting them together in a design could make for an eyewateringly uncomfortable result.

We usually use the word "monochrome" to refer to a black and white palette, but what it actually means is colors from a single color family—any family. You can have a monochrome green palette. Tint green with white to make a pastel, with gray to make a tone, or with black to make a shade, and produce a range of colors that you could pick a palette from.

However, if you want to choose colors from a single family to work together in a design, you can't just pick any greens as they won't all sit happily beside each other. This is because as well as tinting, toning, and shading the primary color, you can mix other colors into a color family to create undertones. And it is these undertones that can cause problems when you are trying to pick two balls of yarn in different colors to work together in a design.

Usually a cool color will have a warm undertone, and a warm color a cool undertone (see opposite for more on cool and warm colors), and mixing the undertones can make your palette look distinctly uncomfortable.

To detect the undertone of a ball of yarn of a particular color, find another ball that is as near to a primary of that color as you can get. Hold the two together and the undertone of the first ball should be obvious; narrowing your eyes and squinting at the colors can help.

So if you are trying to pick a perfect brown to go with a green that has a warm yellow undertone, you could try a brown with a warm red undertone. The undertones are both warm, so that is promising, and the two undertone colors are analogous—they sit beside one another on the color wheel (see page 159)—which will also help them work together well.

Tints, tones, shades, and undertones from the green color family.

Tints, tones, shades, and undertones from the blue color family.

COOL AND WARM COLORS

These groups may not be quite what you expect: red and blue might be obviously warm and cool respectively, but yellow and purple might surprise you. In terms of warm and cool, you can use the way that some colors recede and others dominate to introduce a three-dimensional effect into color work such as Fair Isle patterns.

From the left: red-violet, red, red-orange, orange, yellow-orange, and yellow are the warm colors.

From the left: violet, blue-violet, blue, blue-green, green, and yellow-green are the cool colors.

The color wheel can be split into two groups, the cool colors and the warm colors. The colors in the warm half are the red and yellow primaries, their secondary, orange, and the tertiaries that are made from just that group, plus red-violet, which only has a very small amount of cool blue in it. The colors in the cool half are primary blue and all the other secondaries and tertiaries.

How warm and cool colors work visually is that warm colors stand out while cool ones recede, so if you have equal amounts of, for example, warm red-orange and cool blue-green in a palette, the red-orange will dominate the blue-green. To balance the palette you need proportionally less of the warm color compared to the cool color.

You can take advantage of this visual effect to make a design appear more three-dimensional; a red heart will bounce out against a green background. Or you can use a warm color as a very effective accent, as you only need

small details in it to make a statement. A teal jacket could have pocket linings and the bind-offs of collar and cuffs in burnt orange and the accent orange would really stand out.

People are sometimes surprised that yellow is a warm color and that most of the purple colors come into the cool half of the wheel. But if you put warm yellow next to cool blue, you will easily see how dominant the yellow is, and likewise if you put cool purple with warm red (a color combination that really isn't one I personally like at the best of times).

Tinting cool colors by adding white makes them even chillier; pale greens and pastel blues are as cold as colors can get. And shading warm colors by adding black makes them more intense, so a dark red and a pale green will always be hard to balance.

COMPLEMENTARY AND ANALOGOUS COLORS

Complementary colors are those that are opposite one another on the color wheel, while analogous colors lie next to one another. These two categories of color and the relationships between them will have an enormous influence on any color palette.

Complementary colors sit directly opposite one another on the color wheel, so in a pair, one will be a warm color and the other a cool color: red is the complementary of green, blue is the complementary of orange, and so on. We have already discussed problems of proportion with warm and cool colors (see page 161), but if you do want to use these pairings, putting complementary colors together will often—but not always, remember undertones (see page 160)—be successful.

The complementary colors of each of the three primaries—red, yellow, and blue—are each made by mixing the other two primaries. So, to complement primary blue you need to mix primary red and primary yellow to create secondary orange. Similarly, the complementary of primary red is green (primary blue and primary yellow mixed), and the complementary of primary yellow is purple (primary red and primary blue mixed).

All the colors—the secondary and tertiary colors as well as the primaries—have a complementary color, and it will always be the one directly across from it on the color wheel. And all complementary pairs will always contain between them all three primary colors, but in varying degrees. So the complementary of yellow-orange is blue-violet, and that of blue-green is red-orange.

If you want to use two complementary colors and you are having a hard time finding the perfect balance, look at tones of those colors, the versions where the hue has been muted by adding gray. These less saturated tones will often be more harmonious than stronger versions of the same color.

From the top: orange and blue are a complementary pair, as are violet and yellow-green, and purple and yellow.

Top: red, red-orange, and orange are analogous, as are blue, blue-green, and green.

Analogous colors are those that lie beside one another on the color wheel, plus the tints, tones, and shades of those colors. The classic analogous pair will be a primary color and its secondary, such as red and orange. Introducing their tertiary, red-orange, will make a classic analogous group. But these groups can be very subtle, and if you enjoy pleasing contrasts then you will need to explore further.

You can spice up an analogous group by introducing a color that lies next to the others on the wheel—and so is analogous to them—but that includes the third primary; so red, red-orange, and orange could be joined by red-violet. However, it can be very tricky to make combinations work that include all three of the primary colors. Introducing a stronger shade of one of the original colors would be more easily successful.

Another way to introduce contrast into an analogous group is to include a neutral color, such as gray or brown. The red, red-orange, and orange example we've been looking at would benefit from a rich chocolate brown to add depth.

COLOR VALUES

A color's value is its comparison to that color on the gray scale and is represented by a number. Don't be daunted by the idea of this if it seems difficult to understand; it's basically just a question of darks and lights, and our eyes automatically register color values.

On the right are the colors, and on the left are their gray-scale values.

Color values are a notion that can seem like just one more thing to worry about, but actually they are simple to assess, and important in creating a balanced palette. This is because when you look at a group of colors, one of the main things your eye registers is the difference in their values; your eye doesn't tell your brain this in so many words, so you don't consciously see the group in terms of values, but that is part of what you are registering.

The value of a color is given as a number that signifies the percentage of black that has to be mixed into white to achieve that color's value on the gray scale. The color with the lightest value is yellow, which has a number of 10, signifying that only ten parts of black have to be added to 100 parts of white to make the gray equivalent of yellow. Violet has the darkest value, with a number of 80, so 80 parts of black have to be added to 100 parts of white to make the gray equivalent of violet.

A harmonious color palette has a good balance of values, with two or three in the mid-range, and one darker and one lighter value. And it's incredibly easy to establish this; you just need a black and white photocopy of your yarn selection. You can either wrap strands around a strip of card (wrap about a ½in-wide section of each color so you can see them clearly) and take the strip to a copy shop, or, if you have a computer and photo software, you can take a picture of the balls together and turn it to black and white on the screen.

STARTING COLOR KNITTING

For many beginner knitters, the most intimidating aspects of colorwork are the multiple strands of yarn that need to be managed, and the charts that need to be understood. However, charts are just an extension of the language of knitting patterns, and multiple yarns simply need a strategy, and these pages will help you master both.

WORKING FROM A CHART

Color knitting designs—whether they are for slip stitch knitting (see pages 174–175), intarsia (see pages 176–179), or stranding (see pages 180–188)—are very often given as charts. These make it easy to see how the pattern will develop, and simple to spot any mistakes early on.

Pages 65–67 have information and general advice on working from knitting charts, so if using charts is completely new to you, do read those pages first, then come back to here for more advice on using them specifically for color knitting.

One thing to be aware of is the style of graph paper that the chart you are following is drawn on. While this doesn't in any way affect how you follow the chart, it does affect the shape of the finished motif. Because a knitted stitch is wider than it is tall (so, not square), a chart drawn on squared graph paper will not accurately show what the motif or pattern will look like when knitted up. But if proportional graph paper has been used, as it has on these pages, then the knitted result will look like the chart. So, if the motif you are going to knit looks curiously elongated and it is drawn on squared paper, don't worry; the designer will have compensated for the shape of the knitted stitch when drawing out the motif, and when knitted up it will look fine. For more on using this specialist type of graph paper, turn to page 282, and for blank sheets of the paper that you can photocopy, turn to page 314.

Usually a chart will show a repeat section of a stranded or a slip stitch pattern, or individual motifs for an intarsia design, and the written pattern will tell you how to place the chart within the knitting. Depending on how they are set out, charts for stranding and slip stitch can require a bit of working out if you are a beginner at these forms of color knitting, but charts for intarsia motifs are fairly straightforward to deal with.

INTARSIA

This color knitting technique is used to work individual areas of color (see pages 176–179), rather than an all-over or repeated pattern. At each color join, the yarns are twisted around one another to prevent holes forming. It is well worth spending time practicing the twists with scrap yarn before you start a project, as there are very slightly different techniques depending on the direction the line of color is traveling in, and making the twists smooth and neat will greatly improve the look of the finished knitting.

Motifs can be complex, requiring a number of different colors, and the best approach is to work out exactly how many different areas of color there actually are—each needing its own supply of yarn—before you start knitting; you might be surprised at how many separate areas even a simple-looking, two-color motif actually has. The chart below shows a blue heart on an orange background; the different tones of the colors represent areas that will need separate bobbins of yarn.

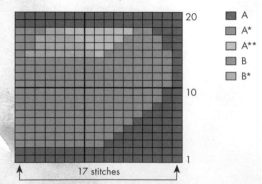

20

10

1

17 stitches

- ■ A
- ■ A*
- □ A**
- ■ B
- ■ B*

You will need to make a bobbin with enough yarn in it for the required number of stitches (see page 168), for each separate area. If the orange background yarn is called yarn A, and the blue yarn is called yarn B, then you will need the main ball of yarn A (the darkest orange) that is being used to knit with before the heart is placed. You will also need a bobbin of yarn A with enough yarn in it to knit 49 stitches (the mid-tone orange; call this bobbin A*), and a second bobbin of yarn A with enough yarn to knit 16 stitches (the palest orange; bobbin A**). You will need one bobbin of yarn B with enough yarn for 140 stitches (the darker blue; bobbin B), and a second bobbin of yarn B with enough yarn for 18 stitches (the paler blue; bobbin B*). So this relatively simple motif needs five separate supplies of yarn.

Bear in mind that if this heart was being placed in a piece of knitting wider than the number of stitches shown on this chart, there would need to be more yarn in bobbin A*, though the amount needed for bobbins A**, B, and B* will always be the same.

If this motif was being worked in stockinette, and using the bobbin names above, a breakdown of the chart in writing would read as follows.

Row 1 (RS): Knit 17 stitches in A.

Row 2: Purl 17 stitches in A.

Row 3: Knit 8 sts in A, join in bobbin B and knit 1 st in B, join in bobbin A* and knit 8 sts in A*.

Row 4: Purl 7 sts in A*, purl 3 sts in B, purl 7 sts in A.

Row 5: Knit 6 sts in A, knit 5 sts in B, knit 6 sts in A*.

Row 6: Purl 5 sts in A*, purl 7 sts in B, purl 5 sts in A.

Row 7: Knit 4 sts in A, knit 9 sts in B, knit 4 sts in A*.

Row 8: Purl 3 sts in A*, purl 11 sts in B, purl 3 sts in A.

Row 9: Knit 2 sts in A, knit 13 sts in B, knit 2 sts in A*.

Row 10: Purl 2 sts in A*, purl 13 sts in B, purl 2 sts in A.

Row 11: Knit 1 st in A, knit 15 sts in B, knit 1 st in A*.

Row 12: Purl 1 st in A*, purl 15 sts in B, purl 1 st in A.

Row 13: Knit 1 st in A, knit 15 sts in B, knit 1 st in A*.

Row 14: Purl 1 st in A*, purl 15 sts in B, purl 1 st in A.

Row 15: Knit 1 st in A, knit 7 sts in B, join in bobbin A** and knit 1 st in A**, join in bobbin B* and knit 7 sts in B*, knit 1 st in A*.

Row 16: Purl 2 sts in A*, purl 5 sts in B*, purl 3 sts in A**, purl 5 sts in B, purl 2 sts in A.

Row 17: Knit 2 sts in A, knit 4 sts in B, knit 5 sts in A**, knit 4 sts in B*, knit 2 sts in A*.

Row 18: Purl 3 sts in A*, purl 2 sts in B*, purl 7 sts in A**, purl 2 sts in B, purl 3 sts in A.

Row 19: Knit 17 stitches in A.

Row 20: Purl 17 stitches in A.

Obviously the chart presents all this information in a concise and clear way, though if this was a chart given in a commercial knitting pattern, there wouldn't be tints of the different colors to signify separate bobbins: it would be up to the knitter to work out what was needed. It may seem complicated, but if you photocopy the chart and mark off sections with a pencil to break the motif down into separate areas, it will be easy to work out how many bobbins you need.

STRANDING

This is the technique to use for a color pattern that is repeated across the knitting (see pages 180–187). This type of colorwork is often referred to as Fair Isle, though that is actually a specific style of stranded knitting that was developed in the eponymous Scottish island.

When you work stranding, the color of yarn that is not making stitches is carried across the back of the work, and correctly tensioning these loose strands, which are called "floats," is key to working the technique well. There are four different ways of holding the yarns (although the way the strands interlace on the back is always the same), and while there is a method that is usually easiest for beginners (see page 181), it's worth experimenting with all the methods shown to find the one that is most comfortable and efficient for you.

A repeated pattern will usually be shown as a single pattern repeat, plus any extra stitches, such as edge stitches, that are needed to complete the pattern and place it correctly in the knitting (for more on working pattern repeats, turn to page 67).

When you are working a repeat pattern using the stranding technique, you must strand the yarns right across the back of the knitting, from edge stitch to edge stitch, even if the final stitch in a given color is several stitches in from an edge. Carry the float across the back and use one of the weaving-in techniques (see pages 185–187) to catch it into the edge stitch. You must do this because the floats running across the back of the knitting make the fabric double-thickness, and if the stranding doesn't run right across, the last stitches in a given color will pull and distort, and the uneven thickness will affect the look of the knitting, and the way the fabric hangs.

If shaping needs to be worked within a patterned area, then increase stitches are usually worked into plain-color knitting at either end of the row, and you must remember to strand the floats across the back of the whole increase section. If there are a lot of increases to be worked, then in order to avoid what can become unsightly areas of plain color, parts of a pattern repeat can be worked into the increased stitches as enough of them are made to accommodate it. The principles of doing this are exactly the same as for lace repeats, and are explained on page 140.

WORKING IN THE ROUND

If a chart is laid out for straight knitting, but you would like to work in the round (see pages 108–109), then, depending on the color pattern, you may be able to do this, but you will need to follow the chart in a different way.

Stranded patterns can easily be worked in the round, and indeed, this can be an easier option because every row will be a right-side row. This means that you are always looking at the right side of the work, and only using the knit row techniques for interlacing the yarns (see pages 181–184), which for many knitters will make it easier to keep an even gauge of the floats and stitches.

As every row is a right-side row, you need to follow every row of the chart from right to left, rather than following the alternate purl rows from left to right. And you will need to work out how many stitches to cast on to make the pattern run continuously around the knitting.

Usually a chart will have been worked out so that once the garment is sewn up (and so the edge stitches are taken into the seam) the repeat pattern is continuous across the seam; in this case you simply need to drop the edge stitches from the number of stitches to be cast on. Remember that if you are casting on for a sweater, this will mean dropping four stitches, one from each edge of both the front and the back pieces.

However, if the charted pattern has not been worked out for the pattern to run correctly, then you will need to make adjustments. The easiest way to check is to photocopy the chart a few times, cut out the repeat sections, cut off the edge stitches, and sticky tape the pieces together to see how the pattern runs. If need be, add in or take out stitches to make the pattern work, but you will need to keep the overall size of the piece in mind, and consider whether the additional stitches will affect any shaping.

Intarsia motifs are not suited to working in the round, because the motif yarn will always be on the wrong edge of the motif. You either have to weave in (see pages 185–187) the motif yarn right around the knitting (in which case you would also weave the main yarn in across the back of the motif to keep the fabric an even thickness), or use a separate length of yarn for every row of the motif, which means an awful lot of ends to try and sew in neatly!

CHOOSING WHICH TECHNIQUE TO USE

In many instances it will be obvious as to whether intarsia or stranding is the appropriate technique to use for a colorwork design, and often a commercial pattern will specify what method to use. However, more complex patterns can often be most successfully worked using a combination of the two techniques.

Although stranding creates a double-thickness fabric and intarsia a single-thickness one, stranding can be the better technique for working just a few stitches in a color, and a small area of thicker fabric within a motif will usually not be a problem if the yarn is no thicker than worsted-weight.

To knit this chart, you could work the heart shape in intarsia, using two bobbins of yarn for the heart and three for the background, as detailed on page 165. As the cluster of green stitches in the center of the heart is so small, you could use a bobbin with enough yarn for 13 stitches to knit it, but strand the blue heart yarn across the central cluster of green stitches to avoid having to join in yet another bobbin of blue yarn, which you would have to do if you used the intarsia technique to knit the green stitches.

The diagonal single lines of green stitches could also be stranded, and if you chose to do that you could use the two ends of yarn technique (see page 188) to knit the upper parts of the two lines. However, it can be tricky to knit single stitches in a color and keep the gauge even so that they match the rest of the knitting, so a better option would be to duplicate stitch the green lines (see pages 189 and 192–193).

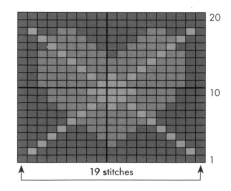

19 stitches

SLIP STITCH CHARTS

As each pattern row is worked twice using one color yarn (so that yarn is returned back to the right-hand side of the knitting, ready to be used the next time it's needed), the charts can be presented in various ways. Stitches can be slipped in different ways (see pages 174–175), and the pattern will specify which one to use.

If you were working a slip stitch pattern in stockinette stitch, then each knit row would set the pattern of stitches worked and stitches slipped, and the subsequent purl row would follow that pattern. So it isn't necessary to show the wrong side rows on a chart, and some designer's charts do and some don't, which can lead to confusion, especially if you are trying slip stitch knitting for the first time.

For example, a pattern might be written out as follows:

Using A, cast on 21 sts.
Row 1 (WS): Purl.
Row 2: Using B, k4, [sl1, k3] to last st, k1.
Row 3: Using B, p4, [sl1, p3] to last st, p1.
Row 4: Using A, k1, [sl1, k3] to end.
Row 5: Using A, [p3, sl1] to last st, p1.
Row 6: Using B, k2, [sl1, k3] to last 3 sts, sl1, k2.
Row 7: Using B, p2, [sl1, p3] to last 3 sts, sl1, p2.
Row 8: Using A, [k3, sl1] to last st, k1.
Row 9: Using A, p1, [sl1, p3] to end.
Rows 2–8 set the patt and are repeated.

Shown in full, this pattern might be charted in three different ways. (Note that stitch 1 and stitch 21 are edge stitches, so these will never be slipped.)

The chart below shows the whole pattern as it is written out, with both the knit and purl rows, and with symbols indicating which stitches are slipped on which rows. You can clearly see the pattern of zigzagging lines that is being formed, but as there is no color, you can't see how the finished pattern looks.

The version below of the chart shows the foundation purl row, but no other purl rows, as they are duplicates of the knit rows. The chart is not more difficult to follow than the fuller version, but as a visual reference, it gives only a clue as to what the finished knitting will look like.

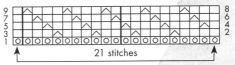

21 stitches

The final version of the chart, shown below, is the most informative, as it not only shows all the rows with symbols for the slipped and purled stitches, but it also shows the colors so the final pattern is clear.

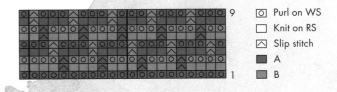

⊡	Purl on WS
☐	Knit on RS
⟋⟍	Slip stitch
■	A
■	B

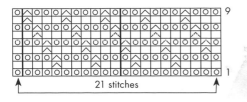

21 stitches

⊡	Purl on WS
☐	Knit on RS
⟋⟍	Slip stitch

BOBBINS

When working with more than two colors across a row it can be very difficult to prevent the yarns tangling. Rather than work with whole balls that roll around, it is better to have little bobbins of color that hang close to the back of the knitting. Hand-made bobbins are called butterflies and are best for small amounts of yarn; you can buy plastic bobbins for larger amounts.

1. To work out how much yarn to make into a bobbin for a particular area of color, count how many stitches are in the area. This is easy enough if you are working from a chart (see page 164), but if you are working from a written pattern, then estimate the number, erring on the side of generosity. Twist the yarn loosely around a needle once for each stitch, and add a little extra for sewing in the ends.

2. With the tail of the yarn in the middle of your palm, wrap the working end in a figure-eight around your thumb and little finger, as shown, until about 4in is left free.

There are various types of plastic bobbins you can buy (see page 27), and these work well if you need larger amounts of yarn for a bobbin. Only unwind a little yarn at a time to keep the working yarns short.

3. Slip the bundle off your thumb and finger and wrap the tail end tightly around the center to tie the bundle, tucking the end into the wrap. Make sure that the free end that was in the center of your palm sticks out of the bundle. Pull this end gently to pull the yarn from the center of the bobbin.

CONTROLLING MULTIPLE YARNS

Even if you are only using two colors, yarns can tangle very quickly, particularly if you are using wool or wool-blend yarns because the fibers tend to stick to one another. With four or five yarns the problem is multiplied. Here are some tips for keeping tangles at bay.

It's best to use the yarn by pulling it out from the center of a ball; this stops the ball rolling around and helps prevent tangling. Find the outer end and tuck it out of the way under some of the outer wraps of the ball. The outer end will usually have been tucked into the opening in the middle of the ball, so turn the ball over and use your fingers to feel inside the opening from the other side to find the loosely wound section in the center, and pull it out. If a lot of yarn comes out along with the center end, just wind the excess around the outside of the ball; it will get used quickly enough.

Most people turn the work in the same direction at the end of each row, and if you do this when working with more than one strand of yarn, the strands will quickly twist around one another. If you are using just two yarns, then getting into the habit of turning the knitting clockwise at the end of one row and counterclockwise at the end of the next will prevent the yarns twisting.

If you are using several colors then it is well worth managing the yarns properly, or you will end up spending hours untangling them. If you are using just short lengths of each color, then you can make bobbins (see opposite).

If you are using whole balls, then placing them in separate containers and arranging those around you is a good solution. The plastic cups with domed lids that juice is sold in are a good size for a ball of yarn, though they are lightweight and fall over easily. Put the ball into the cup, thread the working end of yarn through the hole in the lid, put the lid on, and start knitting. If all the balls are in separate containers like this, then the strands may twist but the balls won't tangle, and you simply have to turn the knitting around as many times as needed to untwist the strands.

If you have an eyelet kit, then you can punch holes in the metal lids of glass jam jars and fit an eyelet (to stop the rough edges of the hole abrading the yarn). Or, if you can crochet, then crocheting a lid with a central hole is a good option. There are patterns on the Internet, though designing your own is simple enough. Work a flat circle the size of the top of the jar, then stop increasing and work several rounds to make the sides of the crochet lid.

Yarn bowls are another popular option, and chopstick bowls stand in for them very well. Or you can put all the balls of yarn into a shoebox, punch holes in the lid, thread the ends through, then put the lid on.

STRIPES

This is the easiest type of color knitting as you are only working with one color at a time, so the most novice of knitters can work stripe patterns. Although stripes are classics, they really don't ever have to be boring as there are so many variations, including texture and blurring.

JOINING IN A NEW COLOR

You can join in colors at a side seam (see page 71) and sew in the ends (see page 227) after you have completed the knitting, and sewn up your seams if appropriate. Or you can weave in the ends on the wrong side as you go, as shown here.

1. On the row before the new color is required, work to about a dozen stitches from the end. Lay the new color over the existing color, as shown, then purl the next stitch in the existing color to catch the end of the new color in against the back of the work.

2. *Lay the new color over the tip of the right-hand needle.

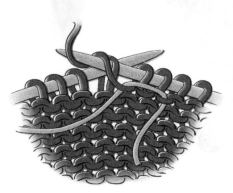

3. Work the next stitch in the existing color, holding the new color high to stop it from going through the stitch.

4. Holding the new color down, work the next stitch in the existing color. Repeat from * to the end of the row. The new color is then secured and ready to work the next row with. You can also weave in the ends of unwanted colors using the same technique.

CARRYING YARN UP THE SIDE OF THE WORK

In repeat stripe patterns you do not need to join in a new color for every stripe. Instead you can carry the colors not in use up the side of the work. The loops that doing this creates will be sewn into the seams, though short loops look tidy enough on unseamed edges, such as the edges of a scarf.

1. If you are working a two-row stripe, then just knit the first stitch of the row after it with the previous color.

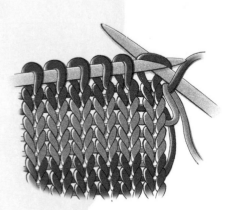

2. If the stripes are wider stripes, catch in the yarn being carried up the side at the start of every third row. Put the right-hand needle into the first stitch, lay the yarn to be carried over the working yarn, and work the stitch in the working yarn.

CARRYING MULTIPLE YARNS

You can carry more than one yarn up the side of the work and so knit multicolored stripe patterns. However, if you carry too many together they will form a thick cord along the side that is unattractive and that can make for bulky seams. Depending on the numbers of rows in each stripe in the pattern, you may be able to carry some colors up each side, thus dividing the bulk.

SINGLE-ROW STRIPES

If you work stripes that are just one-row deep, then the next color yarn won't always be at the right edge, so you have to work these stripes on a double-pointed needle for a narrow project, or back and forth on a circular needle for a wider fabric.

1. Using the first color, cast on the number of stitches required and knit one row. Join in the second color and purl one row. Then slide the stitches along the needle so that the first color is at the working end, ready to be used again. Purl a row in that color and then the second color will be in the right place to knit the next row. Continue in this way, sliding the work along the needle and knitting or purling rows as needed to keep the stripe pattern and stockinette stitch correct.

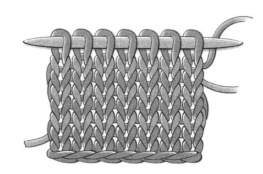

TEXTURE STRIPES

Stripes can be textural instead of colored. Bear in mind that some stitch patterns will pull fabric in widthways, and some will knit up shorter than others, so work a swatch of the patterns you'd like to use before you start a project.

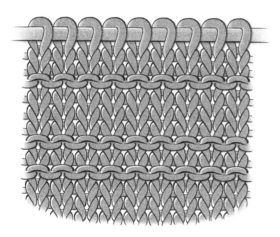

1. This drawing shows stripes of garter stitch and stockinette stitch. Both these stitch patterns knit to the same width, but garter stitch knits up shorter than stockinette, so if you were going to add garter stripes to an existing stockinette pattern you would have to work extra rows to compensate for the shorter garter rows.

BLURRED STRIPES

If a fine yarn is knitted in stripes held together with a thicker yarn, the thicker yarn shows around the thinner one and the effect is a blurred stripe.

1. By carefully choosing tones of colors in thicker and thinner yarns, and changing the combinations of the yarns worked alone or held together, very effective graduated color and soft-edged stripes can be produced. However, the fabric won't be an even thickness, and can become quite bulky in some places.

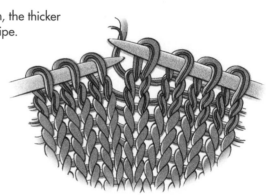

VERTICAL STRIPES

Knitting vertical stripes involves using the intarsia technique, and it can be quite tricky to keep the edges of long vertical stripes neat and firm. The alternative is to knit the piece sideways (if that is possible) so that horizontal stripes become vertical.

1. You need a separate bobbin of yarn for each stripe. Cast on using the technique you prefer (see pages 34–39); here the thumb technique is being used. Start each new color stripe with a slip knot on the needle, and interlink the yarns as shown.

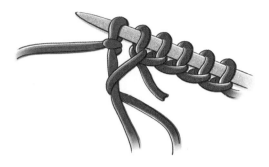

2. Work the stripes, using the method for changing colors in a vertical line (see page 178) to link the yarns between each stripe and so stop holes forming.

CHEVRON STRIPES

Zigzag stripes are maybe more well-known in crochet, but work beautifully in knitting, too. They are very easy to work as they are only horizontal stripes shaped with increases and decreases; there is no complicated color joining to do.

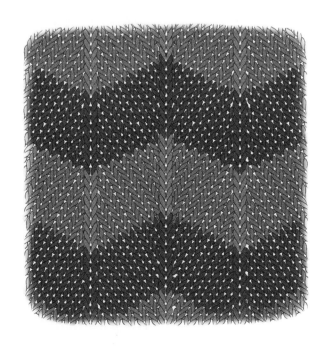

1. There are variations on how the increases and decreases (see pages 80–97) are made for chevrons, and how many stitches there are between them, but here is a typical chevron pattern for two-color stripes.

Using yarn A, cast on a multiple of 14 sts + 2 sts.
Row 1: Purl.
Row 2: K1, inc, k4, ssk, k2tog, k4 *[inc] twice, k4, ssk, k2tog, k4*; rep from * to last 2 sts, inc, k1.
Rep rows 1–2, 3 times more.
Change to yarn B.
Rep rows 1–2, 4 times.
Work in 8-row stripe patt as set.

SLIP STITCH KNITTING

Although the results of this technique look complex, it is actually very simple to work because you are only dealing with one color at a time. The fabric produced will be denser, as slipping the stitches has the effect of pulling in the fabric. Slip stitch knitting can also be worked in one color to create texture patterns.

SLIPPING A STITCH PURLWISE

The only thing that you need to know for slip stitch knitting—other than knitting or purling—is how to slip a stitch. The slipped stitches are most commonly worked purlwise on both knit and purl rows.

1. On a purl row, from right to left, insert the right-hand needle into the next stitch on the left-hand needle and slip it over onto the right-hand needle without purling it.

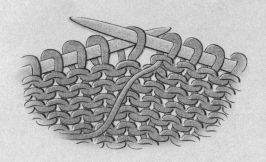

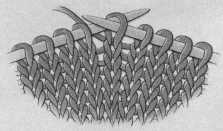

2. On a knit row, from right to left, insert the right-hand needle into the next stitch on the left-hand needle and slip it over onto the right-hand needle without purling it.

SLIPPING A STITCH KNITWISE

This method is used less often, and on both a knit and a purl row the stitch will be turned to face in the opposite direction to the stitches that are not slipped this way.

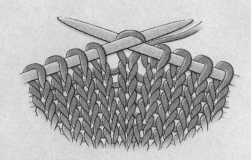

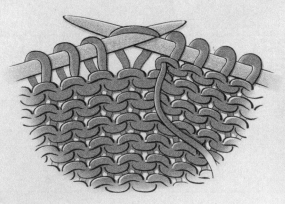

1. On a knit row, from left to right, insert the right-hand needle into the next stitch on the left-hand needle and slip it over onto the right-hand needle without knitting it.

2. On a purl row, from left to right, insert the right-hand needle into the next stitch on the left-hand needle and slip it over onto the right-hand needle without purling it.

SLIPPING A STITCH WITH YARN FORWARD

Sometimes you will be asked to move the working yarn from its natural position when slipping a stitch. This is usually done in textured stitch patterns, but sometimes in color ones. The whole action will usually be abbreviated as "slip wyif." The instruction to "bring yarn forward" is usually abbreviated as "yf," and must not be confused with the "yf" yarnover (see page 136).

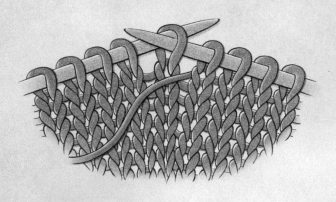

1. On a knit row the working yarn will naturally be at the back, on the side of the work facing away from you. Bring the yarn between the tips of the needles to the front of the work, then slip the stitch as instructed (here it is slipped purlwise), then take the yarn between the needles to the back again, ready to knit the next stitch on the left-hand needle. Slipping the stitch with the yarn forward in this way leaves a little bar of yarn in front of the slipped stitch on the right side of the work.

SLIPPING A STITCH WITH YARN BACK

This is the same principle as slipping a stitch with the yarn forward, but in reverse. The whole action is usually abbreviated to "slip wyib" or "wyb." Here, we are assuming that the right side is stockinette stitch and the wrong side reverse stockinette stitch.

1. On a purl row the working yarn will naturally be at the front, on the side of the work facing you. Take the yarn between the tips of the needles to the back of the work, then slip the stitch as instructed (here it is slipped purlwise), then bring the yarn between the needles to the front again, ready to purl the next stitch on the left-hand needle. Slipping the stitch with the yarn back in this way leaves a little bar of yarn in front of the slipped stitch on the right side of the work.

INTARSIA

This is the method used for larger blocks of color rather than all-over patterns. To keep the fabric as flat and neat as possible, separate balls or bobbins (see page 168) are used for each area of color. When changing color, the yarns are twisted together once to avoid creating a hole. I tug both yarns after twisting to tighten them and avoid loose stitches.

JOINING IN A NEW COLOR

With intarsia you are often not able to join in yarn at the beginning of a row (see page 71). This method lets you join in within a row neatly to avoid a finish that looks untidy or creates a weak spot in the work.

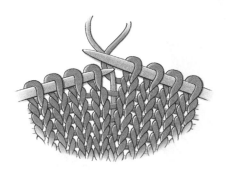

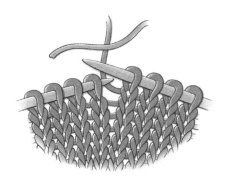

1. On a knit row, work to the color change. Lay the new color over the existing color, with the working yarn to the right and a tail about 4in long to the left.

2. Make a single twist to take the new color under the old color, as shown.

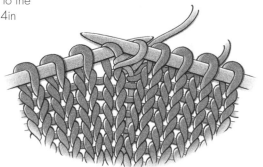

3. Knit the stitch with the new color. Knit a few more stitches, then pull gently on the tail to tighten up the first stitch in the new color. Sew in the tail (see page 227) when the knitting is complete.

4. On a purl row, work to the color change. Lay the new color over the existing color, with the working yarn to the right and a tail about 4in long to the left. Twist the two yarns together with a single twist, as shown.

5. Purl the stitch with the new color. Purl a few more stitches, then pull gently on the tail to tighten up the first stitch in the new color. Sew in the tail (see page 227) when the knitting is complete.

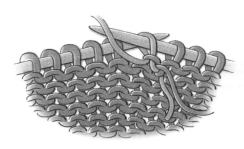

COLOR CHANGE ON A SLANT TO THE RIGHT

Use this method when the line of the new color is moving across and up to the right on the right side of the work. You can see more clearly how the two yarns interlink on the back on the purl row illustrations.

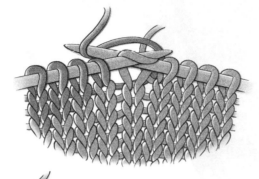

1. On a knit row, work to the second to last stitch in the old color (green in this example). Insert the right-hand needle knitwise into the last stitch, then bring the new color (pink in this example) across under the old color, wrap it around the tip of the right-hand needle, and knit the stitch in the new color.

2. On a purl row, work to the last stitch in the new color (pink in this example), and knit the next stitch in the new color. Insert the right-hand needle purlwise into the next stitch on the left-hand needle, then bring the old color (green in this example) up under the new color, and purl the stitch in the old color.

COLOR CHANGE ON A SLANT TO THE LEFT

This is the method when the line of the new color is moving across and up to the left on the right side of the work. It is a slightly different procedure for the knit and purl rows than on the slant to the right, but the colors end up linked in the same way on the back.

1. On a knit row, work to the last stitch in the new color (gray in this example) and knit the next stitch in the new color. Insert the right-hand needle knitwise into the next stitch on the left-hand needle, then bring the old color (green in this example) up from under the new color, and knit the stitch in the old color.

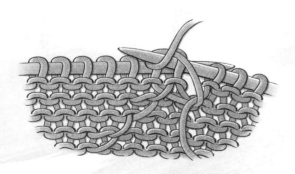

2. On a purl row, work to the last but one stitch in the old color (green in this example). Insert the right-hand needle purlwise into this stitch, then bring the new color (gray in this example) across under the old color, wrap it around the tip of the right-hand needle, and purl the stitch in the new color.

VERTICAL COLOR CHANGE

Vertical lines require careful tensioning and linking of the two yarn colors, because they are prone to either being loose, or for the knit and purl stitches to vary in size, thus making stitches larger and smaller on alternate rows. Tug the working ends of yarn after making the stitches where the yarns are linked, and make sure your gauge in the knit and the purl rows is the same.

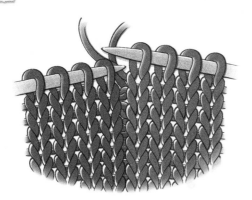

1. On a knit row, work to the last stitch in the old color (blue in this example). Bring the new color (red in this example) under the old color and knit the next stitch firmly.

2. On a purl row, work to the last stitch in the old color (blue in this example). Bring the new color (red in this example) under the old color and purl the next stitch firmly.

CARRYING YARN ACROSS THE BACK

Sometimes you may need to carry a yarn across the back of the work to where it is needed for the next row, and if you have forgotten to weave it in on the previous row (see pages 185–187), you can use this method. Getting the length of the loop right can be tricky, but practice will make perfect. As the technique is worked on the wrong side, you can see what is happening more clearly on the purl row.

1. On a knit row, work to where the new color is needed. Bring the yarn across the back of the stitches, keeping the strand quite loose. Knit the stitch with the new color.

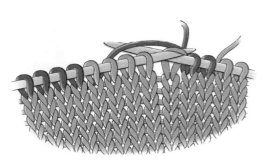

2. Knit the next stitch. *Then insert the left-hand needle into the next stitch and under the strand. Knit the stitch with the new color, but be careful not to pull the strand through the stitch. Knit the next stitch to catch the strand against the back of the work. Repeat from * to catch all of the strand in.

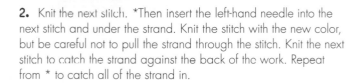

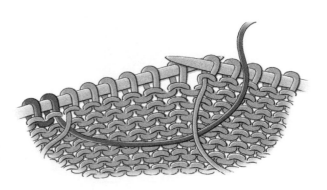

3. On a purl row, work to where the new color is needed. Bring the yarn across the back of the stitches, keeping the strand quite loose. Take it under the old color and purl the stitch with the new color.

4. Purl the next stitch. *Then insert the left-hand needle into the next stitch and under the strand.

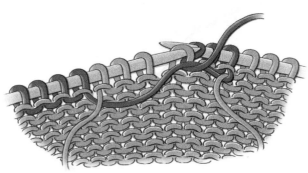

5. Purl the stitch with the new color, but be careful not to pull the loop through the stitch. Purl the next stitch to catch the strand against the back of the work. Repeat from * to catch all of the strand in.

STRANDING

This is the method of color knitting for all-over patterns. It is often referred to as Fair Isle, and is associated with particular patterns from the Scottish island, but Fair Isle is actually a style of pattern that is worked using stranding. Scandinavian, or Nordic, knitting is also a type of stranding, as is Bohus. Traditionally, Fair Isle is worked using only two colors in a row, as shown in these illustrations.

JOINING IN A NEW COLOR

New yarns are usually joined in at the start of a row (see page 71), and carried right across the fabric, but sometimes you may have to join in in the middle of a row if only a section is being stranded.

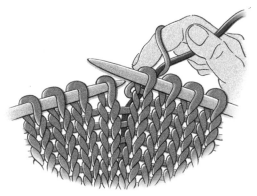

1. On a knit row, work to the color change. Lay the new color over the existing color, with the working yarn to the right and a tail about 4in long to the left. Make a single twist to take the new color under the old color, as shown.

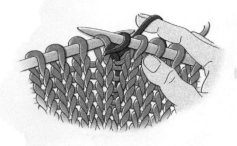

2. Knit the stitch with the new color. Knit a few more stitches, then pull gently on the tail to tighten up the first stitch in the new color. Sew in the tail (see page 227) when the knitting is complete.

3. On a purl row, work to the color change. Lay the new color over the existing color, with the working yarn to the right and a tail about 4in long to the left. Twist the two yarns together with a single twist, as shown.

4. Purl the stitch with the new color. Purl a few more stitches, then pull gently on the tail to tighten up the first stitch in the new color. Sew in the tail when the knitting is complete.

HOLDING ONE YARN AT A TIME

This is the least efficient method of managing the yarns, but is usually the easiest for beginners. The technique is simple enough, it's getting the gauge right that takes practice. The float (the strand of the second color yarn coming across the back of the first color stitches) should lie flat against the back of the knitting without being stretched, or it will pull the fabric in.

1. On a knit row, knit the stitches in color A (red in this example), bringing it across over the strand of color B (brown in this example) to wrap around the needle.

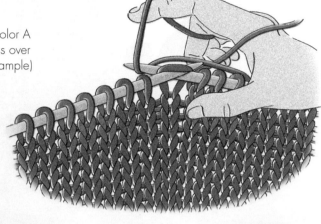

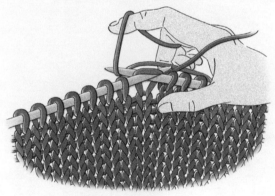

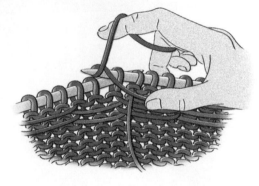

2. At the color change, drop color A and pick up color B, bringing it across under the strand of color A to wrap around the needle, and making sure not to pull it too tight. Knit the stitches in color B. When you change back to color A, bring it across over the strand of color B.

3. On a purl row, purl the stitches in color A (red in this example), bringing it across over the strand of color B (brown in this example) to wrap around the needle.

4. At the color change, drop color A and pick up color B, bringing it across under the strand of color A to wrap around the needle, and making sure not to pull it too tight. Purl the stitches in color B. When you change back to color A, bring it across over the strand of color B. You can clearly see how the strands interlace at the back of the work; color A (red) always comes across over color B (brown), and color B always comes across under color A.

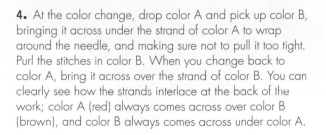

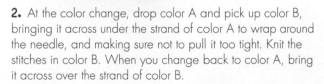

HOLDING BOTH YARNS IN YOUR RIGHT HAND

As you are not dropping the yarn every time you change to work with the other color, this method can be quite quick when you get used to it, but you need to practice tensioning the yarn for the stitches and floats with the second finger. The float (the strand of the second color yarn coming across the back of the first color stitches) should lie flat against the back of the knitting, but without being too tight. This is a good method for those who find any left-hand use difficult.

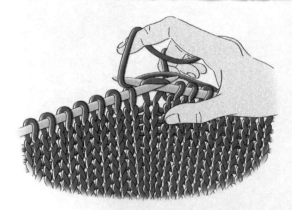

1. Place the color yarn to be used first, color A (red in this example), over your index finger, and the second color, color B (blue in this example), over your second finger, then tension them both together around the other fingers of your right hand in your preferred way (see page 30). On a knit row, using your index finger, knit the stitches in color A, bringing it across over the strand of color B to wrap around the needle.

2. At the color change, lift your index finger high and out of the way and bring your second finger forward to knit the stitches in color B, bringing it across under the strand of color A to wrap around the needle, and making sure not to pull it too tight.

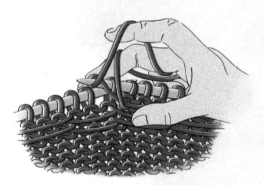

3. On a purl row, arrange the colors in your right hand as for a knit row, with color A (red in this example), over your index finger, and color B (blue in this example), over your second finger. Using your index finger, purl the stitches in color A, bringing it across over the strand of color B to wrap around the needle.

4. At the color change, lift your index finger high and out of the way and bring your second finger forward to purl the stitches in color B, bringing it across under the strand of color A to wrap around the needle: this is usually the trickiest bit of the process to do and get the tension on the strand of yarn correct. You can clearly see how the strands interlace at the back of the work; color A (red) always comes across over color B (blue), and color B always comes across under color A.

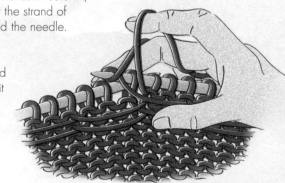

HOLDING BOTH YARNS IN YOUR LEFT HAND

This is a particularly good technique if you knit Continental style (see pages 46–47), because the yarns are always wrapped around the right-hand needle as for that method, and it will probably come more naturally to you. You work the color changes as for holding both yarns in your right hand (see opposite), but there are three possible ways of holding the yarn in your left hand.

1. Place the color yarn to be used first, color A (red in this example), over your index finger, and the second color, color B (pink in this example), over your second finger, then tension them both together around the other fingers of your left hand in your preferred way (see page 31). Use your index finger to knit the stitches in color A, and your second finger to knit the stitches in color B.

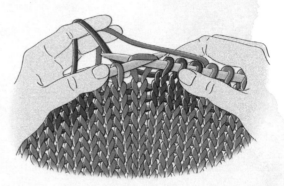

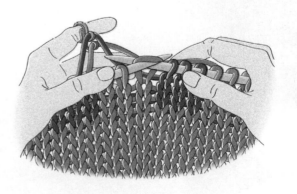

2. This method requires you to catch the yarn with the tip of the needle rather than moving your left-hand fingers very much. Place both color yarns over your index finger, with the color to be used first, color A (red in this example), to the left of the second color, color B (pink in this example), then tension them both together around the other fingers of your left hand in your preferred way.

3. This method involves wearing a yarn ring (see page 27), and also requires you to catch the yarn with the tip of the needle rather than moving your left-hand fingers very much, but your index finger can be more relaxed than in method 2. Place the yarn ring on your index finger with the loops hanging down, as shown. Thread the color to be used first, color A (red in this example), into the left loop, and the second color, color B (pink in this example), into the right loop, then tension them both together around the other fingers of your left hand in your preferred way.

HOLDING ONE YARN IN EACH HAND

This is the fastest and, with some practice, most even way of holding yarns. Try working with your non-dominant hand only on test swatches to get better at controlling yarn with it. The color to be used first goes in the dominant hand, and the following illustrations assume that the knitter is right-handed. The interlacing of the strands happens automatically because of the hand positions.

1. Place the color yarn to be used first, color A (blue in this example), in your right hand, and the second color, color B (green in this example), in your left hand, tensioning each yarn around the other fingers in your preferred way (see pages 30–31). On a knit row, using your right hand, knit the stitches in color A, which will automatically come across over the strand of color B to wrap around the needle.

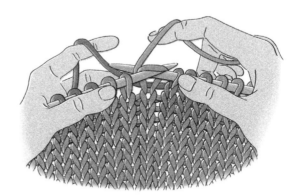

2. At the color change, insert the right-hand needle into the next stitch then draw a loop through from color B held in your left hand, which will automatically come across under the strand of color A to wrap around the needle. Make sure not to pull color B too tight.

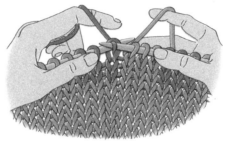

3. On a purl row, arrange the colors in your hands as for a knit row, with color A (blue in this example), in your right hand, and the second color, color B (green in this example), in your left hand. Using your right hand, purl the stitches in color A, which will automatically come across over the strand of color B to wrap around the needle.

4. At the color change, insert the right-hand needle into the next stitch then draw a loop through from color B held in your left hand, pushing the strand down with your left index finger to tension it around the needle. Color B will automatically come across under the strand of color A to wrap around the needle. Make sure not to pull color B too tight. You can clearly see how the strands interlace at the back of the work; color A (blue) always comes across over color B (green), and color B always comes across under color A.

WEAVING IN USING ONE HAND

You want to avoid having floats at the back of the work that are too long or they will snag. If there are more than four stitches between colors, then you need to catch the floats of the yarn not in use against the back of the knitting on every second or third stitch as you work, but not the same stitches on every row to avoid puckers on the front. Do not pull floats too tightly. Use this method if you are not holding one yarn in each hand.

1. On a knit row, insert the right-hand needle into the stitch you need to weave the yarn into (brown in this example). Lay the yarn to be woven in (red in this example) over the working yarn, then knit the stitch. Make sure the woven in yarn does not appear through the stitch; it should just be held firmly against the back of the work.

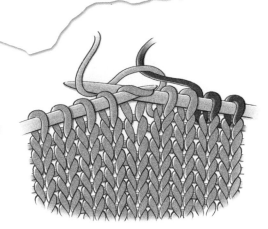

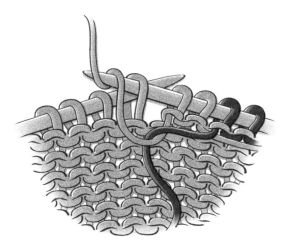

2. On a purl row the principle is the same as for a knit row. Lay the yarn to be woven in over the working yarn, then purl the stitch, holding the woven-in yarn against the back of the work.

WEAVING IN USING BOTH HANDS

This is the method for catching long floats against the back of the knitting if you are stranding with one yarn held in each hand (see page 184). As with one-hand weaving in (see page 185), catch the yarn every two or three stitches, and do not pull the floats too tightly.

1. Place the color yarn you are knitting with, color A (pink in this example), in your right hand, and the yarn to be woven in, color B (green in this example), in your left hand, tensioning each yarn around the other fingers in your preferred way (see pages 30–31). On a knit row, insert the right-hand needle into the stitch you need to weave the yarn in to, and lay the yarn to be woven in over the tip of that needle.

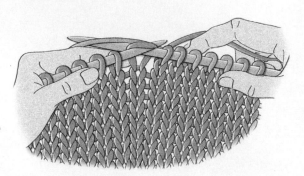

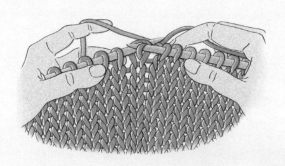

2. Wrap yarn A around the tip of the needle ready to knit; it will automatically slide under yarn B.

3. Knit the stitch in yarn A, making sure that yarn B doesn't come through the stitch at the same time. Knit the next stitch in yarn A to hold the float of yarn B in place against the back of the work.

4. On a purl row, arrange the colors in your hands as for a knit row, with color A in your right hand, and the yarn to be woven in, color B, in your left hand. Insert the right-hand needle into the stitch you need to weave the yarn into, and lay the yarn to be woven in over the tip of that needle.

5. Wrap yarn A around the tip of the needle and purl the stitch, making sure that yarn B doesn't come through the stitch at the same time. Purl the next stitch in yarn A to hold the float of yarn B in place against the back of the work.

CONTINUOUS WEAVING IN

This technique makes a very thick, firm knitted fabric by weaving the floats above or below alternate stitches. The woven-in yarn has a tendency to show through on the front. You can hold the yarn in one or both hands, though both is easier and faster.

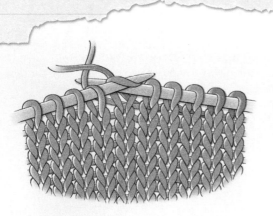

1. The yarn is woven under and over alternate stitches. On a knit row, insert the right-hand needle into a stitch you need to weave the yarn over, and lay the yarn to be woven in over the tip of that needle, then knit the stitch with the working yarn. Make sure the woven-in yarn does not appear through the stitch.

2. To weave the yarn under the next stitch in the row, knit the stitch with the working yarn, keeping the yarn to be woven in under the needle.

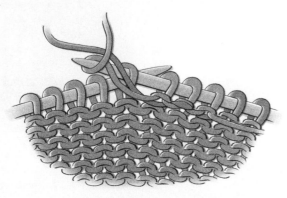

3. The same principles apply on a purl row. Insert the right-hand needle into a stitch you need to weave the yarn over, and lay the yarn to be woven in over the tip of that needle, then purl the stitch with the working yarn. Make sure the woven-in yarn does not appear through the stitch.

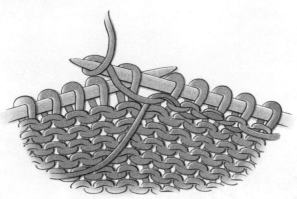

4. To weave the yarn under the next stitch in the row, purl the stitch with the working yarn, keeping the yarn to be woven in under the needle.

USING TWO ENDS OF YARN

Sometimes you can use both ends of a length of yarn to knit part of a motif or start a bit of stranding, and this saves on sewing in ends afterward (see page 227). Look carefully at a pattern before you start and see if this technique is applicable anywhere. Here, it's used at the bottom of a V shape.

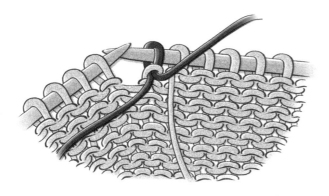

1. Work to where you can start the contrast color; in this example it's the center stitch of a V shape. Cut a length of contrast color yarn long enough to complete the pattern or motif and fold it in half. Work the center stitch with the contrast color at the halfway point.

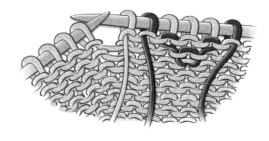

2. As you work the rows, use both ends of the length of contrast color yarn to work the appropriate stitches. The background yarn is stranded across the back of the contrast stitches (see pages 181–184).

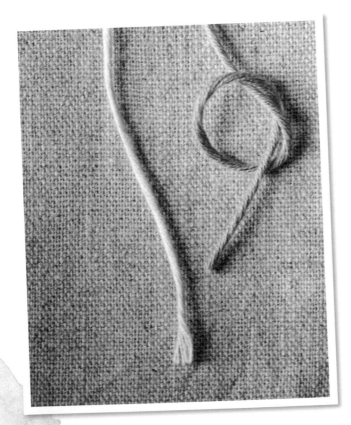

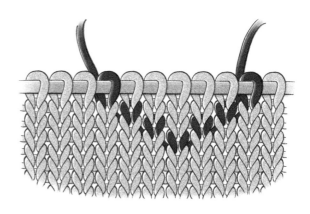

3. Once the shape is complete, you only have the two ends to sew in, not the two extra ends that would have been at the base of the V if you had used two strands of contrast color yarn.

DUPLICATE STITCH AND COLOR KNITTING

Single lines, or single or small groups of stitches, can be difficult to knit neatly in either stranding or intarsia, so sew them on afterward using duplicate stitch (see pages 192–193). The embroidered stitches will be a bit fatter and feel slightly embossed, but can look very neat. This can also be a great way to cover up an error in color knitting.

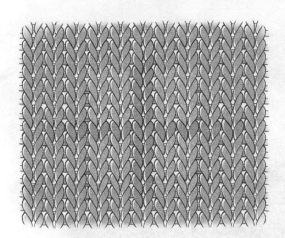

1. To work this motif the green square could be knitted in to the blue background using the intarsia technique (see pages 176–179). Then the pink cross is duplicate-stitched onto the knitted fabric (see pages 192–193).

EDGE STITCHES IN COLOR KNITTING

Even experienced knitters can struggle to get edge stitches perfect where the colors change in stranding and intarsia. Here are two ways of improving edges, both shown on intarsia but the techniques can be used for stranding, too. Also, do check your technique and practice on swatches, as you just might need more practice to get better.

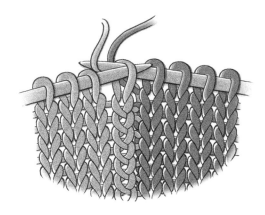

1. Edge stitches can be knitted through the back loops (see page 77). This will twist the stitch, which will show, but a twist can look neater and less obvious than a baggy stitch. You may find that you need to knit the edge stitches of both colors through the back loops, or, as here, just those of one of the colors; it does vary from knitter to knitter.

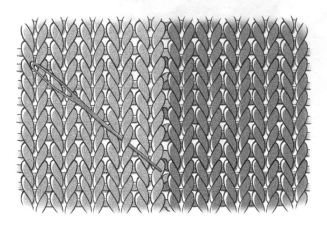

2. The other option is to spend time fixing all the baggy stitches once the knitting is complete. Slide a blunt-pointed sewing needle under the leg of a stitch next to a baggy one and gently ease some of the fullness out of the troublesome stitch. You may need to repeat this in more than one adjacent stitch across the row to even all the stitches out, but if you have the patience, this is a very effective solution.

EMBELLISHED KNITTING

There are a variety of color and texture embellishments that can be added
to a knitter's toolbox of techniques, some methods that are worked as you
knit, and others that can be added to a project once it is complete. The
latter can be useful if a knitted item turns out a little plainer than
you thought it might. While the flat surface of stockinette stitch is
usually the most suitable for embellishing, you can, and should,
experiment with other stitch patterns; your old gauge swatches will
make excellent practise pieces.

EMBROIDERY

Adding embroidery to a knit can turn a plain design into something special. Try a decorative stitch inside cables for a Folkoric effect, or blanket stitch the edge of a pocket or collar. Remember, it is easier to embroider pieces before sewing up.

DUPLICATE STITCH

This technique is also referred to as "Swiss darning" and is worked on stockinette stitch using the same weight yarn as the knitted fabric so that it covers the stitch underneath. You can use this stitch to decorate your knitting, but also to hide mistakes in color work, or to provide extra color definition (see page 189). Try out a motif on a swatch before committing yourself to it on your actual project.

WORKING HORIZONTALLY

1. Thread a blunt-tipped sewing needle with yarn the same weight as that used to knit with, and work from right to left. From the back, bring the needle out at the base of a knitted stitch to be embroidered. Pass the needle around the top of the stitch, going under the "legs" of the stitch above.

2. Insert the needle back through the base of the same stitch and pull the yarn gently taut, so covering the knitted stitch completely. Bring the needle through at the base of the next stitch to the left.

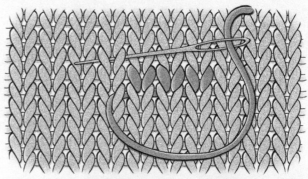

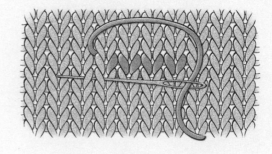

WORKING VERTICALLY

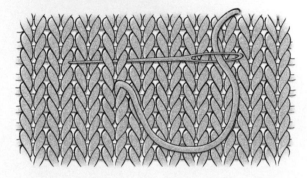

1. Work from bottom to top. From the back, bring the needle out at the base of a knitted stitch to be embroidered. Pass the needle around the top of the stitch, going under the "legs" of the stitch above.

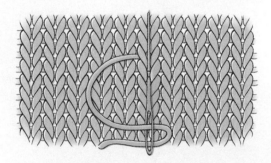

2. Insert the needle back through the base of the same stitch and pull the yarn gently taut, so covering the knitted stitch completely. Bring the needle through at the base of the stitch above.

CHOOSING YARN

For the best results with duplicate stitch, choose a yarn that is the same weight as the yarn used for the knitting. This will allow the knitted stitches to be completely covered by the embroidered ones. The embroidery will feel slightly raised to the touch, and the stitches may look fatter than their knitted neighbors, but if done well, duplicate stitch can be almost indistinguishable from color knitting. Indeed, for thin lines of color, it is often the best option (see page 189).

Also bear laundering in mind: it is best if the embroidery yarn and the knitting yarn are made from the same fibers to avoid any possible shrinkage problems. This applies to all embroidery on knitting.

Thread a tapestry needle with the embroidery yarn and weave in the tail invisibly at the back of the work before you start, or, if the embroidery is a strong color contrast to the knitting, leave a tail and weave that into the back of the completed embroidery stitches.

DECORATIVE STITCHES

There are a variety of embroidery stitches that work well on stockinette stitch, which creates a useful grid pattern for stitches to follow, but the denser fabric of seed stitch or garter stitch can provide a good base, too, and is less inclined to stretch or distort when the embroidery is worked. Blanket stitch in a contrast color is a great way to edge baby knits or afghans. Use a blunt-tipped sewing needle and start by securing the embroidery yarn on the back of the knitting.

BACKSTITCH

As well as being decorative, this stitch can also be used for sewing up certain seams (see page 225).

    Work from right to left. Bring the needle to the front, then take it to the back a backstitch-length to the left (here, over two knitted stitches) and pull the floss through to make the first stitch. Bring the needle to the front a backstitch-length to the left. *Insert it where it last came out, then bring it to the front two backstitch lengths to the left and pull the floss through. Repeat from *.

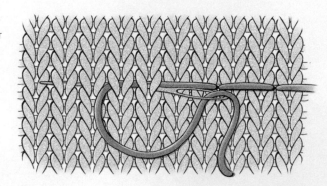

BLANKET STITCH

This stitch may be used along an edge, or on the surface of knitted fabric. Work in either direction; shown here worked right to left.

    *Insert the needle from front to back and bring it back through to the front directly below where it went in, or below the edge of the knitting if you are embroidering along the edge. Pull the floss through, making sure that the working loop goes under the needle. Repeat from *, spacing the blanket stitches evenly.

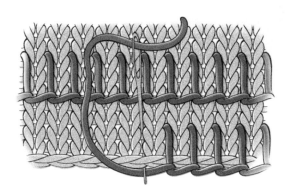

CHAIN STITCH

Work this stitch in lines or curves, and it is very forgiving if you are an embroidery novice.

    Start at the right-hand end of the line of stitches. Bring the needle to the front and pull the floss through. *Insert the needle where it came out and bring it back through to the front a chain stitch-length away. Loop the floss under the tip of the needle, then pull it through. Repeat from *. Secure the last stitch in the chain with a tiny straight stitch over the end of the loop (see Lazy Daisy, page 196).

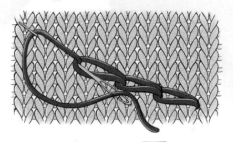

FLY STITCH

This can be worked as single stitches, or in columns or rows.

1. Bring the needle to the front at the top left edge of the stitch. Insert the needle a fly stitch-width away to the right (here, over two knitted stitches), on the same horizontal line, then bring it back through to the front, centered between where it went in and where it came out, on the lower edge of the stitch. Pull the floss through, making sure that the working loop goes under the needle.

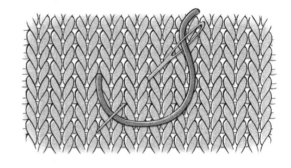

2. Make a straight stitch over the end of the loop to hold it down. This straight stitch can be as long or as short as you want.

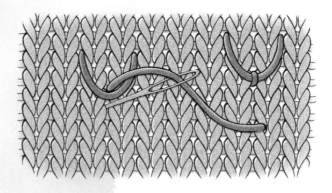

FEATHER STITCH

This is formed in a similar way to fly stitch and is worked in a vertical column.

1. Start at the top left of the column. Bring the needle to the front, then insert it a feather stitch-width away to the right (here, over two knitted stitches), on the same horizontal line. Bring it back through to the front, centered between where it went in and where it came out, at the desired feather-stitch depth. Pull the floss through, making sure that the working loop goes under the needle. *Insert the needle a feather stitch-width to the left, on the same horizontal line, and bring it out a feather stitch-depth lower and vertically in line with the left edge of the stitch above. Pull the floss through, making sure that the working loop goes under the needle.

2. Make the next stitch in the same way, but insert the needle vertically in line with the right-hand edge of the stitch that is two above, and bring it to the front vertically in line with the right-hand edge of the stitch that is immediately above. Repeat from *. Secure the last feather stitch loop with a straight stitch, as for fly stitch (see above).

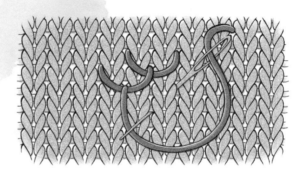

CROSS STITCH

Made from simple straight stitches, work crosses so that the top stitch always slants in the same direction. Crosses can be in a continuous row, or spaced apart, and can be worked over as many knitted stitches and rows as needed.

    *Bring the needle to the front at the top left of the cross. Make a diagonal stitch down to the right, then bring the needle to the front again on the same horizontal line, immediately below where it first came out, and pull the floss through. Make a second diagonal stitch up to the top right to complete a cross. Repeat from *.

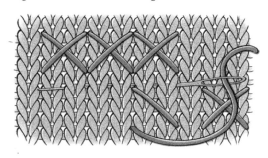

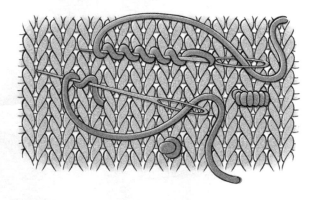

KNOTS

Small, round French knots (at the bottom in the illustration), and longer bullion knots are worked in a similar way.

    For a French knot, bring the needle to the front and pull the floss through. Wind the floss twice around the needle, as shown. Insert the needle half a knitted stitch away from where it came out (so that it spans one strand of yarn) and slowly pull the floss through to form a small knot on the right side. Holding the twists of yarn flat against the knitting with your thumb as you pull the floss through will help the knot form without tangles.

    For a bullion knot, wind the floss around the needle several times and insert the needle one or one-and-a-half knitted stitches away, then pull the floss slowly through to form a longer knot.

LAZY DAISY

These are individual chain stitches grouped together to make a flower. You can vary the number and spacing of the petals.

    *Bring the needle to the front in what will be the center of the flower and pull the floss through. Insert the needle where it came out and bring it back through to the front a stitch-length away. Loop the floss under the tip of the needle, then pull it through. Make a small straight stitch over the end of the loop to hold it down. Repeat from * to form as many petals as required.

RUNNING STITCH

This is the simplest of all embroidery stitches, especially when you have the natural grid of the knitted fabric to guide you.

Bring the needle out to the front and insert it again, going over and under knitted stitches to make straight stitches of the required length.

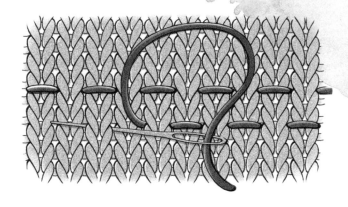

SATIN STITCH

It can take a bit of practice to work this stitch evenly and at the right tension so the knitting doesn't pucker. Practice on your gauge swatch before embroidering a project.

Bring the needle to the front, then insert it a satin stitch-length to the right (here, over four knitted stitches). Bring it back to the front very close to where it last came out. Make all the stitches this way, ensuring they lie flat and close together.

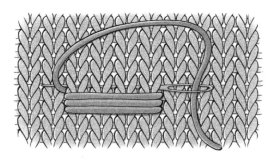

STEM STITCH

This is formed in a similar way to backstitch (see page 194), but creates a thicker embroidered line.

Work from right to left. Bring the needle to the front, then take it to the back a stem stitch-length to the left and pull the floss through to make the first stitch. Bring the needle to the front halfway along that stem stitch and immediately below it. Insert the needle a stem stitch-length to the left, then bring it to the front immediately below the start of the previous stem stitch, making sure the needle goes under the working floss. Repeat from *.

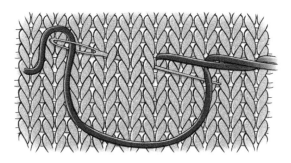

BEADED KNITTING

Beads add glamour and can turn a plain cardigan into a vintage-style star. Pop a pearl in the center of a cable, sprinkle beads on a collar, or use them all over on an evening clutch. A firm gauge is always needed so the beads don't slip to the wrong side.

CHOOSING BEADS

There are a variety of different shapes and materials of bead available to choose from: rounded, oval, rectangular, or made from glass, ceramic, wood—the list is endless. I like to marry up the fiber to the same aesthetic of bead; a chunky, rustic-style yarn lends itself to a wooden or ceramic bead, a silky fiber to crystal or glass. If your bead stockist doesn't have what you want, look in vintage or thrift stores, or garage sales.

The hole in the bead (or sequin) must be large enough for the yarn to go through. The best way to ensure this is to thread up a sewing needle, as explained below, and take that and a length of the project yarn to the bead store. Explain to the staff what you need to check and they should be happy to help.

The beads need to be the right weight for the yarn: heavy beads will stretch knitting done in a fine yarn, and a lot of beads can distort the whole shape of a project. If you are unsure, knit a beaded swatch before starting the project.

The beads need to be smaller than a knitted stitch, or they will distort the shape of the stitches.

If the project is going to need laundering and ironing, check that the beads can withstand that treatment: the store should be able to advise you. Most beads are made of glass, and though they are not very fragile, hand-washing will usually be the best option.

Sequins are usually made of plastic and often do not react well to being either washed or ironed. Even a cool iron used on the back of the knitting can make them curl up. So these are best used on projects that can be gently hand-washed and do not require ironing.

THREADING BEADS ONTO YARN

Trying to thread a cut and fraying end of yarn through the hole in a bead is a frustrating experience, and usually a needle with an eye that is large enough to take the yarn, is too large to fit through the bead. The technique explained here allows you to thread thicker yarns through a bead.

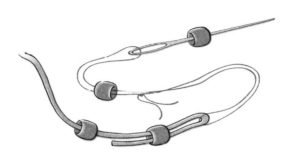

1. Thread a sewing needle with a length of sewing cotton and knot the ends to form a loop. Thread the end of the knitting yarn through the loop of sewing cotton and fold it back on itself.

2. Arrange the loop of cotton so that the knot is clear of the yarn (so that the beads have less bulk to pass over at any single point). Thread the beads along the needle, down the sewing cotton, and onto the yarn until you have the required number of beads on the yarn.

THREADING FOR A CHART

If you are threading on different colored beads to follow a charted design, remember that the bead that is threaded on last will be the one that is used first. So you have to thread on all the beads in reverse order, following the chart backward from the end (see also pages 65–67).

In this diamond motif chart, each colored dot represents a bead, so to knit it you would need 13 purple beads and 12 pink beads. The last row—the top one—is a right-side row, so you start following the bead sequence backward from the top left of the chart.

You would thread the beads onto the yarn in the following order: two purple, one pink, two purple, three pink, two purple, two pink, one purple, two pink, two purple, three pink, two purple, one pink, two purple. You would knit the motif using the knitted-in beading technique (see page 201).

HOW MANY BEADS?

It is important to thread the right number of beads onto a ball of yarn before starting the project, because once the ball is started you cannot add more beads unless you unwind the ball and add them from the other end, or break the yarn.

A pattern will usually tell you how many beads to thread on to each ball of yarn, and it's usually safest to thread on a few more, just in case. If the pattern doesn't give a number, then thread more beads than you will need onto one ball and count the number used when the ball is finished.

SLIP–STITCH BEADING

This is an easy technique to work and is perfect for when you want to create a quite sparsely beaded surface, as you can only place a bead on every alternate stitch, and beads can't sit on the same stitch in every row. Each bead hangs from a strand of yarn that lies in front of a stitch that is slipped purlwise, so beads sit at the base of stitches in a row.

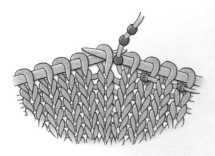

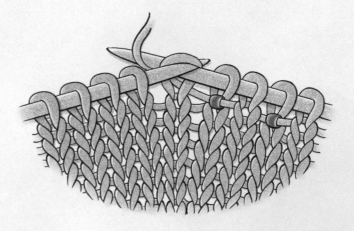

1. On a knit row, knit to the position of the bead, then bring the yarn forward between the needles. Slide a bead down the yarn to sit right in front of the knitting, then slip the next stitch purlwise (see page 77) from the left-hand to the right-hand needle.

2. Take the yarn between the needles to the back, making sure the bead stays in front of the slipped stitch. Knit the next stitch firmly.

3. On a purl row, purl to the position of the bead, then take the yarn back between the needles. Slide a bead down the yarn to sit right in front of the knitting, then slip the next stitch purlwise (see page 77) from the left-hand to the right-hand needle.

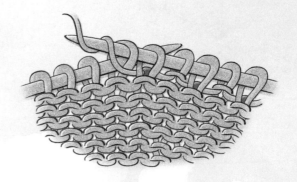

4. Bring the yarn between the needles to the front, making sure the bead stays in front of the slipped stitch. Purl the next stitch firmly.

KNITTED-IN BEADING

This method provides a denser beaded surface because, as the stitches are knitted and not slipped, the technique allows you to bead on every stitch and every row. The beads lie at an angle on one leg of the stitch, but you need to maintain a tight gauge or the beads can have a tendency to disappear through to the wrong side of the fabric. If this is a problem, you can try twisting the stitch by working into the back loop (see page 77).

1. On a knit row, knit to the position of the bead. Slide a bead down the yarn to be close to the needles, then put the tip of the right-hand needle knitwise into the next stitch.

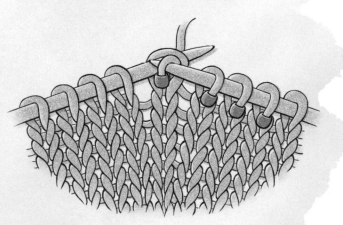

2. Knit the stitch, bringing the bead through it on the new loop of yarn.

3. On a purl row, purl to the position of the bead. Slide a bead down the yarn to be close to the needles, then put the tip of the right-hand needle purlwise into the next stitch.

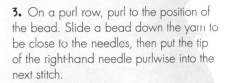

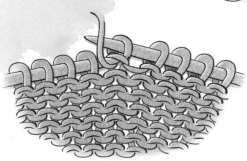

4. Purl the stitch, bringing the bead through it on the new loop of yarn, but making sure that the bead stays on the right side of the knitting.

BEADING WITH TWO YARNS

This technique is perfect for when you want to use smaller beads than will thread onto your yarn. The beads are threaded onto a fine yarn that is knitted together with the main yarn—either in the same shade or a contrast one for a color-mix effect (see page 170). This method is similar to the slip-stitch technique (see page 200), as the bead is held in front of the work on the fine yarn, while the stitch behind is knitted in the other yarn.

With both yarns held together, work to the position of the bead. Separate the two yarns and leave the fine yarn with the beads on the right side of the work. Work the next stitch in the main yarn only. Slide a bead down the fine yarn to sit in front of the stitch just worked, then work the next stitch with both yarns held together.

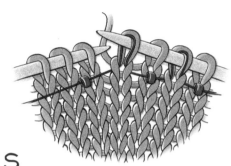

BEADING BETWEEN STITCHES

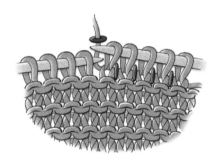

This technique is sometimes called purse knitting as it was used in 17th, 18th, and 19th centuries to create intricate beaded purses and small bags. It is perfect if you want a very decorative item, as you can virtually cover the whole knitted fabric with beads. It works particularly well on garter stitch.

Knit to the position of the bead. Slide a bead down the yarn to sit tight next to the last stitch, then knit the next stitch.

REMOVING OR ADDING AN EXTRA BEAD

However carefully you count and thread beads for a color sequence (see page 199), you can make a mistake, or thread on a misshapen bead without noticing until you come to knit it.

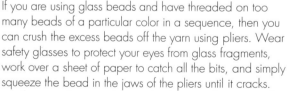

If you are using glass beads and have threaded on too many beads of a particular color in a sequence, then you can crush the excess beads off the yarn using pliers. Wear safety glasses to protect your eyes from glass fragments, work over a sheet of paper to catch all the bits, and simply squeeze the bead in the jaws of the pliers until it cracks.

If you can't correct the mistake this way, then you will have to unravel to the start of the row the mistake is on, cut the yarn—leaving a tail to sew in later (see page 227)—rethread the beads, then rejoin the yarn (see page 71).

If you have forgotten a bead in a threading sequence, then, if the hole in it is large enough, you can add it with a crochet hook. Slip the bead onto the shaft of the hook. Slip the stitch you want to add the bead to off the needle without working it, then catch the stitch with the hook and slide the bead down onto the stitch. Replace the stitch on the left-hand needle and work it, or slip it onto the right-hand needle and skip it; whichever works best for the pattern. Note that the bead will sit at a different angle to the other beads, no matter which technique you have used to place them.

BEADED CAST ON AND BIND OFF

These techniques can create a beautiful decorative edging on a garment or accessory, and the added weight gives some swing to a flared shape, such as an A-line knit. For full instructions for the cable cast on turn to page 37, and for the thumb cast turn to page 36. For instructions for binding off, turn to page 50.

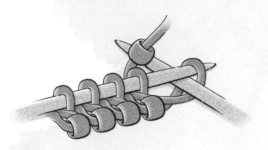

BEADED CABLE CAST ON

The principle is similar to knitted-in beading (see page 201).

Slide a bead down the yarn to be close to the needles, then put the tip of the right-hand needle between the last two stitches on the left-hand needle and pull a loop through, bringing the bead through on it. Push the bead down to the base of the stitch, then put the stitch on the left-hand needle.

BEADED THUMB CAST ON

The principle used here is similar to beading between stitches (see opposite).

Slide all the threaded-on beads along the yarn to past the position of the slip knot. Make the slip knot, then slide one bead along the yarn to sit next to it. (If you are going to seam the edges, then leave the slip knot and the last cast on stitch without beads.) Cast on the stitches, sliding one bead along to sit next to each one.

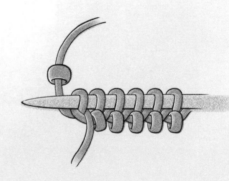

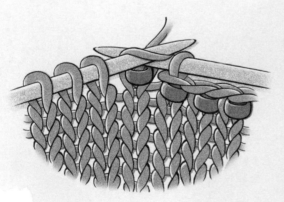

BEADED BIND OFF

This bind-off uses knitted-in beading (see page 201) and the standard bind off technique.

Knit and bead two stitches, then pass the first stitch over the second so that the beads sit just under the bound-off edge. If you are beading only the bind off in a project, then work with plain yarn to the bind-off row and cut the yarn leaving a tail at least four times the width of the knitting. Thread on the beads and work the bind off.

ADDING SEQUINS

Sequins can create stunning effects on knits; as the light catches them they add shimmer to the plainest of garments. They can be worked all over on a simple but glamorous evening tank top, or around the edges of a knit for a more subtle effect. Use any of the three techniques here depending on the size of sequin. Some sequins will have the hole placed at the top rather than the center so they will lie on the knitted fabric differently. Try the techniques on a swatch to see which you prefer.

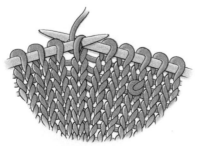

SMALL SEQUINS

Use the knitted-in beading technique (see page 201) to place small sequins on knit and purl rows.

Knit or purl as appropriate, easing the sequin through the stitch as you form it.

MEDIUM SEQUINS

If the sequins are too large to slip through a stitch, use this method to place them.

1. On a knit row, knit to the position of the sequin. Bring the yarn forward between the needles and slide a sequin down the yarn to sit right in front of the knitting.

2. Purl the next stitch, then take the yarn between the needles to the back to complete the row.

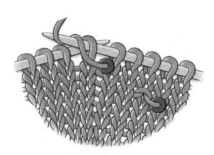

3. On a purl row, purl to the position of the sequin, then take the yarn back between the needles. Slide a sequin down the yarn to sit right in front of the knitting, then knit the next stitch through the back loop (see page 77). Bring the yarn between the needles to the front to complete the row.

LARGE SEQUINS

Use the slip-stitch beading technique (see page 200) to place large sequins on knit and purl rows.

On a knit row, you can either knit the stitch after the slipped stitch, or if the sequins show an inclination to slide between the stitches, purl the next stitch.

TRIMMINGS

Trimmings are a great way to add some decorative interest to a project, and most of them are easy to make. I have a huge fondness for pom-poms, and fringes are a great way to transform a simple scarf, or add some pizazz on the hem of a sweater.

TASSELS

This is the simplest style to work along the cast-on or bound-off edge of a knit. Work out beforehand the thickness and length of tassel you want to prevent being disappointed when you have completed it and found it a bit skinny, or shorter than you wanted.

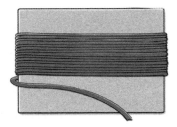

1. Cut a piece of card the desired length of the tassel. Wrap yarn around it, bearing in mind that the more wraps you make, the fuller the tassel will be.

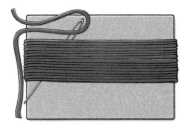

2. Cut a length of yarn long enough to sew the tassel to the project with, and thread it through a blunt-tipped sewing needle. Slip the needle under the wrapped loops, pull the yarn halfway through, and tie it in a very tight knot around the loops at one end of the card.

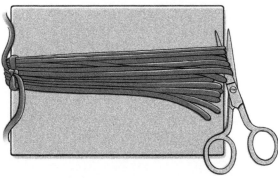

3. Cut through the loops at the other end of the card.

4. Cut another length of yarn and use it to tie off the head of the tassel. Thread the ends of the tying yarn into the sewing needle and take them over the tying yarn and down inside the tassel. Trim the ends of the tassel if need be.

SIMPLE FRINGE

This is a very easy way to add detail to any edge of a piece of knitting. It's shown here on a cast-on edge, but the same principles apply on a bound-off edge. To add a fringe to a row-end edge, loop the strands through the spaces where you would pick up stitches from (see page 76).

1. Cut strands of yarn a little longer than twice the required finished length of the fringe. From the back, slip a large crochet hook through the knitting where you want to attach a tassel of the fringe. Fold as many strands as needed for the tassel in half and lay them over the hook.

2. Pull the strands through the knitting to the back to form a loop.

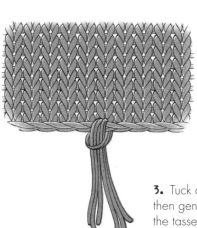

3. Tuck all the cut ends of the strands through the loop, then gently pull on the ends to tighten the loop. When all the tassels are attached, trim the ends of the fringe.

KNOTTED FRINGE

This style is more decorative and is an interesting variation on the usual fringe. Works particularly well on heavier yarns.

1. Make a fringe (see above) with long tassels spaced apart. Divide each tassel in half and knot each half to half of the adjacent tassel using an overhand knot. If you make the tassels very long, you can divide and knot them again to create a netting effect.

BEADED FRINGE

The extra weight of the beads can make this type of decorative fringe hang really well. Worked in brightly colored beads, it can also add an ethnic touch to a project.

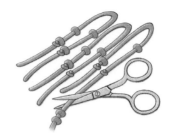

1. Thread beads onto the fringe yarn as for knitted beading (see page 199). Cut the yarn into strands a little longer than twice the required finished length of the fringe, with as many beads as required on each strand. Tie knots in the ends of each to stop the beads from falling off. Make the fringe in the same way as a simple fringe (see opposite).

UNRAVELED FRINGE

This type of fringe needs to be worked as you knit the project. It will hang down from the row edge—what is usually the side of a piece of knitting. It works best in garter stitch as stockinette stitch can become a bit loose along the edge of the knitting; though blanket stitching the edge will fix that. If you don't like the crinkles from the unraveled stitches, you can steam and gently stretch the loops straight.

1. Cast on the required number of stitches for the project, plus the required number for the fringe: each stitch will produce a double strand of fringe that is three times as long as the stitch was wide. Knit the project, knitting all the fringe stitches on every row. On the last row, knit the fringe stitches, then bind off the remaining stitches. Use a blunt-tipped sewing needle to help unravel the fringe stitches right along the edge.

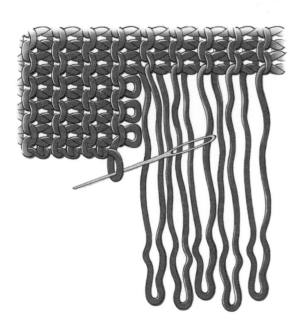

TWISTED CORD

A twisted cord can be slotted through the knitted fabric—or through eyelets (see page 252)—as a drawstring to gather up the top of a bag, or underneath the yoke of a dress. You can use two or three different colors to make striped cord. Ideally, you need a friend to help by holding one end of the strands.

1. Cut strands that are three times the required finished length of the cord, bearing in mind that it will be double thickness; two strands of yarn will make a cord four strands thick. Knot the strands together at each end. Slip a knitting needle into each end, as shown. Ask a friend to hold one end, and turn the needles in opposite directions until the strands are tightly twisted. You can anchor one end over a door handle and twist the other end if there is no-one to help you.

2. Holding the cord in the middle with one hand, bring both ends together, keeping the two halves taut. Release the middle and allow the cord to twist up, then smooth out any small loops. Knot the free ends together.

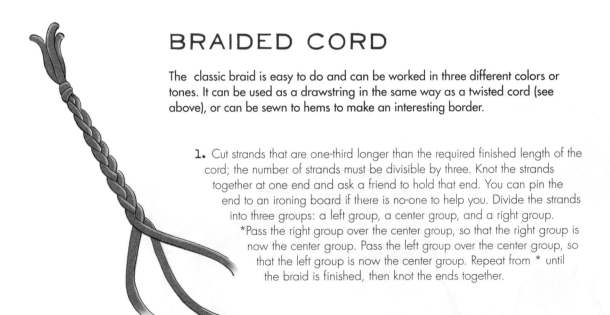

BRAIDED CORD

The classic braid is easy to do and can be worked in three different colors or tones. It can be used as a drawstring in the same way as a twisted cord (see above), or can be sewn to hems to make an interesting border.

1. Cut strands that are one-third longer than the required finished length of the cord; the number of strands must be divisible by three. Knot the strands together at one end and ask a friend to hold that end. You can pin the end to an ironing board if there is no-one to help you. Divide the strands into three groups: a left group, a center group, and a right group. *Pass the right group over the center group, so that the right group is now the center group. Pass the left group over the center group, so that the left group is now the center group. Repeat from * until the braid is finished, then knot the ends together.

FRENCH KNITTING

I used to do this on a wooden cotton reel with nails hammered into the top of it, but cotton reels are made of plastic now... But fortunately you can buy knitting dollies. You can get big ones with more than four prongs, but the principle remains the same. They are a good way to introduce children to the idea of making a fabric.

1. Thread the tail end of a ball of yarn down through the middle of the knitting dolly. Wind the ball end clockwise around one of the prongs in the top of the dolly, then take it across to the next prong, moving counterclockwise around the dolly itself.

2. Wind the yarn clockwise around each prong in turn until each has a loop of yarn over it.

3. Repeat the process so that each prong has two loops over it. Using a thin knitting needle (or some dollies will come with a tool), lift the lower loop on the first prong over the upper one.

4. Do the same on each prong, so that they all have just one loop of yarn on them again.

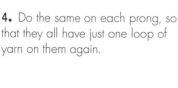

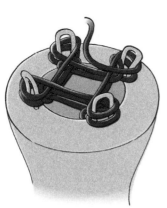

5. Repeat Step 2 to add a second loop of yarn to each prong. Then lift the lower loop on each prong over the upper one.

6. Repeat Step 5 until the cord that spools out of the middle of the dolly is the required length. Cut the yarn and thread the end through the final loops on the prongs to fasten off the cord.

TRADITIONAL POM-POM

My favorite embellishment of all. Whether they are big pom-poms on beanies, small ones decorating mittens, or the giant ones on the ends of a scarf, there is something fun and joyous about pom-poms. They are easy to make in the traditional way with card, but make sure that the card is stiff enough not to split when you are cutting through to divide the two sections.

1. Cut two circles of card slightly wider in diameter than the required size of the finished pom-pom. Cut a smaller hole in the center of each circle, about half the size of the original diameter. Holding the two circles together, wind yarn around the ring until it is completely covered. You can use several strands of yarn held together for speed. Continue winding layers of yarn around the ring until the hole in the middle is almost filled. As the hole gets smaller, you may find it easier to use a sewing needle to pass the yarn through it.

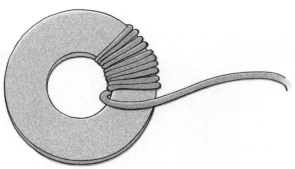

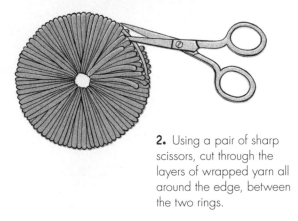

2. Using a pair of sharp scissors, cut through the layers of wrapped yarn all around the edge, between the two rings.

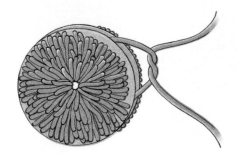

3. Separate the rings slightly. Wrap a length of yarn tightly around the center of the pom-pom, between the rings, and tie the ends in a firm knot, leaving tails long enough to sew the pom-pom in place.

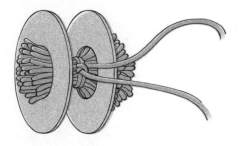

4. Pull or cut the rings off the pom-pom.

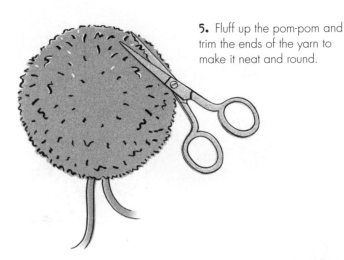

5. Fluff up the pom-pom and trim the ends of the yarn to make it neat and round.

USING A POM-POM MAKER

A pom-pom maker is very quick to use as you don't need to cut your own card circles, and winding the yarn on is a speedier process. As they are made out of plastic, you don't have the worry of splitting the card, and of course they are reusable. Pom-pom makers come in different sizes, and you can even get heart-shaped ones.

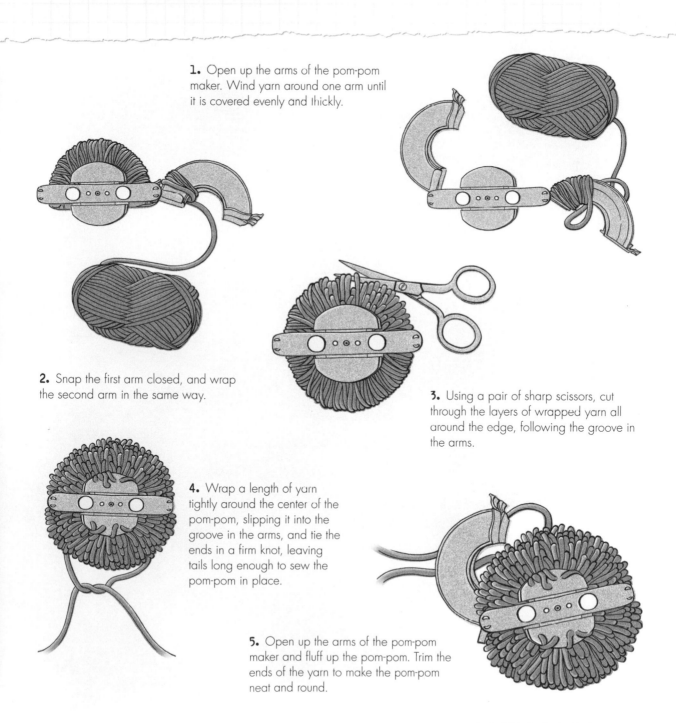

1. Open up the arms of the pom-pom maker. Wind yarn around one arm until it is covered evenly and thickly.

2. Snap the first arm closed, and wrap the second arm in the same way.

3. Using a pair of sharp scissors, cut through the layers of wrapped yarn all around the edge, following the groove in the arms.

4. Wrap a length of yarn tightly around the center of the pom-pom, slipping it into the groove in the arms, and tie the ends in a firm knot, leaving tails long enough to sew the pom-pom in place.

5. Open up the arms of the pom-pom maker and fluff up the pom-pom. Trim the ends of the yarn to make the pom-pom neat and round.

KNITTED LACE

Plain knits can be embellished by adding lace borders after the main piece has been completed. Rather than work a standard rib, for example, you could add a lace trim to the cuffs or hem of a tunic, or around the edges of a throw.

KNITTING LACE TO FIT

Lace trims can be worked from the bottom up, from the top down, or, as is most often the case, lengthwise. A top-down lace can simply be added to the bottom edge of a main piece, though you will need to work out stitch counts to be sure of the lace repeat fitting neatly along the edge.

Similarly, bottom-up lace patterns can be worked and then the main knitting continued from them, as long as the lace repeat fits the required size of the knitting.

Lace worked lengthwise will need to be worked to the right length, then sewn onto the finished main piece. The best way to do this is to knit a section of the lace, including at least three pattern repeats, and measure that. Stretch the lace very slightly when you measure, as it will need to be stretched slightly as it is sewn on to make it lie flat and smooth. Then measure the edge you need to fit the lace to. If a multiple of the lace swatch measurement will fit the edge to within an inch, then you should be able to ease the pieces to fit neatly. Otherwise it would be better to choose a different lace pattern.

GRAFTING ON LACE

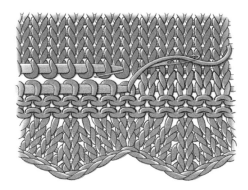

If you know that you want to add a border or lace trim to a piece of knitting, but haven't decided exactly what before you start work, then use a provisional cast on (see page 43) to keep the stitches live. That gives you the option of knitting on from the piece later, or grafting a trim onto the stitches.

As long as the gauges are compatible, a lace border knitted from the bottom up can easily and very successfully be grafted (see page 228) onto the live stitches once they have been placed on a needle. It's worth swatching a section of the lace and making sure it will match the gauge of the main knitting before you cast on for a long length.

SEWING ON LACE

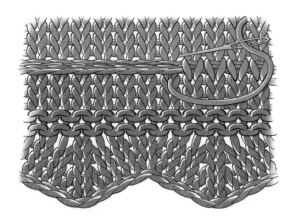

If the gauges are reasonably compatible, the neatest way to sew on a lace trim is with mattress stitch (see pages 220–224). Here, the bound-off edge of the lace is being sewn to the cast-on edge of the plain knitted fabric, but you can also easily sew row ends (so the top edge of lace knitted lengthwise) to a cast-on edge. If the gauges of the trim and the main knitting are not at all similar, then sew the lace on with backstitch or oversewing (see page 225).

CROCHET ON KNITTING

Crochet can be worked around the edges of knitting to create a neat border; it works particularly well on seed stitch or garter stitch. It can also be a quick and easy alternative to embroidery for surface decoration on stockinette fabric.

SURFACE CROCHET

This technique can be used with fancy yarns, although very textured yarns can be difficult to pull through the knitting, and the texture can obscure the individual stitches. The crochet chain can move in any direction on the knitting, but be careful not to pull it too tight and pucker up the fabric.

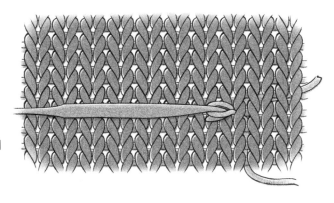

1. With the crochet yarn at the back of the work, push a crochet hook through the knitting where you want to start the chain. Wind the crochet yarn around the hook and pull a loop through. Leave a 4in tail at the back to sew in later (see page 227).

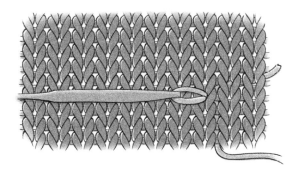

2. *Keeping the loop on the shaft of the hook, push the hook down through the fabric a crochet-loop length away. Wind the working end of the crochet yarn around the hook and pull a loop through the fabric and through the loop on the hook.

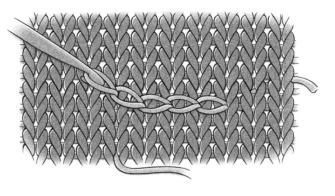

3. Repeat from * to make a crochet chain that sits on the surface of the knitting.

SLIP STITCH EDGING

Slip stitch in crochet is abbreviated to "ss" or "sl st." It makes a very shallow edging on knitting that lends stability and neatens rather than adding width, and it can be worked in a different color yarn for an accent. The technique is shown here on a cast-on edge, but the same principles apply to all edges.

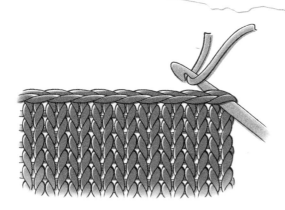

1. Push the crochet hook through the knitting where you want the edging to start. You can go through a stitch, or into the space between stitches, as you prefer. Wind the crochet yarn over the hook and pull a loop through.

2. *Push the hook through the next stitch or gap, wind the yarn over the hook, and pull a second loop through.

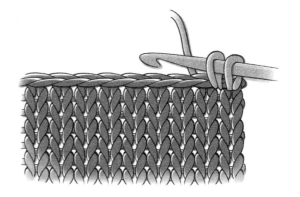

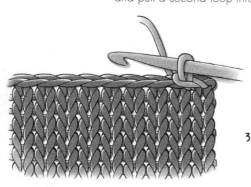

3. Pull the second loop through the first loop.

4. Repeat from * to make the slip stitch edging.

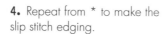

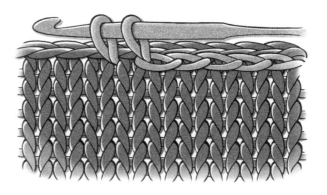

SINGLE CROCHET EDGING

This method creates a more decorative edge than slip stitch crochet (see opposite). It adds a little width to the knitting, as well as stabilizing the edges and neatening them very effectively. Try adding this edge to pocket openings, cuffs and collars, scarves, and afghans, but be careful that it isn't too tight and so pulls the edge in, or too loose and so flutes unattractively.

1. Push the crochet hook through the knitting where you want the edging to start. You can go through a stitch, or into the space between stitches, as you prefer. Wind the crochet yarn over the hook and pull a loop through. Wind the yarn over the hook again.

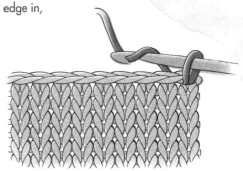

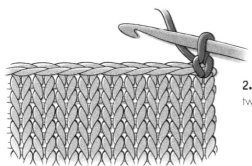

2. Pull a second loop through the first one to make a two-stitch chain to start the edging at the right height.

3. *Push the hook through the next stitch or gap and pull a loop through.

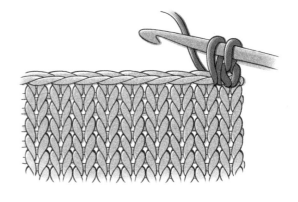

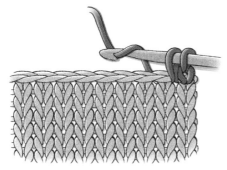

4. Wind the yarn around the hook again and pull a loop through both the loops on the hook.

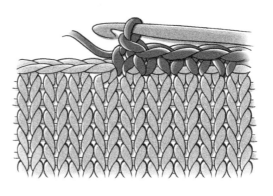

5. Repeat from * to make the single crochet edging.

FINISHING

This aspect of knitting is one of the most important to master, and yet it seems to be something that many knitters find rather intimidating. I meet quite a few who would prefer to move on to another project in preference to finishing the one they have just completed knitting. Perfect picking up and sublime seaming are the way forward in creating professional-looking knits: however beautifully you have knitted the pieces of your project, sewing them up badly or working an untidy neckband can ruin all your hard work.

BLOCKING

Because of the elastic nature of knitted fabric, and variations in gauge from your initial small swatch to that over multiple stitches in your project, you may find that there is a slight variation in the measurements of your pieces to those quoted in the pattern. The best way to fix this is to pin out the pieces and block them.

MAKING A BLOCKING BOARD

An ironing board can be used for blocking, but unless the pieces are very small, the chances are that they will be bigger than the width of the board. Making a special blocking board is surprisingly easy, and has the advantage of letting you leave things pinned out. Gingham fabric is an excellent choice for a board, as it helps you keep the pinned pieces straight. For blocking very large pieces, you can use a mattress or towel.

YOU WILL NEED

A square or rectangle of chipboard
  or MDF
Medium-weight wool or cotton batting,
  1in larger all around than the board
Cotton fabric (gingham is ideal), 2in
  larger all around than the board
Staple gun

Lay the batting flat and lay the board right-side down on top of it, positioning it centrally. Fold the batting over the edges of the board, mitering the corners neatly, and staple it in place with the gun. Do one edge at a time, making sure that the batting remains smooth and taut across the front of the board.

Turn under and press a ½in hem on all edges of the cotton fabric. With the board and fabric right-side up, lay the fabric over the batting, arranging it so that the edges overlap the edges of the board equally all the way around. If you are using gingham fabric, make sure that the pattern is square to the edges. Fold the fabric over to the back of the board, miter the corners, and staple the edges in place as for the batting.

PINNING OUT KNITTING FOR BLOCKING

All you will need are a blocking board, long dressmaking pins that don't have plastic heads that will melt when pressed, a tape measure for measuring your pieces, and a good steam iron. Use distilled water in the iron to avoid calcification and the unloading of white grains all over your work.

Lay out the knitted pieces right side down on the blocking board. If you have covered your board with gingham, then use the checked pattern to make sure that edges that are supposed to be straight, are straight. Ease the pieces to the correct sizes, following any measurements in the pattern. You won't be able to stretch pieces too much without damaging them, but small discrepancies in size can be made up.

Using dressmaking pins, pin each knitted piece out, sliding the pins through the edge stitches of the knitting and into the batting on the blocking board. You can start by pinning out corners, and then pin out the edges between them, placing pins about ½–1in apart. You need to pin out the edges carefully, easing them into shape so that lines are smooth and the pieces are symmetrical. Be careful not to stretch ribbing as the blocking process can ruin the elasticity if you do (see top right).

If a piece is badly pinned out—so that the edges are irregular and not symmetrical (see right)—and then the piece is blocked, the poor shaping can become permanent.

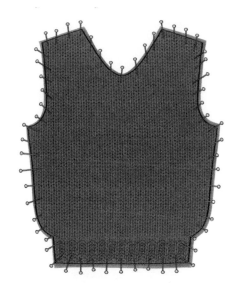

BLOCKING METHODS

Check advice on the ball band as to which of the following pressing methods to use. Block lightly and repeat if necessary, but make sure that you don't over-press as this will make the fabric limp. Also be aware of the stitch patterns used: too firm blocking can destroy a delicate pattern such as seed stitch, or flatten a cable.

STEAMING

Use a steam iron and a dry cloth, or a damp cloth if the piece is very curled. Or try a dry iron and a damp cloth.

Pin the pieces out (see above). Lay the cloth over the work and hold the iron just above it and press the steam button, allowing the steam to penetrate the knitting. Leave the knitting to cool completely before unpinning it from the board.

PRESSING

Use a steam iron and a dry cloth, or a damp cloth if the piece is very curled. Or try a dry iron and a damp cloth. For delicate yarns, use a dry, cool iron and a dry cloth.

Pin the pieces out (see above). Do not slide the iron over the knitted fabric; instead, place it on one area for a few seconds, lift it off, and place it on another area. Repeat until you have pressed the whole piece. Leave the knitting to cool completely before unpinning it from the board.

SPRAYING

Pin the pieces out (see above), but pin them right-side up. Using a spray bottle (the kind used to spray plants is ideal), dampen the piece thoroughly with cool water. Or dab it gently all over with a clean, wet sponge. Leave the knitting to dry completely before unpinning it from the board.

SEAMS

MATTRESS STITCH ON STOCKINETTE: STITCHES TO STITCHES

Mattress stitch is extremely neat, and it is my preferred method for almost every type of seaming. As it is worked from the right side, you can see exactly what you are doing, and as it matches stitch to stitch and row to row, it is the most accurate method of joining pieces together, and is virtually invisible. This is how to join cast-on and bound-off edges.

1. Right-sides up, lay the two pieces to be joined edge to edge. Thread a blunt-tipped sewing needle with a long length of yarn. Secure the yarn on the back of the lower knitted piece, then bring the needle up through the middle of the first whole stitch in that piece. Take the needle under both loops of the first whole stitch on the upper piece, so that it emerges between the first and second stitches.

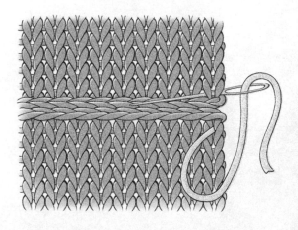

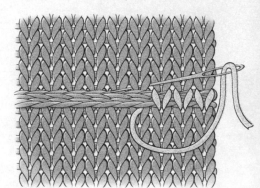

2. *Go back into the lower piece and take the needle through to the back where it first came out, and then bring it back to the front in the middle of the next stitch along. Pull the yarn through.

3. Take the needle under both loops of the next whole stitch on the upper piece. Repeat from * to sew the seam. You can either gently pull the sewn stitches taut but have them visible, as shown, so that they continue the stockinette stitch pattern, or you can pull them completely tight so that they disappear, in a similar way to mattress stitching row ends together (see opposite).

MATTRESS STITCH ON STOCKINETTE: ROW ENDS TO ROW ENDS

You can take a whole stitch in for the edge for neatness as here, or half a stitch if you are working with a fairly thick yarn and don't want the seam to be too bulky. Closing up the seam where half a stitch is used makes a whole stitch that is not quite symmetrical, so this doesn't create such an invisible join as when taking in a whole stitch.

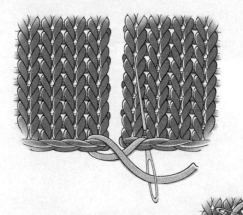

1. Right-sides up, lay the two edges to be joined side by side. Thread a blunt-tipped sewing needle with a long length of yarn. Secure the yarn on the back of the right-hand knitted piece. To start the seam, from the back bring the needle up between the first and second stitches of that piece, immediately above the cast-on edge. Take it across to the left-hand piece, and from the back bring it through between the first and second stitches of that piece, immediately above the cast-on edge. Take it back to the right-hand piece and, again from the back, bring it through one row above where it first came through, between the first and second stitches. Pull the yarn through and this figure-eight will hold the cast-on edges level.

2. Take the needle across to the left-hand piece and, from the front, take it under the bar of yarn above where it last came out on that side, between the first and second stitches.

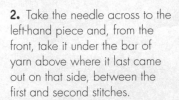

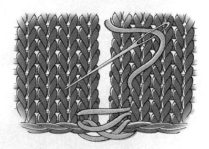

3. *Take the needle across to the right-hand piece and, from the front, take it under the next two bars of yarn between the first and second stitches. Pull the yarn through. Then take the needle back to the left-hand piece and, from the front, under the corresponding two bars between the first and second stitches.

4. Repeat from * to sew the seam. When you have sewn about 1in, gently pull the stitches up tight to close the seam, and then continue.

PATTERNED KNITTING

When the knitted pieces are patterned, precise matching is even more important. For greater accuracy, take the needle under one stitch bar at a time as you sew the seam. This is also a good option when seaming thicker yarns.

MATTRESS STITCH ON STOCKINETTE: STITCHES TO ROW ENDS

This is a combination of the techniques for sewing stitches to stitches (see page 220) and row ends to row ends (see page 221). The spacing of the sewn stitches on the row-end edge might take some experimentation, but the aim is to get the sewn stitches all lying flat without puckering. This seam is used when sewing the top of sleeves to the body in a dropped shoulder or square set-in sleeve.

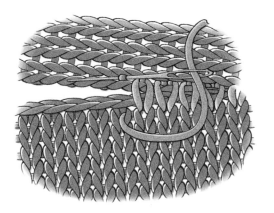

1. Right-sides up, lay the two edges to be joined touching one another. Pin them together at the halfway point to help space the sewn stitches neatly. Thread a blunt-tipped sewing needle with a long length of yarn. Secure the yarn on the back of either piece. On the row-end edge, take the needle under one bar of yarn either a whole stitch in from the edge, or half a stitch, as shown here (see also Which Stitch?, below).

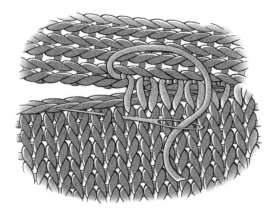

WHICH STITCH?

If your row edge stitches are baggy, then work a whole stitch in from the edge. For a less bulky seam, work half a stitch in, taking the needle through the center of the first stitch and under the bar of yarn. On the cast-on or bound-off edge, you can work under both loops of a single stitch, or one loop each of two adjacent stitches, as shown here, depending on how the two edges need to be positioned together.

2. On the cast-on or bound-off edge, take the needle under two stitch loops (see also Which Stitch?, left).

3. However, as a stitch is wider than it is long, on approximately every third stitch along the row-end edge, take the needle under two bars instead of one.

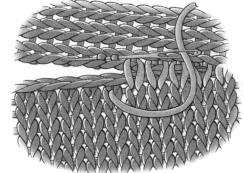

MATTRESS STITCH ON REVERSE STOCKINETTE

Use this method of mattress stitching if reverse stockinette stitch is used at the edges on the right side of the work, for example, in a traditional cable pattern.

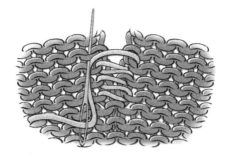

1. Use the same technique as for sewing stockinette stitch row ends to row ends (see page 221), but take the needle under only one bar of yarn at a time on each knitted piece for a neat finish.

OTHER RIB PATTERNS

The same principles apply no matter what the rib pattern is: always make sure that the knitted pieces start and end with identical stitches so that you can work a half or whole stitch (as works best for the pattern) in from the edge and keep the rib pattern continuous across the seam.

MATTRESS STITCH ON SINGLE RIB

Both pieces must start and end with the same stitch, which will usually be a knit stitch, as shown here. You will be taking in half a stitch on each side, which when the edges are drawn together will create a whole stitch, thus keeping the rib pattern continuous across the seam.

1. Use the same technique as for sewing stockinette stitch row ends to row ends (see page 221), but take the needle through the center of the first stitch on each knitted piece, instead of between the first and second stitches.

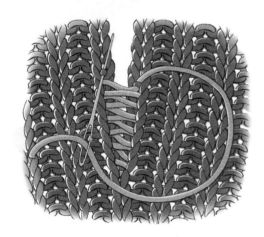

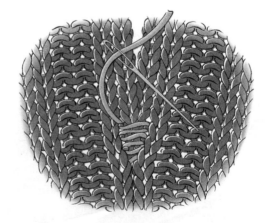

MATTRESS STITCH ON DOUBLE RIB

This method is the same principle as sewing up single rib (see above), but each piece will start with two of the same stitches, and you'll take one in on each side to make the pattern continuous and create an invisible seam.

1. Use the same technique as for sewing stockinette stitch row ends to row ends (see page 221), taking the needle between the first and second stitches in from the edge on each knitted piece.

MATTRESS STITCH ON SEED STITCH

With this method the pieces need to start and end with the same stitch, and you work half a stitch in. The seam is not quite as invisible as it can be on stockinette (see pages 220–222) or rib (see page 223), but it is still very neat.

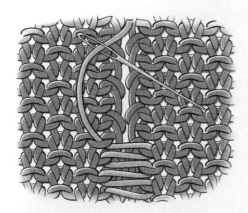

1. Use the same technique as for sewing stockinette stitch row ends to row ends (see page 221), but take the needle through the center of the first stitch on each knitted piece, instead of between the first and second stitches, and under only one bar of yarn at a time.

MATTRESS STITCHING OTHER STITCH PATTERNS

The great advantage of mattress stitch is that you are working from the right side of the fabric, so you can clearly see where the needle is going and so match up patterns effectively. Most fairly dense stitch patterns can be mattress stitched, you just have to work out the edge stitches on each piece to make the seam as invisible as possible. You can add a plain knit edge stitch to each piece to make mattress stitching simple on more complex patterns. Openwork lace patterns don't generally work well with mattress stitch and you are better to backstitch the seams (see page 225), unless there is a selvedge edge.

MATTRESS STITCH ON GARTER STITCH

This takes in one stitch from each side, and if you don't pull too tightly when you draw the edges together it produces quite a smooth seam. If you prefer you can use a flat seam for garter stitch (see opposite).

1. Use the same technique as for sewing stockinette stitch row ends to row ends (see page 221). Take the needle under the lower loop on each ridge on one knitted piece, and under the upper loop on each ridge on the other piece.

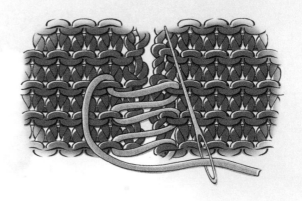

BACKSTITCH SEAM

This is worked from the wrong side so it's not so easy to match stitch for stitch and row for row well, but it can be a good seam for curves, such as on a fitted sleeve head. Worked approximately one stitch in from the edge, it can make a fairly bulky seam. It is best to pin the pieces together right along the length before sewing, but it still does not have the accuracy of mattress stitch.

1. Pin the two pieces to be joined right-sides together. Thread a blunt-tipped sewing needle with a long length of yarn and secure the yarn on the piece at the back, at the right-hand end of the seam. Bring the needle through both layers to the front, then take it back through both layers a sewn stitch-length to the left and pull the yarn through to make the first stitch. Bring the needle to the front a sewn stitch-length to the left. *Insert it where it last came out, then bring it to the front two sewn stitch lengths to the left and pull the yarn through. Repeat from * to sew the seam.

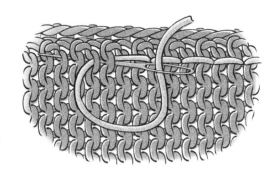

FLAT SEAM

This seam is particularly good for babies as there is no bulky seam to rub against skin. However, it is not a very strong seam and the stitches can stretch. It is worked on the wrong side.

1. Wrong-sides up, lay the two edges to be joined side by side. Thread a blunt-tipped sewing needle with a long length of yarn and secure the yarn on the back of one piece. Take the needle through the bump of the first edge stitch on one side, then through the same bump on the side of the other piece. Continue in this way, zigzagging between the stitch bumps, as shown, and pulling the seam gently tight as you work.

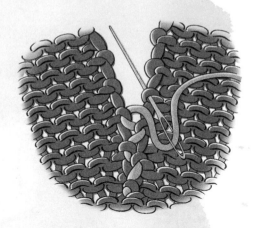

OVERSEWING

This is another seam without much bulk, but it can be untidy. It is worked on the wrong side about one stitch in from the edge.

1. Pin the two pieces to be joined right-sides together. Thread a blunt-tipped sewing needle with a long length of yarn and secure the yarn on the piece at the back, at the right hand end of the seam. Bring the needle through both layers to the front, *then take the needle over the top of the edges of the fabric and, from the back, go through both layers to the front again. Repeat from * to sew the seam.

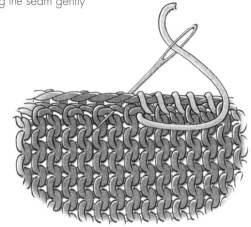

SLIP STITCHING

There are two methods for slip stitching, one with an invisible seam—which is particularly good for attaching pockets to the front of a project—and one that uses live stitches, which can be used as a good way of attaching a previously knitted neckband.

TWO PIECES

This stitch can be used to sew one piece on top of another and the stitches will be invisible.

1. Lay one piece on top of another, matching the finished edge of the upper piece to a column of stitches on the lower piece. Thread a blunt-tipped sewing needle with a long length of yarn and secure the yarn on the back of the lower piece. Bring the needle through the lower piece, going under a bar of yarn between stitches, *then through the back of the stitch loop on the corresponding stitch on the upper piece. You may have to move the upper piece aside a little, or lift it, to do this. Pull the stitch tight. Take the needle under the next bar of yarn along on the lower piece, and repeat from * to sew the pieces together.

LIVE STITCHES

Rather than binding off an edge, you can work a provisional bind off (see page 57), then slip stitch the live stitches in place later. The method is best used on the wrong side of the work and is shown here on a neckband.

1. Position the live stitches where they need to be attached, pinning the layers together if necessary. Thread a blunt-tipped sewing needle with a long length of yarn and secure the yarn on the wrong side of the work. Take the needle through the first live stitch, *then slip that stitch off the waste yarn holding it. Take the needle under the back of a stitch loop just below the live stitch and pull the yarn through. Take the needle through the next live stitch, and repeat from * to sew all the live stitches in place. Do not pull the sewn stitches too tight or the edge will pucker and lose its elasticity.

TAPING A SEAM

This method is particularly useful for strengthening shoulder seams on heavy garments where you are concerned that the weight of the garment might stretch the seams. Use tape that can be laundered with the yarn; if you are not sure pre-wash it first.

1. Cut a length of tape ½in longer that the seam. Fold under ¼in at one end and pin that to the wrong side of the work at the right-hand end of the seam, positioning it so that the tape lies over the seam itself. Using sewing thread to match the yarn and a standard sharps sewing needle, whip stitch (see page 243) both edges of the tape to the back of the work. Make the stitches small and firm for maximum support.

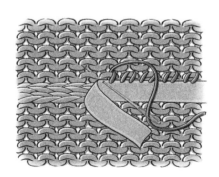

SEWING IN CAST—ON AND BOUND—OFF ENDS

When casting on and binding off, leave the yarn tails as long as possible and use them to sew up the seams (see pages 220–226). But if an edge is not being seamed, then sew it tidily into the back of the knitting.

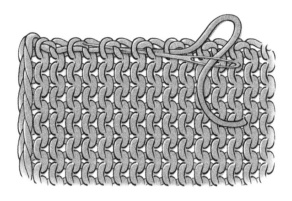

1. If the edge is not going to be taken into a seam, then thread the end into a blunt-tipped sewing needle. Take the needle under a few stitches along the edge of the knitting, then skipping the last stitch, take it back through the stitches. If the yarn is bulky, then go through the stitches in one direction only. Trim the end close to the knitting. If the edge is going to be taken into a seam, but you are not going to use the end to sew up with, then sew the seam first. Then use the method above to sew the end into the stitches that were taken into the seam.

SEWING IN INTARSIA OR STRIPE ENDS

If you find it difficult to obtain very neat stitches at the color changes in intarsia (see pages 177–178), you may find that you can fix the stitches when you sew in the ends, as you can fill gaps or tighten stitches at the same time. If you have small motifs that use quite a few colors, do not be tempted to run ends along the main part of the work, it will make the fabric look uneven; always sew in ends along the contrast color at the color changes.

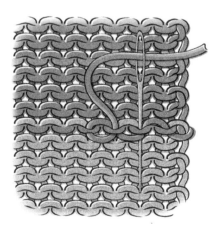

1. Thread a blunt-tipped sewing needle with one end of yarn at a time. Weave the needle up and down through the backs of three or four stitches that are the same color as the end, and pull the end through, keeping it at the same tension as the knitted stitches.

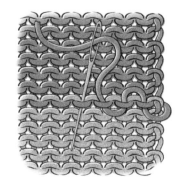

2. Weave the needle back through the stitches in the opposite direction, as shown, pushing it through the yarn to split it. This will help stop the ends from working themselves free. Trim the end close to the knitting.

GRAFTING STOCKINETTE: STITCHES TO STITCHES

Use this method when you are joining two pieces of knitting, both of which have the same number of live stitches and one of which has a long end of yarn. The stitches could have been provisionally cast on (see page 43), or provisionally bound off (see page 57), but this technique is easier to work if the stitches are put onto knitting needles, rather than being on waste yarn.

1. Right-sides up, lay the two pieces to be joined on a flat surface with the needles parallel and pointing in the same direction. Measure out the working yarn from the lower piece to four times the width of the knitting, cut the yarn and thread a blunt-tipped sewing needle with the end. From the back, bring the sewing needle through the first stitch of the lower piece and then, from the back again, through the first stitch of the upper piece. Take the needle through the front of the first stitch of the lower piece, then from the back, through the second stitch of the lower piece.

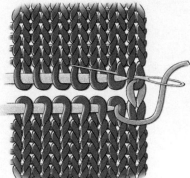

2. From the front, take the needle through the first stitch of the upper piece and then from the back through the second stitch on the same piece.

3. Continue in this way across the row, taking the sewing needle through a stitch from the front and then through the adjacent stitch on the same piece from the back. Take the needle across to the other piece of knitting and take it from the front through the stitch it last came out of, then through the back of the adjacent stitch on the same piece. Adjust the sewn stitches as you make them so that they have the same gauge as the knitted stitches.

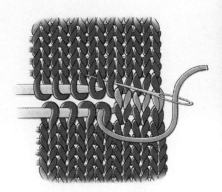

GRAFTING STOCKINETTE: STITCHES TO ROW ENDS

This is a good way of joining live stitches to a row-end edge as it creates a fairly flat seam with little bulk, that is also elastic. Spacing the live stitches along the row-end edge may take some experimentation, as both pieces of knitting need to lie flat without puckering. This method can be used for sewing the top of a dropped shoulder or square set-in sleeve to the body of a garment.

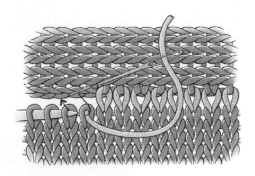

1. Right-sides up, lay the two pieces to be joined on a flat surface, as shown. Measure out the working yarn from the piece on the needle to four times the width of the knitting, cut the yarn and thread a blunt-tipped sewing needle with the end. Take the needle in and out of the live stitches on the needle in the same way as for grafting stockinette stitches to stitches (see opposite). On the row-end edge, take the needle under one bar of yarn a whole stitch in from the edge.

However, as a stitch is wider than it is long, on every third or fourth stitch along the row-end edge, take the needle under two bars instead of one. Adjust the sewn stitches as you make them so that they have the same gauge as the knitted stitches.

GRAFTING GARTER STITCH: STITCHES TO STITCHES

This is the same principle as for grafting stockinette (see opposite), but to keep the stitch pattern correct in garter stitch, one of the pieces of knitting must finish with a right-side row and the other with a wrong-side row.

1. Right-sides up, lay the two pieces to be joined on a flat surface with the needles parallel and pointing in the same direction. The piece that finished with the wrong-side row must be the lower piece. Measure out the working yarn from the lower piece to four times the width of the knitting, cut the yarn and thread a blunt-tipped sewing needle with the end. From the back, bring the sewing needle through the first stitch of the lower piece and then, from the back again, through the first stitch of the upper piece. Take the needle through the front of the second stitch of the upper piece, then from the front, through the first stitch of the lower piece. Then from the back, bring it through the second stitch of the lower piece.

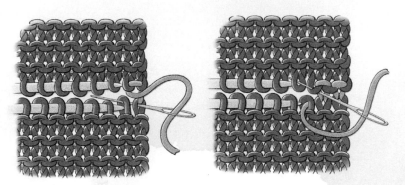

2. Continue in this way across the row, bringing the needle through each lower stitch from the back first and then the front, and each upper stitch from the front first and then the back, as shown, forming a ridge on the upper piece that will look like a row of garter stitch. Adjust the sewn stitches as you make them so that they have the same gauge as the knitted stitches.

GRAFTING RIB: STITCHES TO STITCHES

This is the technique for joining two pieces of rib worked in opposite directions, such as for seaming front bands or a shawl collar at the back of the neck. You need two pairs of knitting needles the same size. The finished result is not as invisible as other grafting, but the seam does lie flat and smooth.

1. Leave both of the two pieces of rib on the needles until you are ready to join them. On each piece, slip the purl and the knit stitches onto separate needles, as shown.

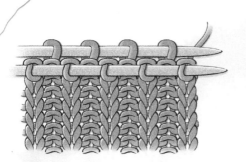

2. Right side up, lay the two pieces to be joined on a flat surface, so the needles holding the knit stitches are uppermost, parallel and pointing in the same direction. (Roll the needles holding purl stitches to the back to keep them out of the way.) Measure out the working yarn from the lower piece to four times the width of the knitting, cut the yarn and thread a blunt-tipped sewing needle with the end. From the back, bring the sewing needle through the first stitch of the lower piece and then, from the front, take it through the first stitch of the upper piece and then through the adjacent stitch on the same piece from the back. Take the needle across to the other piece of knitting and take it from the front through the stitch it last came out of, then through the back of the adjacent knit stitch on the same piece. Take the needle across to the other piece of knitting and take it from the front through the stitch it last came out of, then through the back of the adjacent stitch on the same piece. Continue in this pattern across the row, taking the sewing needle through a stitch from the front and then through the adjacent stitch on the same piece from the back. Slide the knitting needles out of the knitted stitches as you graft them, and adjust the sewn stitches as you make them so that they lie flat and do not pull the rib in.

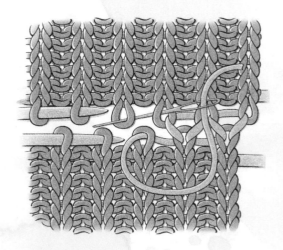

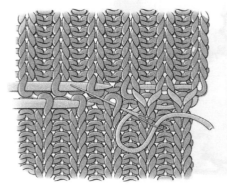

3. Turn the joined pieces over so that the stitches that were purl are now uppermost and are seen as knit stitches. Repeat Step 2 to graft these stitches together.

CROCHET SEAM

This technique can be used to make a pleasingly chunky, decorative, visible seam on cast-on or bound-off edges, as well as a more conventional, although bulky, seam on the wrong side of the work. Use a hook to suit the thickness of the seaming yarn. On the right side, you could use a contrast yarn for added decorative detail.

1. For a visible seam on cast-on/bound-off edges, lay the two edges to be joined right-side up and touching one another. From the front, slip a crochet hook under a stitch in the finished edge, then under the corresponding stitch in the finished edge behind. Wrap the seaming yarn around the hook and pull a loop through both edges. *Slip the hook under the next stitch along on both finished edges and wrap the yarn around it.

2. Pull a loop through both edges and through the loop on the hook.

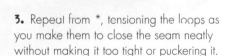

3. Repeat from *, tensioning the loops as you make them to close the seam neatly without making it too tight or puckering it.

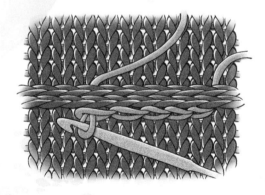

4. To join two pieces with a crochet seam on the wrong side, hold or pin them wrong-sides together. On a cast-on/bound-off seam, follow Steps 1–3. On a row end seam, as shown here, work the crochet loops in the same way, putting the hook through the layers one stitch in from the edge.

CROCHETING TWO PIECES TOGETHER OFF THE NEEDLES

This method is similar to a three-needle bind off (see page 53). It is quick to work, but you do need to be careful not to make the seam too tight. The working yarn should be left on the piece that will be at the front, the one that will have the right side facing away from you. Use a crochet hook that is the same size as the knitting needles.

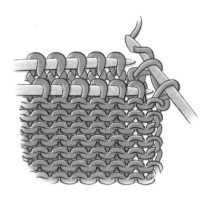

1. With the right sides of the work together, hold both needles in your left hand, the tips facing in the same direction. The needles are shown spaced apart here to make it easier to see what's happening, but you would hold them so they were touching. Put the crochet hook into the back of the first stitch on the front needle and then into the front of the first stitch on the back needle and slip them off the needles. Wrap the yarn around the hook.

2. Pull a loop through both stitches on the hook. *Put the hook into the next stitch on each needle, slipping them off the needles, and wrap the yarn around the hook.

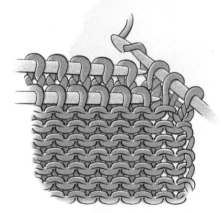

3. Pull a loop through all three loops on the hook. Repeat from * until just one loop remains on the hook. Cut the yarn, put the tail through the loop, and pull it tight.

BINDING OFF TWO PIECES TOGETHER

This is a way of binding off two pieces together that some people find easier than a standard three-needle bind-off (see page 53). Although you do need a third needle, because you are not trying to slip live stitches off two needles at the same time without dropping any other stitches (which can be all too easy to do), this method can be less fiddly to work.

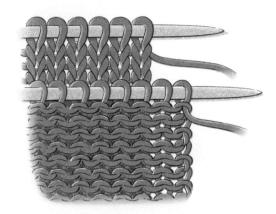

1. With the right sides of the work together, hold both needles in your left hand, the tips facing in the same direction. The needles are shown spaced apart here to make it easier to see what's happening, but you would hold them so they were touching.

2. Hold a third needle in your right hand. *Put the point of the right-hand needle into the back of the first stitch on the front left-hand needle and then into the back of the first stitch on the back left-hand needle. Slip both stitches onto the right-hand needle, then use the tip of the front left-hand needle to lift the first stitch over the second stitch and off the needle, leaving just one loop. Repeat from * until all the stitches have been worked onto the right-hand needle.

3. Slip all the stitches onto another needle so that the working yarn is ready to use at the end of the row. Bind off all the stitches in the usual way (see page 50).

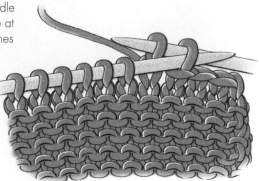

KNITTING OFF ONTO A ROW END

This is another way of joining live stitches on a needle to a row-end edge, but doesn't involve grafting (see page 229). If you find it tricky to pull the live stitches through the knitting, then use a crochet hook instead, but be careful not to make the seam too tight.

1. Hold the pieces right-sides together in your left hand, with the piece with the stitches on the needle at the back and the needle pointing to the right. The pieces are shown spaced apart here to make it easier to see what's happening, but you would hold them so they were touching. Hold a second needle in your right hand. *From the back, put the right-hand needle through the row edge, either a whole or a half stitch in from the edge, as you prefer. Then knit the first stitch on the left-hand needle.

2. Bring the right-hand needle, and the stitch on it, back through the row-end piece.

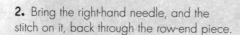

3. Repeat from *, putting the right-hand needle through the next space in the row-end piece and knitting the next stitch on the left-hand needle. There are now two loops on the right-hand needle.

4. Use the tip of the left-hand needle to lift the first stitch on the right-hand needle over the second stitch and off the needle. Repeat Steps 3–4 until all the stitches have been worked off the left-hand needle and just one loop remains on the right-hand needle. Cut the yarn, bring the tail through the row-end piece and through the loop, and pull it tight.

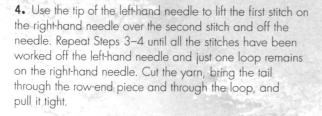

POCKETS

I love pockets on my clothes, and they can have both practical and decorative elements. On children's knits, I will often knit the lining or top band of an inset pocket in a contrast shade to add a pop of color, or work a "kangaroo" pocket on a hoodie. If there are large areas of a simple stitch pattern, pockets can also add detail and break up these areas.

SEWN-ON PATCH POCKET

This is the simplest type of pocket to make, but it can be tricky to sew them on neatly. Attach them after blocking all the knitted pieces (see pages 218–219), but before making up the garment, as this will make it much easier to sew the pocket on.

1. Pin the patch pocket in position on the garment. Using contrast color yarn, sew a line of running stitch around the side and bottom edges of the pocket, keeping the line straight and half a stitch beyond the edge of the pocket piece.

2. Using matching yarn and a blunt-tipped sewing needle, sew the pocket to the garment, using the running stitch lines as a guide to keep it square and in position. You can whip stitch the pocket, as here, which is a simple way of sewing it on, but the stitches will be visible. Alternatively, you can slip stitch the pocket in place (see page 226), or mattress stitch it (see pages 220–221), or duplicate stitch it (see below).

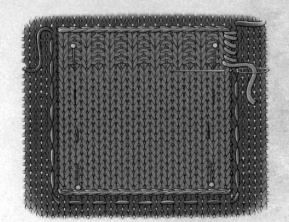

DUPLICATE-STITCHED PATCH POCKET

This way of sewing on a pocket is strong and can be very neat. Use the main yarn or the pocket yarn, as appropriate, so that the duplicate stitches will cover the finished edge.

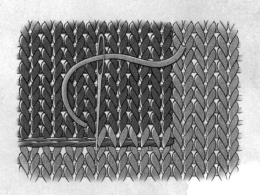

1. Pin the patch pocket in position, matching the edges carefully with rows and stitches of the garment piece. Using a blunt-tipped sewing needle, work horizontal duplicate stitch (see page 192) along the bottom edge of the pocket, sewing over the cast-on edge and through both layers of knitting. Then work vertical duplicate stitch (see page 193) up each side edge, again sewing through all layers.

PICK UP AND KNIT PATCH POCKET

This way of adding a patch pocket to a knitted piece has the advantage of needing no sewing on afterward. The methods are shown here over just a few stitches, but the pocket can be any width. If you are going to work a stitch pattern, such as single rib, at the top edge of the pocket, the edge stitches must be knit stitches.

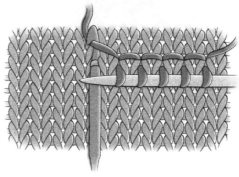

1. Working from right to left across where the bottom of where the pocket will be, and using a crochet hook, pick up and put on a knitting needle (see page 75) the number of stitches needed for the pocket.

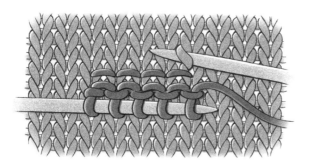

2. *Work one wrong-side row. On the next row, slip the right-hand needle under the left leg of the stitch in the main garment that corresponds with the first stitch of the next row of the pocket piece: this will be every alternate row as you do not attach the pocket piece on wrong-side rows. Lift this stitch onto the left-hand needle and knit it together as one with the first stitch of the pocket piece.

3. Knit the row of the pocket piece to the last stitch, then slip that stitch knitwise (see page 77) onto the right-hand needle. Slip the left-hand needle under the left leg of the stitch in the main garment that corresponds with the last stitch of this row of the pocket piece. Slip the last pocket stitch back onto the left-hand needle and knit it through the back loop (see page 77) together as one with the stitch from the garment. Repeat from * until the pocket is the required size, then bind off on a right-side row, picking up the garment stitches at the beginning and end of the row.

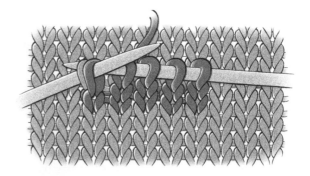

POCKET BORDERS

Pockets don't have to be plain, you can add design detail by working a top border in a contrasting stitch pattern or color. Borders are shown here on patch pockets, but they can be added to inset pockets (see page 238) by working the rows before the bind off in pattern or color.

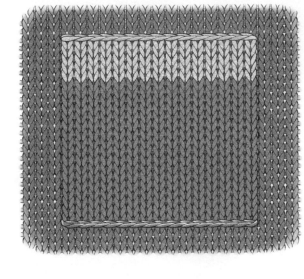

1. An accent color can be picked up on a pocket border by simply working the top few rows in the chosen color. Sew in the color ends (see page 227) before sewing on the pocket.

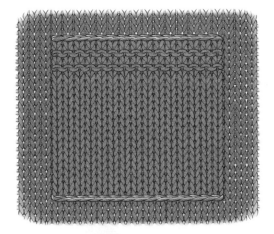

2. Garter stitch (see page 60) makes a neat border for a pocket, but as the stitches are shorter than stockinette stitches, a deep border can look a bit stretched at the sides where the patch pocket is sewn to a stockinette background.

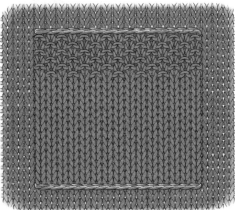

3. Seed stitch (see page 61) is a firm, stable stitch that works very well as a border. The stitches knit up to the same depth as stockinette stitches, so the pocket is easy to sew on.

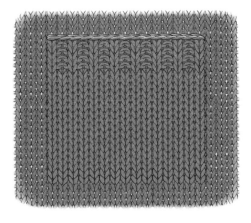

4. Single rib (see page 61) is a classic border pattern, but the elasticity of the stitch can pull the top of the pocket in a bit rather than allowing it to lie flat. You can avoid this by purling every stitch on the wrong-side rows.

HORIZONTAL INSET POCKET

The inset pocket, sometimes called an integrated pocket, is an easy and neat style. A contrast lining can add a flash of color that creates design detail, particularly if you don't add a border at the top edge of the pocket. You can leave the pocket stitches on a stitch holder rather than binding them off, and work a border later; you'll need to sew the edges of the border in place as for a patch pocket (see page 235).

First, make a pocket lining. This should be a piece of knitting two stitches wider than the required width of the pocket opening, and one row deeper than the required depth, and should finish with a right-side row. Leave the stitches on a spare needle or a stitch holder.

1. Work to the row before the position of the top of the pocket, which should be a wrong-side row. If you want a pocket border (see page 237), then work the rows before the pocket top in the required pattern: here they have been worked in single rib (see page 61). On the next row, knit to the position of the pocket. Bind off the required number of stitches for the pocket opening, then knit to the end of the row.

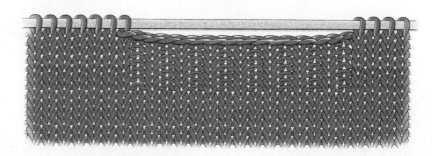

2. On the next row, purl to one stitch before the bound-off stitches. Hold the lining with the wrong-side facing you and purl the last stitch before the bind off together as one with the first stitch of the lining.

3. Purl across the lining stitches to the last stitch. Purl this stitch together with the first stitch on the left-hand needle after the bind off. Purl to the end of the row and complete the rest of the piece. Whip stitch (see page 243) the pocket lining to the back of the piece.

VERTICAL INSET POCKET

This pocket is a similar principle to a horizontal inset pocket (see opposite), but it runs vertically. You will need two spare knitting needles, or one spare needle and two stitch holders. This style of pocket works well on casual, blouson jacket styles.

1. Work to the row before the position of the bottom of the pocket, which should be a wrong-side row. On the next row, knit to the position of the pocket opening. Leave the remaining stitches on the left-hand needle on a spare needle or a stitch holder. Turn the work; these stitches are the front pocket stitches. Work these stitches until the pocket opening is the required depth, finishing with a wrong-side row. To work a border, work a few stitches at the end of right-side rows and beginning of wrong-side rows in the required pattern: here they have been worked in garter stitch (see page 60). Leave the stitches on a spare needle or a stitch holder.

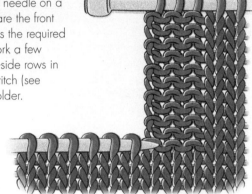

2. Go back to the stitches left earlier (putting them on a needle if need be), rejoin the yarn (see page 71), and using the cable method (see page 88), cast on the number of stitches required for the lining. Work all the stitches to same depth as the front pocket section, finishing with a wrong-side row.

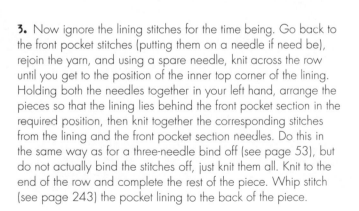

3. Now ignore the lining stitches for the time being. Go back to the front pocket stitches (putting them on a needle if need be), rejoin the yarn, and using a spare needle, knit across the row until you get to the position of the inner top corner of the lining. Holding both the needles together in your left hand, arrange the pieces so that the lining lies behind the front pocket section in the required position, then knit together the corresponding stitches from the lining and the front pocket section needles. Do this in the same way as for a three-needle bind off (see page 53), but do not actually bind the stitches off, just knit them all. Knit to the end of the row and complete the rest of the piece. Whip stitch (see page 243) the pocket lining to the back of the piece.

SELVEDGES, HEMS, FACINGS, & BANDS

The pieces you work first in knitting are usually unstructured, particularly those with front openings, such as cardigans or jackets. They need bands, collars, or edges either knitted in or added afterwards. Hems can replace ribs or collars can be faced. The techniques that follow show you how to make these features look neat and professional.

SELVEDGES

This is mainly useful on edges that are not going to be seamed as they make a neater finish than plain row ends. They are perfect for side vents on tops, although they can cause problems if you decide later to seam the edge or pick up stitches from it. Note that in all these patterns "yf" means "bring yarn forward" and does not mean you should work a yarnover (see page 136).

SLIP STITCH SELVEDGE

This selvedge is a column of longer, slipped stitches on the edge of the knitting.

Slip the first stitch (see page 77) on every row.
Written out for stockinette the pattern would read:
Row 1 (RS): Sl1 kwise, k to end.
Row 2: Sl1 kwise, yf, p to end.

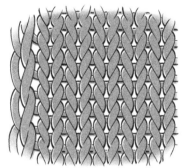

GARTER STITCH SELVEDGE

This creates a textured selvedge that looks slightly different on the left and right edges of the knitting. The illustration on the left shows the left-hand edge, and that on the right, the right-hand edge.

Knit the first and last stitch on every row.
Written out for stockinette the pattern would read:
Row 1 (RS): Knit.
Row 2: K1, yf, p to last st, yb, k1.

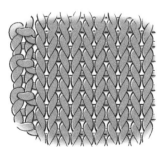

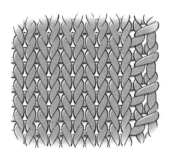

DOUBLE GARTER SELVEDGE

Two-stitch selvedges are a good option for edges that will be very visible as they create a narrow decorative, stable border. This version uses slipped and knit stitches.

Start every row by slipping the first stitch knitwise (see page 77) through the back loop (see page 77) and knitting the second stitch. End every row by knitting the last two stitches.
Written out for stockinette the pattern would read:
Row 1 (RS): Sl1 kwise tbl, k to end.
Row 2: Sl1 kwise tbl, k1, yf, p to last 2 sts, yb, k2.

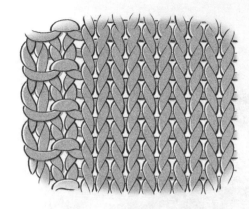

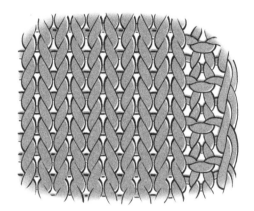

CHAIN GARTER SELVEDGE

This two-stitch selvedge uses a slip stitch and a purl stitch to create a selvedge with a flat outer edge.

Start and end every right-side row by slipping the first stitch knitwise (see page 77) and purling the second stitch. Start and end every wrong-side row by purling the last two stitches.
Written out for stockinette the pattern would read:
Row 1 (RS): Sl1 kwise, yf, p1, yb, k to last 2 sts, yf, p1, yb, sl1 kwise.
Row 2: Purl.

PICOT SELVEDGE

This is a decorative selvedge that is much easier to work than it might look. There is also a picot cast on (see page 41) and a picot bind off (see page 55) that complement this selvedge.

Start every row by using the cable method (see page 88 to cast on the required number of stitches for the picot (here, two stitches), then immediately bind them off before working the row.
Written out for stockinette the pattern would read:
Row 1 (RS): Cast on 2 sts, bind off 2 sts, k to end.
Row 2: Cast on 2 sts, bind off 2 sts, p to end.

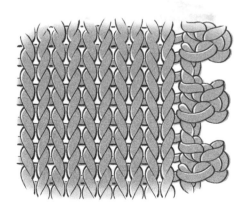

HEM WITH GARTER STITCH FOLD ROW

This is good for a crisper fold on a hem. It gives a slightly bumpy bottom edge because of the nature of garter stitch, but on a chunky yarn you can use this feature in a decorative way. A garter stitch fold row can be worked on the right side or the wrong side.

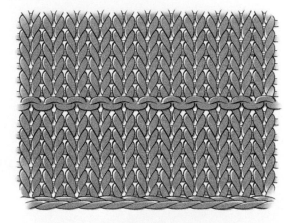

1. Cast on the required number of stitches and work the required depth of the hem in stockinette stitch. Then work the fold row: this will be a purl row if it is being worked on the right side, and a knit row if it is being worked on the wrong side. Complete the piece of knitting.

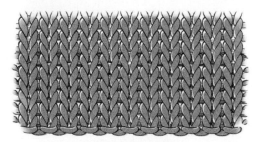

2. Turn up the hem to the back along the fold row and sew it in place (see opposite).

HEM WITH SLIP STITCH FOLD ROW

This also gives a crisper fold on a hem, but the edge is flatter. The method will need an odd number of stitches and can be worked on a right side or a wrong side.

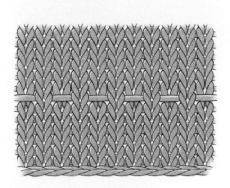

1. Cast on the required number of stitches (this must be an odd number) and work the required depth of the hem in stockinette stitch, then work the fold row. If this is being worked on the right side, then knit and slip purlwise (see page 174) alternate stitches, slipping the stitches with the yarn in front (see page 175), and ending the row with a knit stitch. If the fold row is being worked on the wrong side, then purl and slip purlwise (see page 174) alternate stitches, slipping the stitches with the yarn in front (see page 175), and ending the row with a purl stitch. Complete the piece of knitting.

Written out for a right-side row the pattern would read:
Fold row (RS): [K1, sl1 wyif] to last st, k1.
Written out for a wrong-side row the pattern would read:
Fold row (WS): [P1, sl1 wyib] to last st, p1.

2. Turn up the hem to the back along the fold row and sew it in place (see page opposite).

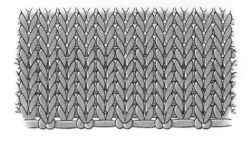

WHIP STITCHING A HEM

The actual stitches holding up a hem should be invisible on the right side, though a bump will usually show in the fabric where the hem is attached. Use the same yarn as the project if it is strong enough, or one that's a close color match; here a contrast color is used for clarity.

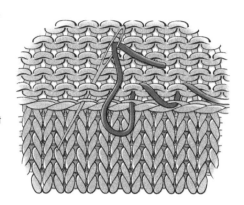

1. Thread a blunt-tipped sewing needle with a long length of yarn and secure the yarn on the back of the piece, at the right-hand end of the seam. Turn up the hem and pin it in place if need be. *Working from right to left, take the needle from top to bottom under the loop of the back of a stitch just above the top edge of the hem, and then take it through one stitch loop in the finished edge of the hem. Pull the stitch gently taut but not tight. Repeat from *, taking the needle through every alternate stitch loop.

HERRINGBONE STITCHING A HEM

This technique is more time-consuming to sew than whip stitch (see above), but it creates a more stable hem. This is a good technique for chunky yarns, but it's best to do the actual sewing using a thinner yarn that's a close color match.

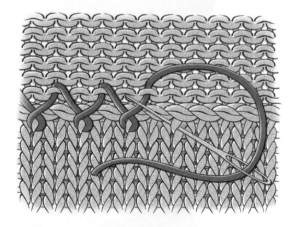

1. Thread a blunt-tipped sewing needle with a long length of yarn and secure the yarn on the back of the piece, at the left-hand end of the seam. Turn up the hem and pin it in place if need be. *Working from left to right, take the needle from bottom to top under the loop of the back of a stitch just above the top edge of the hem, and then take it from right to left through the right-hand loop of a stitch just under the finished edge of the hem. Repeat across the hem until it is sewn in place. Pull the stitch gently taut but not tight. Repeat from *, taking the needle through every alternate stitch loop.

KNITTED-IN HEM

This avoids having to sew up the hem later, but does mean that the hem is permanently fixed, it can't be let down. You will need a spare knitting needle the same size as the project needles. This technique works well for items without side seams, such as blankets or pieces knitted in the round.

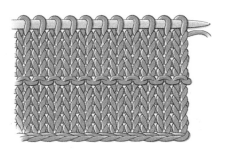

1. Cast on the required number of stitches and work the required depth of the hem in stockinette stitch. Then work the fold row if required—here it's a garter stitch fold (see page 242). Work rows until the knitting above the fold row is the same depth as the hem below it, ending with a wrong-side row.

2. Make sure the live stitches can't fall off the needle (a point protector is good for this), and turn the work upside down. Using the spare knitting needle, pick up and knit one stitch from every cast-on stitch (see page 76). When you have picked up right across the row, the tip of the needle must be pointing in the same direction as the needle holding the main live stitches.

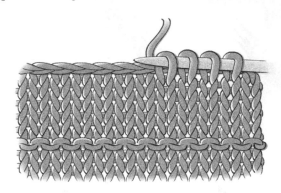

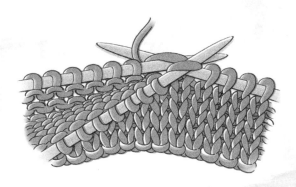

3. Fold the hem along the fold row so that the wrong sides are together and hold the needles together in your left hand. Using the spare needle, knit the corresponding stitches from each left-hand needle together. Do this in the same way as for a three-needle bind off (see page 53), but do not actually bind the stitches off, just knit them all. Complete the knitted piece.

GRAFTING A HEM

Because there's no cast-on edge, a hem that has been grafted in place lies flatter on the wrong side of the knitting, so there will be less of a bump visible on the right side. Use the project yarn to do the grafting.

1. Cast on using the provisional cast on (see page 43) and work the whole piece. If there are seams to sew, then sew them before turning up the hem. Unpick the cast on and put the live stitches on to a needle.

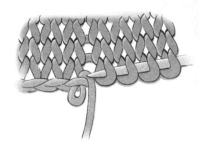

2. Turn up the hem and pin it in place if need be. Thread a blunt-tipped sewing needle with a long length of yarn and secure the yarn on the back of the piece, at the right-hand end of the hem. Working from right to left, bring the needle from the back through the first live stitch. *Then take the needle up under the loop of the back of a stitch just above the top edge of the hem.

3. Take the needle back down through the loop of the back of the next stitch to the left, then from the front into the live stitch it last came out of. From the back, take the needle through the next live stitch to the left. Slip the knitting needle out of the live stitches as you sew them in place, and pull the sewn stitches gently taut but not tight. Repeat from * to graft the hem in place.

GARTER STITCH FOLD FACING

A facing is particularly good on an edge-to-edge jacket worked in one stitch, so front bands are unnecessary, but you want to reinforce the front edges. The garter stitch fold gives a crisp fold and a slightly bumpy edge, and can be used to complement a garter fold hem (see page 242).

1. Cast on as many stitches as are needed for the piece, plus one stitch for the fold row, and the number of stitches needed for the facing. Knit all the right-side rows, and on the wrong-side rows, purl all the stitches other than the fold stitch, which is knitted.

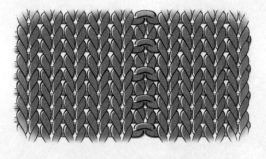

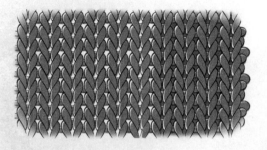

2. When the piece is complete, turn the facing to the back along the fold line and whip stitch it in place using the same principle as for a hem (see page 243). The garter stitches will define the outer edge of the facing.

SLIP STITCH FOLD FACING

This is an alternative to the garter stitch fold facing and gives a smoother fold line. Buttonholes can be worked on any facing to create a hidden button fastening.

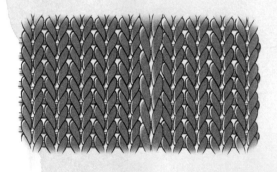

1. Cast on as many stitches as are needed for the piece, plus one stitch for the fold row, and the number of stitches needed for the facing. On the right-side rows, knit all the stitches other than the fold stitch, which is slipped purlwise (see page 77). On the wrong-side rows, purl all the stitches.

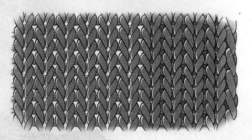

2. When the piece is complete, turn the facing to the back along the fold line and whip stitch it in place using the same principle as for a hem (see page 243). The slip stitches will define the outer edge of the facing.

MITERED FACING AND HEM

This is a combined facing and hem with a mitered corner to make it all sit as flat and neat as possible. It is shown here with a garter hem fold (see page 242) and a slip stitch facing fold (see opposite), but you can make the folds the same if you prefer.

1. Decide on the depth in rows of the hem; here, it is six rows deep. Cast on the number of stitches needed for the piece, minus six (one stitch for each row of the hem). Work the hem in stockinette, increasing by one stitch at the front edge on every row, so that when you reach the hem fold row the right number of stitches are on the needles. On the hem fold row, increase by one stitch to make the facing fold row. Work the piece, increasing by one stitch at the front edge on every row for the number of rows that the hem is deep; here, that is six stitches.

2. When the knitting is complete, turn the hem and facing to the back along the fold lines and whip stitch them in place. Make sure the mitered corner lies flat and whip stitch the edges of it together.

3. On the right side, the fold lines will define the outer edge of the facing and bottom edge of the hem.

PICKED-UP BAND

This is my favorite band to work; it provides a neat edge and after you have knitted it, you can work fewer or more rows if you are not happy with the width. The band stitches run at right angles to the body stitches and the buttonholes, although worked horizontally, will appear as vertical buttonholes in the finished band. Be careful not to pick up too many stitches as this will make the band wavy.

1. To help you pick up the right number of stitches, evenly spaced, first measure and mark with pins equal-sized sections along the front edge. Divide the number of stitches to be picked up by the number of sections marked out and the resulting number is how many stitches need to be picked up in each section. Pick up the stitches along the row edge, skipping every third or fourth stitch (see page 76) so that the band will lie flat.

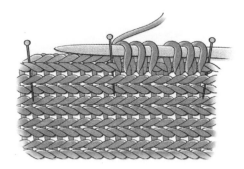

2. Work the band in the required stitch pattern; here it is single rib. Work buttonholes on the buttonhole band using your preferred method (see pages 252–255).

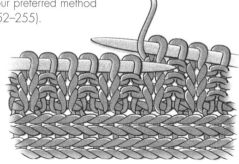

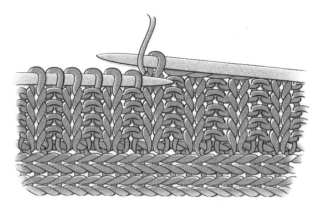

3. Bind the band off in pattern, being careful not to bind off too tightly.

KNITTED-IN BAND

This band runs in the same direction as the main body, so buttonholes worked horizontally will be horizontal. Work the buttonholes on the buttonhole band (the right band for girls, the left band for boys) using your preferred method (see pages 252–255). Knitting-in the band like this—rather than just knitting the band stitches as you work the main piece—creates a more defined edge to the band, and keeps that edge consistent around shaped areas, such as the neckline. And you can knit the welt and the band in a different color to the body.

1. For both fronts, cast on the stitches for the band and the bottom rib: on the right side, the last stitch of the band must be a knit stitch. Work the bottom rib across all the stitches, finishing with a right-side row, then put the band stitches on a holder and work the main part of the piece, starting with a wrong-side row.

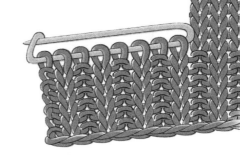

2. On the left band, slip the stitches onto a needle, re-join the yarn and start with a wrong-side row. Work to the last stitch, which will be a purl stitch. With the yarn forward, put the right-hand needle into the purl stitch and purlwise into the first stitch on the edge of the garment. Purl the two stitches together (see page 91).

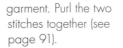

3. Turn the work. Slip the first stitch purlwise (see page 77) and rib to the end of the row. Work the whole band in this way.

4. On the right band, slip the stitches onto a needle, re-join the yarn and start with a right-side row. Work to the last stitch, which will be a knit stitch. With the yarn in back, put the right-hand needle into the knit stitch and knitwise into the first stitch on the edge of the garment.

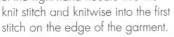

5. Knit the two stitches together (see page 90). Turn the work. Slip the first stitch purlwise (see page 77) and rib to the end of the row. Work the whole band in this way.

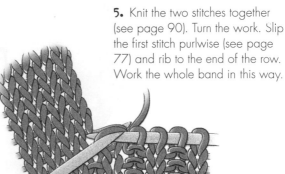

SEWN-ON BAND

This band runs in the same direction as the main body, so buttonholes worked horizontally will be horizontal. The seam creates a defined and firm inner edge to the band, which can be an asset if the knitted fabric is soft and fluid.

1. For both fronts, cast on the stitches for the band and the bottom rib: on the right side, the last stitch of the band must be a purl stitch. Work the bottom rib across all the stitches, then put the band stitches on a holder. On the first row of the main piece, increase by one stitch on the front edge, then complete the piece. Re-join the yarn to the band stitches and, starting with a wrong-side row, increase by one stitch, which will be a purl stitch, on the inner edge. Complete the band, slightly stretching it to fit neatly around the shaping and to the center back neck.

2. Right sides together, pin the band to the main piece and sew in place, taking a one-stitch seam allowance and using backstitch (see page 225).

REINFORCING A BUTTONBAND

Sometimes a front band, particularly if it is worked at the same time as the main part, can be slightly floppy, and stiffening it with grosgrain or petersham ribbon will lend structure. Reinforcing bands is also a good way to prevent them gaping between buttons in a close-fitting cardigan. Ribbon can be added to just the straight bit of the band, leaving the shaped section free. Choose a color that won't show through the knitting. Alternatively, add ribbon to the front of the band in a contrast color and make a feature of it.

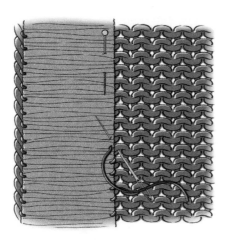

1. Cut a piece of grosgrain or petersham 1in longer than the section of the band to be reinforced. Turn under and finger press ½in at each cut end. Pin the ribbon to the back of the band, pinning it just inside the front edge. Using a sharp sewing needle and sewing thread to match the yarn, sew the ribbon in place with tiny whip stitches.

FASTENINGS

There are many ways to fasten your knits, with buttons and buttonholes being the most commonly used. But you can also use buttonloops with buttons, or choose a zipper, which can give a contemporary feel. Elastic is also included in this section.

POSITIONING BUTTONHOLES

You need to position buttons carefully to match buttonholes so that the bands lie smoothly without pulling or bulging out. There may be different methods depending on the information given in your pattern but you will usually be told to work one at the top and bottom of the band and the others positioned evenly between. The most important thing is to make sure the bands don't gape between buttons on cardigans or jackets and if unsure of how many are needed, I will always go for more buttonholes rather then fewer.

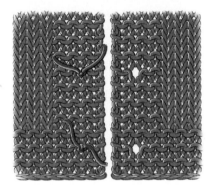

1. If the pattern gives specific instructions for working the buttonholes, then complete both bands and block and finish the garment. Arrange the finished garment so the buttonhole band and the buttonband are side by side. Count the rows between the buttonholes. On the buttonband, count out the same numbers of rows and mark the position of each button with a length of contrast yarn knotted through the appropriate stitch. Check the positions by laying the buttonhole band over the buttonband and pulling all the contrast strands through the buttonholes.

2. If you are not following a pattern, or the pattern doesn't give specific instructions, then knit the buttonband first. Lay it flat and measure and mark out the positions you want the buttons to be. The lowest button should not be more than ½in up from the hem, and the top button no more than ½in down from the neck, or placed accurately at the base of the V if the cardigan has a V-neck. The other buttons should be spaced equally between these two. Measure the spaces and mark them with pins, then count the rows between each button to space them completely evenly, and mark the final positions with lengths of contrast yarn knotted through the appropriate stitches.

When working the buttonhole band, a vertical buttonhole should begin a row or so below the marker and end a row or so above it. Horizontal buttonholes should be made directly opposite the markers. All buttonholes should be centered on the band.

Spend time carefully working out the spacing you need, taking into account the number of rows you are going to work each buttonhole over, and write out a pattern for yourself. It can be a good idea to knit a section of the band with two buttonholes in to make sure it will fit against the button markers before knitting the whole buttonhole band.

EYELET BUTTONHOLE

This is the smallest buttonhole you can make, so it is particularly good for items such as baby clothes. It also works well with chunkier yarns where other methods would produce too big a buttonhole. This is also the way to make eyelets for threading cord or ribbon through. It's shown here on stockinette stitch, but it can be worked in any stitch pattern.

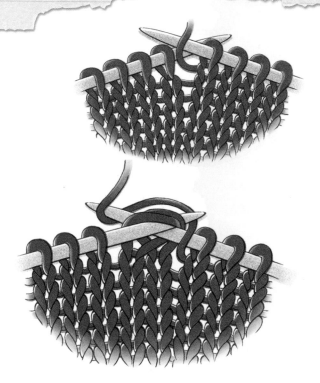

1. On a knit row, work to the position of the buttonhole. Bring the yarn forward between the needles ready to make a yarnover (see page 136).

2. Make the yarnover and knit the next two stitches together (see page 90) to maintain the original stitch count.

3. On a purl row, work to the position of the buttonhole. Wrap the yarn around the right-hand needle to make a yarnover (see page 136).

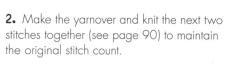

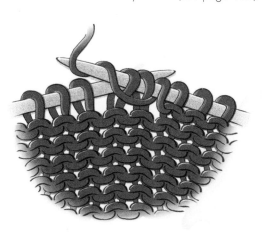

4. Purl the next two stitches together (see page 91) to maintain the original stitch count.

HORIZONTAL BUTTONHOLE OVER ONE ROW

This method is worked over one row like the eyelet buttonhole (see opposite), but it can be as large as is needed; the number of stitches bound off depends on the size of the buttonhole required. The technique is shown here on stockinette stitch, but it can be worked in any stitch pattern.

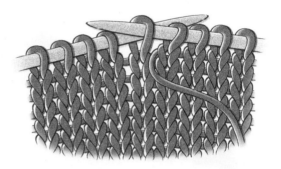

1. Work to the position of the buttonhole. Bring the yarn forward between the needles and slip the next stitch purlwise (see page 77).

2. Take the yarn back between the needles to the back of the work. Slip the next stitch purlwise then use the tip of the left-hand needle to lift the wrapped stitch over the top of the stitch just slipped and off the needle. *Slip the next stitch purlwise then use the tip of the left-hand needle to lift the first slipped stitch over the second one. Repeat from * until you have bound off the number of stitches required for the buttonhole.

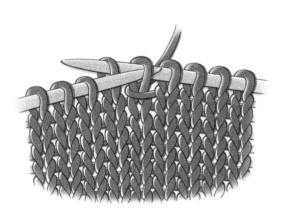

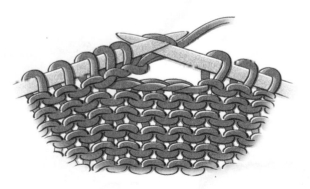

3. Turn the work and using the cable cast on increase technique (see page 88), cast on the number of stitches that were bound off, plus one extra stitch.

4. Turn the work so that the right side is facing and take the yarn to the back. Slip the next stitch from the left-hand needle onto the right-hand needle. Using the tip of the left-hand needle, lift the extra stitch on the right-hand needle over the top of the slipped stitch and off the needle. Knit to the end of the row.

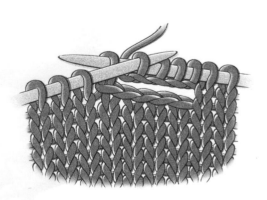

HORIZONTAL BUTTONHOLE OVER TWO ROWS

This is the most commonly used type of buttonhole, and the number of stitches bound off depends on the size of the buttonhole required. There are small variations that claim to give a neater result, but this is the basic principle. It is shown here on stockinette stitch, but it can be worked in any stitch pattern.

1. Work to the position of the buttonhole. Bind off (see page 50) the number of stitches required for the buttonhole. Work to the end of the row.

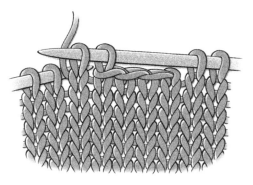

2. On the next row, work to the bound-off stitches.

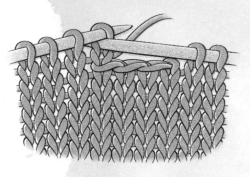

3. Turn the work and put the tip of the right-hand needle into the first stitch on the left-hand needle.

4. Using the cable cast on increase technique (see page 88), cast on to the left-hand needle the number of stitches that were bound off.

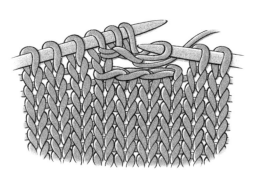

5. Before placing the last cast-on stitch onto the left-hand needle, bring the yarn forward between the two needles to the front of the work, then put the stitch on the left-hand needle. Turn the work again, pull the working yarn tight, and complete the row.

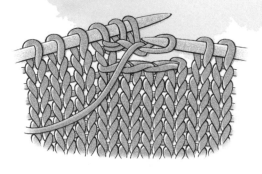

VERTICAL BUTTONHOLE

For this method you will need a stitch holder, a second ball of yarn, and a third needle. A vertical buttonhole needs to be reinforced at the bottom and top of the opening, and the tails of yarn that are left over from making it are ideal for this, so leave them long when joining in and cutting the yarn.

1. Work to the position of the buttonhole. Slip the remaining stitches of the row onto a stitch holder. Turn the work and work on the stitches on the needles until the buttonhole is the required depth, finishing with a right side row. Do not cut the yarn.

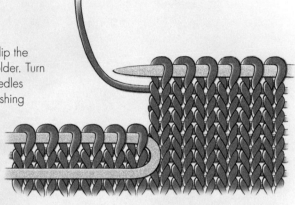

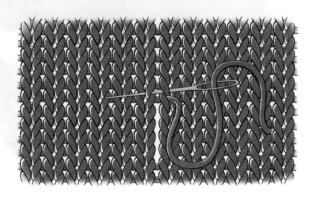

2. Join another ball of yarn to the stitches on the holder (see page 71). Using a third knitting needle, work the second half of the buttonhole to one row less than the first half. With the needle holding the first half in your right hand, knit across the stitches of the second half of the buttonhole.

3. Using the ends of yarn at the top and bottom of the buttonhole, sew across the top and bottom to reinforce them, then sew in the ends (see page 227).

REINFORCING BUTTONHOLES

On yarns with a lot of give, reinforcing can help prevent buttonholes from stretching more than they would with constant use alone. Individual buttonholes can be reinforced, or the whole buttonhole band can be stabilized using the same principle as on a buttonband (see page 250); this also helps prevent gaping openings.

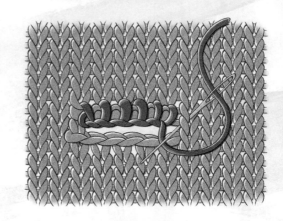

1. Reinforce individual buttonholes by sewing around them using blanket stitch (see page 194). You can use the project yarn, or a toning or contrasting color yarn for detail.

2. To reinforce a whole buttonhole band, cut a piece of grosgrain or petersham ribbon 1in longer than the section of the band to be reinforced. Turn under and finger press ½in at each cut end. Pin the ribbon to the back of the band, pinning it just inside the front edge. Turn the piece over and using a fabric marker, carefully draw through the knitted buttonholes onto the ribbon to mark the position and size of each buttonhole. Unpin the ribbon and sew the buttonholes in it, either by hand using blanket stitch (see page 194), or using a sewing machine. Pin the ribbon to the back of the band again, lining up the knitted buttonholes with those in the ribbon. Using a sharp sewing needle and sewing thread to match the yarn, sew the ribbon in place with tiny whip stitches. Then sew the layers together around each buttonhole.

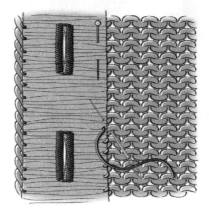

BUTTONLOOPS

Instead of making buttonholes, you can make little loops to fasten buttons through. These can be knitted, crocheted, or made from loops of yarn blanket-stitched together. I prefer to crochet mine.

1. Work a crochet chain by making a slip knot on the hook. *Wind the yarn around the hook and pull another loop through the one on the hook. Repeat from * until the loop is the required length. Cut the yarn, leaving a long tail, put the tail through the last loop, and pull tight. Use the tails at the start and end of the crochet chain to sew it to the edge of the knitting to form a loop.

ELASTIC IN A CASING

This is the classic elastic waistband—a hem folded over to the inside with elastic threaded through. The elastic is shown hanging down here so that you can see how it is sewn together. This method works best on fabrics knitted in fine yarns, because the casing can end up being quite bulky.

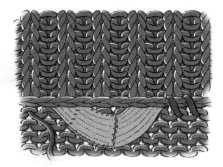

1. A casing for an elastic waistband is essentially a hem at the top of the garment. You can use a fold row (see page 242) for a flatter top edge. Whip stitch (see page 243) the edge of the casing in place, leaving a small opening. Measure the elastic, attach a safety pin to one end and use that as a bodkin to thread the elastic through the casing. Overlap the ends, making sure the elastic isn't twisted, and sew them firmly together.

STITCHING IN ELASTIC

This method is less bulky than a casing (see above) as there is only a single layer of fabric, so works well when knitting with thicker yarns.

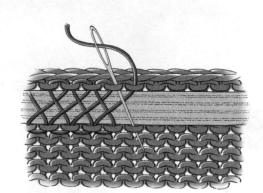

1. Measure the elastic, overlap the ends, making sure the elastic isn't twisted, and sew them firmly together. Pin the loop of elastic in place on the wrong side of the garment, just below the top finished edge. Thread a blunt-tipped sewing needle with a long length of yarn and secure the yarn on the back of the piece above the elastic. *Working from left to right, take the needle under the loop of the back of a stitch just below the elastic, and then take it up under the stitch loop immediately to the left. Take the needle over the elastic and across to the right making a diagonal stitch, then take it up under the loop of the back of a stitch just above the elastic, and then down under the stitch loop immediately to the left. Make a diagonal stitch down across the elastic to the next stitch loop to the right of the last one with a stitch in below the elastic and repeat from *. Pull the stitches gently taut but not tight.

THREADING IN ELASTIC

Sometimes a rib is not as stretchy as you would like, or it can lose its elasticity over time. Threading through shirring elastic can improve it.

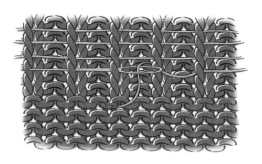

1. Thread a blunt-tipped sewing needle with a long length of shirring elastic. Fasten one end to the back of the work where you want the elastic to start; you can either knot the elastic in place or sew it on using sewing thread. Thread the elastic under one leg of each knit stitch on the wrong side of the work, pulling it evenly as taut as needed, and threading it through every row of rib for a smooth, snug finish.

INSERTING A ZIPPER

Zippers are a good fastening for jackets and cardigans and are surprisingly easy to sew in as the knitted fabric hides any sewing inadequacies. They can give a modern feel to knits and I particularly like to use them in casual knits for children. Buy good quality zippers; cheap ones stick and don't last.

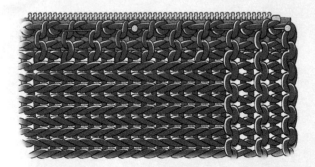

1. Open the zipper and pin it in place, with the edge of the knitting close to the teeth, but not so close as to easily catch in them.

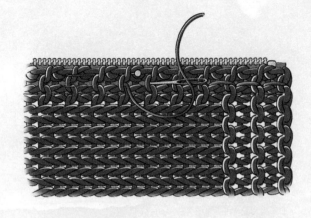

2. Using a sharp sewing needle and sewing thread that matches the yarn, sew the zipper in place using backstitch (see page 194). Make the stitches as small and as discreet as possible.

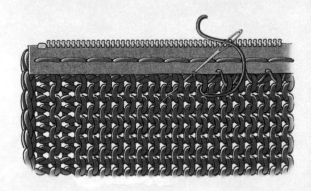

3. On the wrong side, whip stitch the zipper tape to the back of the garment, sewing through the loops of the backs of the stitches so that no stitching shows on the right side.

CROCHET ZIPPER OPENING EDGE

To create a very neat edge for your zipper opening you can work a simple crochet border as an alternative to working the edge in a stitch pattern. This border also stiffens and stabilizes the edge a little, so it's a good solution if a knitted fabric is floppy.

1. Before sewing in the zipper, work a single crochet border (see page 215) along the opening edges. Then sew the zipper in place (see opposite), working the backstitch along the edge of the crochet close to the knitting.

2. If the opening edge is very floppy, you can stiffen it a bit by working an additional row of slip stitch (see page 214) into the single crochet, as shown. This can be done before or after sewing the zipper in place.

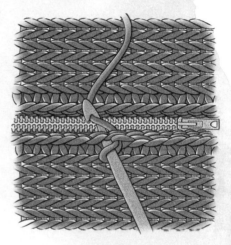

SEWING WOVEN FABRIC TO KNITTING

There may be few times that you will need to sew woven fabric to knitting, but when you do you will need to take into account the difference between the knitted and the woven fabric. One of my favorite designs is one that I created using a floral print skirt attached to a cable and seed stitch bodice.

The first thing to seriously consider is that the knitted fabric will be stretchy and the woven fabric won't be; even if you buy stretch fabric, it is unlikely to have as much elasticity as the knit. So be sure that once the woven fabric is sewn in place, the knit will still be able to stretch as is needed; for example, to get a garment on.

The best way to sew a knitted fabric to a woven one is using a serger. These machines are designed to work with stretch fabrics and have settings that allow for stitching that is strong and has the maximum possible amount of give. Alternatively, most modern sewing machines have a stretch straight stitch that will work well. If your machine does not have this function, then try using a narrow zigzag stitch, which will not produce as neat a seam, but will work with the two fabrics.

If you are sewing by hand, then use a backstitch seam (see page 225), or oversewing (see page 225) if the edge of the woven fabric is already neatened.

DESIGNING KNITS

When I talk to knitters about designing their own projects, many of them will say that they aren't confident enough, that they wouldn't know where to start. But when I enquire further, it often turns out that the very first thing they ever knitted was something they had designed themselves; it was a scarf. And the steps from designing a scarf to designing a sweater are smaller and easier than you might think.

FINDING INSPIRATION

Inspiration is a very personal thing; it's found by people via different routes in different places using different tools. You need to explore and experiment, and don't worry if the results aren't what you expected: when it comes to inspiration, surprises should be relished! Other people's experiences can be useful in helping you consider options, so in that spirit, here are my thoughts on—and some of my ways of finding—inspiration.

PHOTOGRAPHY

Photographs, whether taken by you, found in books or magazines, bought as postcards, downloaded from the Internet, will be high on most people's list of sources of inspiration. Personal photographs don't have to be brilliant; a few quick snapshots will usually be enough to record the shapes, colors, and textures of a scene, and you don't have to show your efforts to anyone else!

Up to five years ago it never occurred to me to be concerned if I left my mobile phone at home; I only took it with me when I was traveling and needed to contact home. When I got a Blackberry I became more phone-conscious, because I could send and respond to e-mails when I was away from my computer, which alleviated the horror of turning it on when I got home and having to answer hundreds of e-mails.

How I have changed now that I have a phone that takes photographs: it has revolutionized the way that I seek out inspiration. Just walking down a busy London street in the very multi-cultural area I live in, I am bombarded by images that can set off a train of thought that leads to a design: from a clash of color in an Indian sari shop to the shape or detail of a garment in a store window. Rather than try to hold the image in my head until I can get it down on paper, I can take a photo and store it forever. And so I can look back at images I took a few years ago and find ideas that are relevant to the collection I am working on now.

On a recent trip to New York I looked out of the hotel window and saw the neon lights of a building reflecting on the windows of a skyscraper opposite; the pinks against the grey ended up in a primarily monochrome Fair Isle that featured just a dash of rose.

MOOD BOARDS, SCRAPBOOKS, AND SKETCHBOOKS

A mood board is essentially a small scrapbook that develops a specific idea or collection of ideas: a sheet of card with images, swatches, sketches, tear sheets, and whatever else you find inspiring stuck to it.

I love mood boards; you can start with just a couple of items, put the board somewhere where you can see it, and add to it as you find new inspirations, so that the ideas grow and develop organically. Or you can use a mood board to arrange a host of materials that you have assembled and that just need structuring to become something wonderful.

I am fascinated by the mood boards put together by other designers, and quite often suffer from sketchbook envy. Recently my colleague Teresa and I pored over the sketchbook of a fashion student we were interviewing for a work placement, and as soon as she had left there were sighs of "did you see what she had done with small twigs?" and "her handwriting!"

Of course, with the Internet there are many ways to source ideas these days, and one of my favorite places to go to is Pinterest. I like to see what other people are inspired by, and I also find it a quick way to create stories, especially while traveling. Pinterest works well for me because I have very little confidence in my ability to sketch well or produce a beautiful mood board, so putting together images on the computer initially is a good option.

But I am still very old-school, so I also need to have a pinboard in the real world, too; I have one that takes up nearly a whole wall in my studio. Images from magazines, bits of fabric, yarn fringes from my yarn lines, swatches that I've knitted can all be swiftly put up and I can then stand back and change things around, add or take away.

CREATING A COLLECTION

You may think that the notion of "a collection" only applies to professional designers, and if that isn't you, then why would you consider your knitting in those terms? But most people have a favorite color palette, preferred items to knit, favorite yarn fibers, and as you start to create your own knit designs, they will often quite naturally become "a collection."

While I am working on a range of garments, I want the "story" behind the designs to come through, so photographs of landscapes, backgrounds, and colorways are integral to the theme. They also help when I'm talking through the shoot with the stylist and the photographer. I look on websites such as style.com, because it's good to be aware of fashion looks coming through the following season. If you are designing for yourself rather than as a professional, it is still nice to be aware of what shapes, styles, colors, or even stitches are going to be popular.

Having said all this, looking through my sketches I realize just how many have been drawn on napkins! While I try to carry a notebook around with me to pin down an idea (they can come at any time, anywhere), there are too many occasions when I don't have one, so the thought gets put down on any piece of paper to hand, although judging by the number of napkins, ideas always seem to strike me in a restaurant! But however and wherever you record these initial garment shapes and ideas, keep them carefully as these are the start of the design process.

DESIGNING TO FIT

There are a couple of things to consider before starting to design a garment, and the first is to consider your body shape, or that of the person you are knitting for.

SIZING

If you pick the pattern size of a knit you want to make based on the size you take in store-bought clothes, and you have always been dissatisfied by the fit of the end result, it may simply be that you are not making the right size.

I love the fact that I have the opportunity to design for children as well as produce collections of fashion knitwear for women, and occasionally men. The process of designing for all three is different—and I approach it in a different way—but I am particularly interested in addressing women's body shapes in my collections. Women's shapes are often categorized as pear, apple, rectangle, and hourglass. At various times in my life I have been each of the first three of these shapes, but sadly, never hourglass.

One of the privileges of traveling round to various stores to present new collections and yarns is that I get the opportunity to try the garments on knitters. Larger-sized women are usually reluctant to try the knits on when I tell them that they are the same garments that were used in photography and that they are all a 34-inch bust. However, when they do slip them on they are always amazed to find that their perception of the size they should knit is rather skewed and that they may only need to knit one size up.

There are a couple of primary reasons for this: the hand-knitted fabric is an elastic and forgiving one, so there will always be a certain amount of stretch in it. Almost all designs, unless they are completely figure-fitting, will have a certain amount of ease, at least 2in for a fairly close fitting garment, and usually more depending on the style. Check the actual measurements of the pattern, not the bust size, to see how much ease there is; you may prefer the measurements of a size other than the one you have chosen.

Knitters have asked me in the past why my patterns don't go up to the larger sizes (over 48-inch bust) but I feel very strongly that there has to be a point when grading up or down from the standard sizes must stop. This is because people do not necessarily size up incrementally; you may have a 42-inch bust, but be small with narrow shoulders. If designers grade up their patterns by adding more to each and every measurement—width, length, back neck, etc—you may find that your project resembles a small tepee. It will droop off your shoulders so that your sleeves are too long, the neckline will sag, and you will feel frumpy. So many knitters I have met have stopped knitting for themselves because they feel unattractive in their knits, and quite often that is down to them making garments that are simply too big for them.

BASIC GARMENT SHAPES

When it comes to sweaters, cardigans, and jackets, there are some simple, classic shapes that will suit different shaped bodies. You don't have to stick to these ideas when developing a design, but they are worth considering.

Knitters take a tremendous leap of faith when they choose a project to knit. I rarely buy clothes online because I like to try everything on. Dresses can be a nightmare because what fits me on top is too tight around the hips. As a designer and someone with my own brand of yarns, I never take for granted the faith that a knitter has put in me when they choose one of my patterns and buy my yarn, because until you have completed the project you will not know if it fits you well.

As we all have slightly different body shapes, designers have to work to standard shapes: we can't design for all idiosyncrasies, but we can address them by thinking about shape rather than just creating a huge range of sizes by adding or subtracting numbers when pattern writing.

For example, if am designing a long-line top or tunic, I very often add some flare for a subtle A-line, as there is nothing worse than a sweater that has a rib at the bottom that brings it in as it cuts across your hips or bottom. Most of us notice that as we get older our shape changes (I said goodbye to my waist many years ago), but rather than try and hide what we don't like by wearing shapeless garments, it's better to create shape by wearing knits that have slight tailoring.

A boxy jacket is much more flattering if it is slightly shaped at the sides, or if it goes down to a smaller needle size at the waist. Those with bigger busts look great in simple knits with a V-neck, or longer-line tunics that are slightly flared from under the bust rather than the big, generous, boyfriend sweaters.

Remember that what makes the knitted fabric great is also what can make it rather treacherous; the stretch that can be flattering can also make some women look rather shapeless, so choose your knits with care!

Once you have decided upon a shape you like, make a rough sketch—it really doesn't have to be more than that at this stage—so that you are ready to tackle the next stage in the process.

MEASURING FOR FIT

Having got an idea of the style of garment you want to knit, you now need to establish the size it must be in order for it to fit you beautifully. Spend time doing this so that your measurements are really accurate, or the time spent knitting will be wasted.

When you are designing a garment for yourself, it is a good idea to measure both your body and other garments you already own that you like the fit of. If you own a garment in a shape that is similar to the project you want to design, then so much the better. It doesn't have to be a knitted garment, but if you are measuring a fabric garment that doesn't stretch (such as a linen shirt), then bear in mind that the knitted garment will stretch and so will naturally provide more ease than the linen one.

You also need to remember seam allowances. You will be measuring the existing garment from seam to seam, but the sizes of the pieces you are going to knit will need to have one stitch/row added for seam allowances. You can turn a garment inside out and that will enable you to measure right up to the sewn seam lines. You can also measure the seam allowances, but be aware that they may be a different width to a single stitch or row in your knitted fabric.

Start by trying on garments you own until you find one that you like the fit of and that is as similar a shape as possible to the project you want to design. Lay this garment out flat, without stretching it. Photocopy your rough garment sketch to a larger size, so you have plenty of room to write on it. Use a cloth tape measure (not a ruler or a metal tape measure) to measure the garment; the diagram opposite shows you which measurements you might find useful. Using a colored pen, write the appropriate measurements on the sketch.

MEASURING A GARMENT

The example shown here is a sweater, but the principles apply to any item of clothing. If you are measuring a garment like the waterfall jacket shown opposite, where the fronts overlap, then lay it flat with one front folded back out of the way so that you can measure the other front without distorting it. Fronts will usually be symmetrical, but if not, then just fold the first one out of the way and measure the other one as well.

This diagram shows an ideal, complete set of measurements for a sweater with waist shaping, but the measurements you will need will depend on the style of garment you are making.

A Length from back neck (below collar or neckband) to waist.

B Length from waist to hem.

C Depth of armhole (from shoulder seam to underarm seam).

D Width of back neck (don't include collars or neckbands).

E Depth of back neck (don't include collars or neckbands).

F One shoulder width (from edge of neck below neckband to shoulder seam).

G Width across the shoulders (from shoulder seam to shoulder seam).

H Width of front neck (don't include collars or neckbands).

I Depth of front neck (don't include collars or neckbands).

J Width at bust (usually about 1in below the armhole).

K Width at waist (from side seam to side seam).

L Width at hips (or hem, if appropriate; from side seam to side seam).

M Length of sleeve (from shoulder seam to cuff).

N Length of underarm seam.

O Bicep width.

P Cuff width.

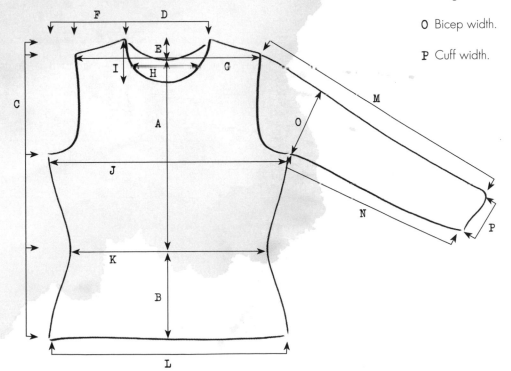

MEASURING YOUR BODY

Do be honest when measuring yourself—no holding your tummy in—or the knitting may end up being a waste of time and effort!

Double-check measurements on your own body, asking a friend to help you do this because the twisting and stretching you will need to do to get the tape measure in the right place will distort the measurements you take. If you need additional measurements that you can't take from the existing garment (because, for example, it isn't long enough), then take those from your body, too. The figure drawings below show you where to take various body measurements.

These diagrams shows whereabouts on the body to take specific measurements.

A Bust (measure around the widest point of your bust, making sure the tape measure stays level across your back).

B Natural waist (to find your natural waist, put your hands on your waistline and bend sideways; the point at which your body bends is your natural waist).

C Hips (measure around the widest point of your hips).

D Front length from shoulder to waist (from the top of your shoulder, over your bust, to your natural waist).

E Length from center of back neck to natural waist.

F Length from waist to hips.

G Width across the shoulders (from shoulder tip to shoulder tip).

H Arm (from shoulder tip to wristbone).

I Bicep (measure around the largest part of your upper arm).

J Wrist (measure around the narrowest part).

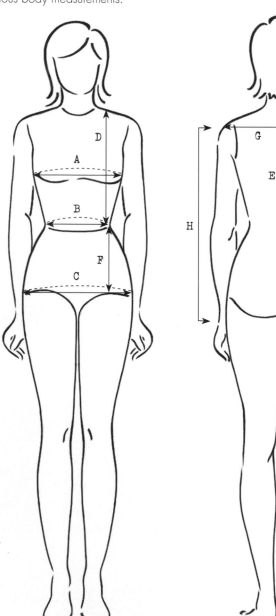

A SCALE DIAGRAM

Once you have all of the measurements you need, it is a good idea to re-draw your rough diagram to scale. Use a ruler for straight edges, and sketch in curves freehand, or use a French curve if you already have one.

Choose a simple scale, maybe 1:10, so that 20in becomes 2in. You want something that will fit onto a standard-size piece of paper. Your diagram doesn't need to be perfectly accurate at this stage as you aren't going to be working from it as such; it's just there to help you refine the idea and map out the shapes.

At this stage you may well find that an element you thought would work well becomes quite a different, and maybe less appealing, shape when it is drawn out at the right size.

Measuring for accessories such as scarves or beanies, or homewares such as pillows or throws, is simpler than for garments, but it can still be worthwhile to draw a diagram and write in all the measurements, just to be sure you haven't missed anything before you start knitting.

Drawing and measuring like this is also a great way of deciding which size of a commercial pattern to knit. You can use the pattern diagram as a starting point, add on your own measurements, then read the knitting pattern through quickly to see if any additional useful measurements are given in the text: for example, sometimes a pattern will tell you to work straight until the armhole measures a certain depth from the start of the shaping.

Once you have as complete a set of measurements as possible, you can see which pattern size is the best match. Remember that it is straightforward to add a little extra length to a sleeve or body of a simple, plain garment, but if there is a lot of shaping, or a stitch pattern to take into account, then pattern alterations can be trickier.

DEVELOPING
A DESIGN

Once you have decided on a shape and size, you can start on the really exciting, creative part of the design process. This is easily my favorite stage in developing a design, and I sometimes spend days refining small details, coming back to them time and again.

CHOOSING COLOR

Choosing a color is usually the first stage in developing your design idea into an actual knitted item. We are surrounded by color every day, some of our own choosing, some chosen by others, and some from nature, so there is plenty of inspiration to help make a choice.

Color plays an important part in memory with me: where some people can be transported back to the past by a certain smell, for me it is much more likely to be a shade that will remind me of a new dress for Easter when I was

five, or a stripe on the wooden handles of my skipping rope. When I first watched the Walt Disney Sleeping Beauty animation, the most memorable sequence to me was when the fairy godmothers used their wands to keep changing the colors of the dress they had made for the princess until they had found the perfect shade; greens turned to blues to mauves to pinks and reds, and for me it was the most enchanting part of the whole film.

Not all memories are good, of course; there is a shade of pink that I will forever associate with the calamine lotion that was liberally applied when I had chicken pox as a child.

Color is very subjective, we all have favorite shades. I will always lean toward blues and grays and struggle with oranges and reds. When I am choosing a color palette for my new yarns, I will be informed by the fiber when I am swatching. The feel of the yarn as it runs through my fingers will make me think of certain shades: a soft cotton may make me think of sorbets, ice-cream shades of mints and raspberry pinks; a silk will lead me to color-saturated brights.

When I am choosing new colors to add to an existing range, I will choose ones that harmonize with the other shades, but also look at future trends. I am fascinated by the fact that our attitude toward color changes with context; a fuchsia or orange may not appeal to me when I see it in isolation in a trend forecast, but I know that seen in an accessory such as a great scarf and put against gray or a chocolate brown, it has the power to energize the main shade.

USING PATTERN

It may be that you have planned to knit a single-color item, but even if that is your intention, it's always worth giving the idea of pattern a little consideration. It doesn't have to be an all-over, complicated Fair Isle knit; accent colors and color trims come under this heading.

This brings me to proportion. Like me, you may have experienced great disappointment in having selected a beautiful combination of colors for a Fair Isle, but then when knitted up into the pattern the colors don't create the excitement you felt when you saw them in the ball. This is because of proportion; you won't be using an equal amount of each shade and the balance is altered. I usually find that it will take at least two or three attempts at combining colors before I am happy, or I will knit up swatches of stripes in different widths to see if I can work on the balance before I start on the patterning. Duplicate stitch (see pages 192–193) is helpful, too, as it may be only one row that needs to be changed. Save all of your attempts, even if you are not happy with them: I have a library of swatches so I can check what didn't work in the past.

What I particularly like about classic Fair Isle is the way that subtle shading can be used to make the pattern strengthen and fade, creating an almost three-dimensional effect, and I like to use this in my designs where I have enough rows to allow for it.

Traditional Fair Isle can take on a modern twist with bold coloring. Work a pattern in brights to create a design bursting with color, yet still traditional at heart, and experiment with using the same pattern but substitute another background shade. Change the proportion by knitting a swatch using a thicker weight yarn to see how the size of the patterning transforms the look.

You may want to try tints, shades, and tones of one hue to play with depth of color, and great combinations can be made from a palette of black, grays, and white, but adding a pop of color in one row.

Ideas for colorwork palettes can come from anywhere. Many designers are inspired by nature, and a frosty winter garden can be just as dramatic as a summer one with pops of color against earthy grays and browns. However, for me cityscapes often provide wonderful inspiration. I live in a very multi-cultural area of London and just walking down the street I can see dramatic combinations of red, bright pink, and gold in a local sari

store, or the fabulous costumes of African women attending the church near my house.

Find inspiration around you and use it as a reference and starting point for work. Carry a camera around with you: I created a Fair Isle pattern inspired by a shot I took of a block of flats in Greece opposite where I was staying. The building was light gray with dark gray shutters, except for one window where the shutters were peach—and this lead to experimenting with monochrome colorwork combined with terracotta and peachy pink. I often tear pages out of magazines because I have seen colors that I think really work and I want to keep for future reference. Analyze the colors in an image and then use snippets of yarn as a starting point for your colorwork.

PRACTICALITIES OF PATTERN

As well as creative choices, there are some practical and technical issues to consider when choosing a color pattern for a knit.

When you are designing color knits, think about the borders—the ribs or edgings that "frame" the garment. Harmony can be achieved by using some of the colors from the main part of the knitting to work these frames. I am a big fan of a cast on or bind off in a contrast shade, or a picot edge where the points of the picot are in another color. .

Be aware of where the shaping is going to be on your design. As with any patterning, whether it is texture or color, you need to be sure that the neck or armhole shaping isn't going to interfere with the pattern in an unattractive way. With bands of Fair Isle I want to make sure that the neck depth is between the bands, so when the neckband is picked up it doesn't cut across the pattern or pull the stitches up, making the color band "wave."

With separate motifs you need to make sure that they are not placed too near the neckline, or the side and shoulder seams. Again, balance is very important to create harmony within the design, and the space between the motifs is as important as the space that they occupy.

Initially I like to draw the shape of the project on graph paper and then chart out the motifs separately. I cut around the motif leaving some space and then keep moving them within the garment outline until I am completely satisfied with the effect. You can do this on a computer, of course, but I find this method quicker as a starting point, although younger designers may disagree!

Perhaps an obvious point, but one always worth mentioning, is to work in a really good light. Different light sources affect how color is perceived; colors and hues seen under natural daylight will change when seen under a light bulb, lighter colors may look more brown and dark colors even darker. If you do have to work under artificial light, try and work under a daylight bulb—it can make a great difference to your color choices.

If you want to explore color more, turn to pages 157–163 of this book. Also, one of my favorite books (which I have as an interactive app on my iPad) is *Interaction of Color* by Josef Albers. It is a record of an experimental way of studying color and I always find it inspiring.

COLOR-EFFECT YARNS

Another option you might consider are the multicolored yarns that are so widely available these days. These yarns come in a variety of weights and an absolutely enormous selection of colors, and they can produce a range of different effects.

Color-effect yarns range from self-patterning yarns designed especially for socks (they create a kind-of-Fair-Isle pattern when knitted up), to the most wonderful, rich, variegated and self-striping yarns. These can provide instant colorwork without any effort other than plain knitting from you, but do buy a ball and do some careful swatching before you plunge in.

A yarn that looks entrancing in the ball may not look as delicious when it is knitted up. And you should try knitting a swatch that is the width of the planned project, because the pools of color you found so attractive in a 4in-square swatch might become skinny stripes when knitted up over four times as many stitches as the swatch.

Indeed, you may want to knit more than one swatch, because the effect that will be produced over, for example, 80 stitches for the back of a cardigan, will be different to that produced over 45 stitches for a front. And a sleeve that increases in width will end up with different patterns as it gets wider.

These yarns can make for interesting detailing on a project that is knitted mainly in a plain color. Match the plain to one of the colors in the variegated yarn, then use the latter to knit cuffs and collar, or patch pockets.

Ombre yarns, in which the yarn is dyed in different shades of the same color, can make a beautiful knitted fabric, and although the issues of color pooling—where one color makes a large and sometimes oddly shaped or unfortunately placed patch—apply as they do for multicolored variegated yarns, the results are usually not as startlingly obvious.

And don't forget tweed yarns. These can be bold and vivid with flecks of bright color, or softly mottled in the colors of the landscapes of the Scottish and Irish islands that they originate from. A small swatch will give you an accurate idea of how a tweed yarn will look knitted up as a larger piece.

Finally, variegated yarns can make absolutely amazing pom-poms (see pages 210–211) and cords (see pages 208–209).

TEXTURE PATTERNS

Texture can range from simple seed stitch that a beginner knitter can easily deal with, to intricate, twisting cables and bobbles (see pages 121–135) that will have the most skilled knitters reading their patterns very carefully indeed. But whatever form it takes, texture and yarn are perfect partners.

To my mind, texture epitomizes the nature of hand knitting. However beautiful colorwork is—and it can be stunning—it can be reproduced in weave, in print; on most surfaces in fact. But stitch patterns in hand knitting are usually unique to the craft and have been developed over many years. A lot of knitters enjoy the history of the craft and are aware of the provenance of certain stitch patterns through discovering the story of fishermen sweaters, or through reading the fascinating pattern books of Barbara Walker, who invited knitters to submit patterns they loved.

A collection of favorite patterns can be passed down through families, or symbolize the iconography of a trade such as fishing, as with ganseys. And even if the story of the possible link between the Book of Kells and Celtic cables isn't accurate, what a great story it is!

In fact, when I put together textures for a new design, I always feel as if I am creating a new story. In an Aran-style knit, each panel I put together has to harmonize with the others, the balance has to be right, and with each new design I feel as if I am exploring all the possibilities that hand knitting offers. I swatch the different panels separately so that I can switch them around until I feel that the balance is right. I may need to make one larger or smaller, or separate them with a rib rather than reverse stockinette stitch to strengthen the sequence. Sometimes the swatches stay laid out on my table for days, and every time I walk by, I contemplate the patterns, maybe move one element. It's such an enjoyable process for me.

One of the things I really love about hand knitting is that you can put together the same stitch patterns in two separate designs, but by changing their order, trying different weights of yarn, and adding detailing and maybe color, you can create something original every time.

INCORPORATING TEXTURE

You can use a simple stitch pattern as an over-all texture, but when it comes to the more complex patterns, it is well worth taking the time to consider exactly how to place them in your design. Your time and effort will be well-rewarded because carefully placed texture really can transform a knit.

I like to link stitches and shapes. For example, if there is seed stitch in a cable, a selvedge at the sides in seed stitch will pull the design together. The diagonal shape of diamond cables link with chevrons, and a lace panel can be harmonized by using a decorative edge.

Cabled designs look so much more interesting when an alternative to a basic rib is used. A center panel can be run down into the rib, or if bobbles are used in the stitch pattern of the main body of the design, then bobbles can be placed in the purl stitches of a rib, or on the points of a triangular edge. A simple stockinette stitch roll can prevent too tight a welt, which is particularly useful on long-line tops that can stretch over your widest part.

Classic knits can be a great source of inspiration. The plainest of ganseys have a wealth of detail, from the garter stitch edgings with side slits, or picot cast on lower hems, to underarm and shoulder gussets, and button fastenings on the neck band. Ganseys from the island of Eriskay have beautiful patchwork yokes made up of squares of stitch patterns and lace and knitted in a fine wool. Their delicacy belies the practical job they had of protecting people from the harsh elements. Sweaters and jackets from the Aran Islands use a landscape of stitches with intricate cables placed next to simple rope cables, and light and shade produced in honeycomb stitches so the texture has depth and height.

PRACTICALITIES OF TEXTURE

There are a few practical issues to think about when using texture in a knit design, but nothing that will actually inhibit your choice of stitch pattern.

Care has to be taken with the more dense stitch patterns so that the garment doesn't become too heavy and unwearable—too much texture in a heavier yarn can make a knit feel like wearing cardboard. Proportions should be generous enough to make the knit comfy: you want to show the garment who is boss, so make sure you wear the knit, don't let the knit wear you. One of the most important areas for ease is the armhole depth and therefore also the top of the sleeve; too tight here and you won't be able to wear anything underneath, and most of us prefer a layer between skin and knit.

I love big "boyfriend" knits, but as I have grown older and my body has grown chunkier, they don't suit me as much as they did, and now I need some shape. I can still wear the Aran-style knits I love, but now I will introduce some shaping at the waist by either decreasing and increasing stitches at the side, or changing down to a smaller needle at the waist. If I do want to wear a more classic design, I will make it longer to wear as a tunic and do some subtle decreasing between the panels to add some flare.

CHOOSING A STITCH PATTERN

There are some great stitch pattern libraries around these days; my particular favorites are the ones collected by Barbara Walker and those originated by Leslie Stanfield and Melody Griffiths, which contain some fantastic stitch creations (see page 313).

When time allows I love to knit the same pattern, but change details every time I work a new swatch. In this way I can feel confident technically with the stitch, and allow my creative mind to wander and produce a kind of knitting stream of consciousness! I may introduce bobbles into a traveling cable, change garter stitch to seed stitch... there are endless variations. You can also embellish stitches by delineating them with embroidery (see pages 192–197).

You can use the way a stitch pattern behaves to create shape. A traditional gansey has a ribbed yoke that brings the fabric in, giving a slightly flared effect. To be honest, this can look slightly strange on a man to my mind, so I increase on the row before the transition from stockinette stitch to rib to even out the fabric.

However, the difference between stitch patterns can be used if you want to create an A-line, such as on a child's smock-style dress or a flared top. Instead of decreasing at the yoke, use a stitch that brings the fabric in, such as ribs that go into a cable or a trellis stitch with stockinette stitch.

YARNS FOR TEXTURE

The fiber you use is crucial; you will need a smooth yarn that accentuates the stitch and makes it stand out in relief from the background fabric.

Cotton and cotton blends give the best definition, but as the fiber doesn't close up in the way that wool yarns do, the fabric can pull away at the transition between the knit stitches and the reverse stockinette stitch background in cables, leaving an irritating and unsightly "ladder" effect along the edge of the cable. Try different yarns until you find one that gives the best effect; you are looking for one that balances the crispness of cotton for stitch detailing with the elasticity and forgiving quality of wool. Silk, silk blends, and wool/cotton mixes can also work really well. And there are tricks for making the "ladders" less visible (see page 305).

Yarn choice is just as important when using simple texture. A pared-down knit can be enhanced with a neat Peter Pan collar in seed stitch, or a Breton striped top have a traditional vertical panel of a few stitches in garter stitch, but it really needs to show up clearly or your effort will have been wasted.

Texture doesn't always need to be dramatic; fully fashioned shaping a few stitches away from a neckline or the side edges of a top, particularly when worked in a chunky yarn weight so that the stitches stand out, can look really effective.

It is a joy to have the opportunity to design garments where you are also making the fabric, and to use the strengths and qualities of the fiber to create texture and shape custom-designed for a project.

ADDING EMBELLISHMENTS

Embellishments can make classic knits just that little bit more special, and with "upcycling" being a key word for the last few years, it is good to have some knowledge of various techniques that can transform a tired, jaded knit into something splendid, or at least extend its life for much longer than you would have thought.

Embellishments fall into two categories when it comes to adding them to knitting. There are those types that you can add once the knitting is complete, such as embroidery and some trims, and those that you have to work in as you knit, such as beading and integrated trims. The first type is particularly useful if you have spent ages knitting a project, and once you have completed it, sewn all the seams, you realize that it just isn't as interesting as you hoped it might be.

Embellishments that need to be worked as you knit can affect the gauge of your knitting (see pages 68–69), so you must work a gauge swatch using your chosen technique. And embellishments can also affect the drape of a garment; a tunic with a beaded hem can hang quite differently to one with a plain hem, and a lot of embroidery can make knitted fabric very stiff and thick.

BEADING

Usually beads are knitted in as you go, and there are various forms of bead knitting shown on pages 200–203. However, you can sew them onto knitted fabric; use ordinary sewing thread that matches the yarn, and a fine, sharp needle.

Beads are a great way to embellish knits; you can make a swan out of a duckling with pearls or beads with sheen, or go rustic with wooden beads. Beading can transform a plain, fitted cardigan into a vintage style by adding them as yoke detail, or working a floral motif such as a rose in small, straight, colored beads. Or why not both.

I have embellished tired Fair Isles by sewing beads to the points of traditional "stars," and added cross stitch between the Fair Isle bands. Another way to use beads is to sew them on or knit them into a collar or cuffs, and this looks particularly effective on a silk yarn.

There are a few practicalities to consider, a primary one being laundering. Not all beads take washing very well—some are even not proof against the gentlest handwash. Beads sold specifically for knitting should cope, but if you are at all unsure, wash your gauge swatch before starting the project.

You can also add sequins to knitting (see page 204), although they often don't wash at all well.

EMBROIDERY

The natural grid of stitches and rows makes it simple to work many embroidery stitches onto knitted fabric, but you have to be careful to get the stitch tension right or the fabric will pull in and pucker, or your stitches might be loose and untidy. Turn to pages 192–197 for instructions for a range of embroidery stitches.

I have always loved Folkloric knits, particularly the Tyrolean styles that were popular in the 1940s and 1950s, with embroidery worked inside stitch patterns. You can jazz up a cabled sweater with embroidery between the panels or inside a cabled diamond stitch. It doesn't always have to be a floral, such as daisy stitch, either; I love cross stitch and blanket stitch. You can work the latter as a border along the hems of a garter stitch jacket, for example, or around a baby blanket. The other advantage of embroidery is that you don't have to be that great at it; if your stitches aren't perfect then you merely describe your technique as being deliberate in order to achieve a folk, rustic look!

Embroidery is also good for personalizing a knit, particularly if it is a gift. I love to embroider initials or the date of birth on a baby blanket, and everyone appreciates those kinds of details because the recipient knows you have made the effort to do something special.

TRIMS

You can make all sorts of trims to embellish your knits with, and there are a variety of techniques on pages 205–212. You can, of course, also add purchased trims to knitted fabric, but do check that the trim and the yarn are compatible when it comes to laundering. Sew a length of trim to your gauge swatch and wash it to be sure.

Personally I am sucker for a pom-pom—tassels are for wimps. Huge cream versions loop around my mantelpiece mirror, and smaller versions strand across our tree every Christmas. I put them on each corner of blankets, and love gathering the ends of scarves and putting a pom-pom at each end. And to my mind, no pom-pom is too big to attach to the top of a hat.

One word of warning, make sure your pom-poms are made as tightly as possible; there nothing worse than a shedding pom-pom, and loose strands can be a safety issue for children and babies.

I still prefer to make pom-poms the old-fashioned way with cardboard (see page 210) so I can get the size I want. And although some people swear by the fork method (not as daft as it seems, check out online videos), to my mind they just don't have the firmness and density you need.

Fringing goes in and out of fashion on clothes, but it will always be a great way to finish off a scarf or throw. I have also used fringing on big collars and on the hems of tunic tops. Buttons can make or break a garment—cheap ones can ruin the look of your knit. If I can't find the right shade to match up to my garment, then a safe bet is usually mother-of-pearl, as the beautiful sheen on them picks up the light and reflects the color of the yarn. Buttons don't always have to be functional, they can be put anywhere; tiny ones can add delicacy to a fine knit, and metallic ones give a military edge to a shirt-style top.

CHOOSING AND SWATCHING YARNS

There is such a huge range of yarns available today that choosing just one to knit a project in can be a real trial. The good news is that to make this choice you are perfectly justified in spending a lot of time swatching in whatever yarns take your fancy.

When fifteen years ago I was first given the opportunity to have my own brand of yarns, my knowledge of fiber and fiber blends was pretty much restricted to the yarn that was available at home in the UK. This could be more or less summed up as wool, cotton, and wool with nylon. On a visit to the US to meet my American distributor, Knitting Fever, I was taken around the New York yarn stores by one of their reps. The retailers may have been aware of a middle-aged Brit wandering up and down the aisles muttering "you can get a wool/alpaca/silk blend, and camel hair !!!!", while feverishly feeling the balls of yarn.

I was simply stunned, and very excited, by the combinations of fibers and the variety of yarn that was available. Also, the shade range seemed never-ending and sophisticated. Of course, beautiful yarns are now available worldwide, but I have never forgotten my reaction that day, and how it opened up a world of design opportunity.

I think it vital for a knitter to have some knowledge of fibers and how each one performs: every craftsperson should understand the materials they work with in order to produce the finest work. Over the years I have been lucky enough to meet many experts in the yarn manufacturing business, and they have helped me understand more and more how different fibers behave.

Twice a year I go to Pitti Filatti, a trade fair in Florence, Italy, where I can see the yarns produced for the following year by mainly Italian manufacturers. I choose the yarns I initially like, and then wait for them to arrive so I can start sampling them. Often something I have liked in the ball can be disappointing when swatched: for example, perhaps it feels slightly "dead" without enough elasticity. So I might go back to the manufacturer and ask them to add another fiber, or alter the proportion of the fiber blend. Adding wool, for example, will give more bounce, more elasticity to a yarn. Or adding alpaca or silk fibers can soften a yarn that when swatched produces a fabric that is harder than I would like.

Understanding a yarn is necessary when either designing your own knits, or if you want to substitute a pattern yarn (see page 70 for more information on substituting yarns). Generally, I would not substitute a yarn in a commercial pattern without good reason: the designer knows why they married together that yarn and that styling in their design, and the two components are an inherent part of the finished result. However, there are times when you may have to substitute a yarn; for example, if you fall in love with a pattern worked in wool yarn, which is a fiber your skin just can't tolerate.

But substituting is not simply checking that the gauge or weight is the same; you need to ask yourself, how does it behave? A cabled sweater in wool or a wool blend will be completely different if you use cotton yarn instead—the pieces will be wider, the fabric completely different. Does the design call for a fabric that drapes, or will the crisp stitch detail produced by cotton be lost in another fiber. The answer? Swatch, swatch, swatch! Only by seeing the yarn knitted up can you have any idea of what the fabric it produces will look like.

Turn to pages 16–17 for more information on different yarn fibers.

DRAWING OUT A DESIGN

Although I went to art school for four years, I am still rather surprised that I managed to get in at all considering how very weak my drawing skills are. Thankfully, after the first year I realized I was never going to be a graphic designer and I went on to study Fashion and Textiles.

Being able to put down my ideas on paper is essential, but in the early stages I do this in only a very basic way. I make very rough sketches that show the style and overall shape, and some details such as a collar and ribs. Then I add on the yarns, shades, and the stitch pattern that I want to use.

The next stage is a schematic or diagram which shows measurements: these always include width, length, length of sleeve, armhole depth, back and front neck width and depth, and might include more (see pages 266–268) for more on measuring.) I now have all the information I need to start writing the pattern.

It is at this stage that I realize that my original rough sketch was a flight of creative fantasy, and I have to face up to reality. For instance, the style I wanted may not be compatible with the stitch pattern I chose, perhaps the pattern repeat is too large for the width or length I wanted. So either I have to adapt the style or change the stitch pattern.

I may make several sketches and experiment with swatching various stitch patterns (see opposite) before settling on one, and then writing up my pattern (see page 284 for more on knitting pattern writing).

There is a difference between drawing out a design for yourself and taking ideas in to show a client, such as a magazine. What I get away with in the privacy of my own studio, I do not feel is acceptable professionally. There have been times in the past when I have commissioned ideas from designers and I have always taken into account that the best designers do not always have sketching skills. But sometimes the opposite is true; I have been seduced by a wonderful illustration and then been disappointed with the resulting garment.

However, I think it shows respect to have made some effort, and there are excellent books and online resources for fashion illustration. Try *9 Heads* by Nancy Riegelman and *How to Draw Like A Fashion Designer* by Celia Joicey and Dennis Nothdruft; these can help you improve your drawing skills enormously.

Many designers work from a "croquis," which is a rough outline of a figure model in various poses. You can download and print these and draw on your garment, or put it into a drawing software program and work digitally, but this takes some practice.

Also it can be helpful to show a client tear sheets, images from a magazine, or the internet that show the kind of style you were thinking of. And take with you notes of the measurements you were planning to make sure that you are not talking at cross purposes with the client.

USING PROPORTIONAL GRAPH PAPER

Many beginner knitters have carefully worked out a shape for a knitting project on graph paper bought in a local stationery store and been terribly disappointed when the finished result was not the same shape as the drawing.

Some designers will plot out a whole garment on graph paper as part of creating a pattern, others will just plot out areas such as neckline curves or shaping, while some don't work on graph paper at all. But if you are going to work on graph paper—and it can be very helpful when you first start designing your own projects—then you should work on knitter's proportional graph paper, not the standard square graph paper. This is because a knitted stitch is not square—it is wider than it is tall—and if you plot out the shape on square paper, it will be very distorted (see pages 65–67 for more on stitch shape). At the back of this book you will find sheets of proportional

graph paper in two ratios, 4:5 and 2:3 (see pages 314–315). The first ratio has four stitches measuring the same as five rows, and the second has two stitches measuring the same as three rows. Most knitting will fit one of these two ratios, so measure out the stitches and rows on your swatch and photocopy the appropriate sheet. You can also buy sheets of this paper or download it from the internet.

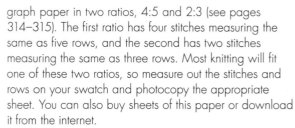

Draw the garment pieces with one block on the paper representing one knitted stitch horizontally, and one row vertically. You can either draw out the pieces once you have written the pattern, or draw them first, to help you write. If you choose to do the former, working from the written pattern, then that is also an excellent way of checking that your pattern does work sensibly!

If you are going to draw out, for example, a whole sweater, then start by drawing out the back. The front can later be drawn on top of the back in a different-colored pen, which will help you see that the front and back shaping match up.

If you are drawing before writing the pattern, you can draw curved shapes onto the paper in pencil, getting the lines right, then re-draw them in pen following the graph paper blocks to translate the curves into stitches and rows. Longer, sloping straight lines—such as the edges of sleeves—can be drawn in pencil with a ruler from the end of the shaping to the start of the cuff, then one side can be translated into stitches and rows, and the other side copied from the first one to create a symmetrical shape.

Probably the most common use of proportional graph paper is for drawing out color motifs and patterns. And if you are placing knitted motifs on a garment, then a graph paper outline of each separate garment piece can be hugely helpful. You can place motifs at full size, precisely and to best effect.

TURNING MEASUREMENTS INTO STITCHES AND ROWS

Don't worry, all the math for this is fairly simple and, with the aid of a calculator, quick to work.

Once you have a drawing and a diagram of your project, all the measurements written out, and all the stitch patterns swatched, you can start compiling your pattern, and the first step is to translate the measurements into stitches and rows.

Start by measuring your gauge very carefully (see page 68). Measure over the appropriate stitch pattern every time: never measure over stockinette and assume that your gauge will be the same over another stitch pattern; it often won't be. For the sake of this exercise, let us say that there are 22 stitches and 28 rows to a 4in square over pattern.

Now you need the project measurements; for a pillow that is 16in wide and 20in long, the sum will be:

Width = 22 (stitch gauge) ÷ 4 (gauge measurement) = 5.5 (stitches to 1in) x 16 (pillow width) = 88. So you need 88 stitches plus one on each side for the seam allowances, making a total of 90 stitches to be cast on.

Length = 28 (row gauge) ÷ 4 (gauge measurement) = 7 (rows to 1in) x 20 (pillow length) = 140. So you will knit 140 rows. The cast-on and bound-off rows will be the seam allowances.

Exactly the same principle applies to more complex shapes, though this is where you may well find it easier to work on proportional graph paper (see opposite). You can start by plotting out the overall length and width of the piece. So if you were working out a tunic back that is 23in wide and 26in long, and using the same gauge as for the pillow, above, you would plot out a rectangle that is 127 blocks/stitches wide and 182 block/rows high. (Note that numbers should be rounded up or down from fractions to the nearest whole number.) You might find it easiest to add on seam allowance stitches where needed after you have plotted the whole piece.

If the back neck is 9in wide, and each shoulder 3in wide, then the neck will take up 50 stitches and each shoulder 17 stitches. Together these come to 84 stitches, so you have 43 stitches to play with for armholes and shaping. You need an even number (so the piece will be symmetrical), so reduce the neck by one stitch, giving you 44 stitches, 22 on each side for armholes and shaping.

Plot the neck and shoulder width centrally on your rectangle, then move on to work out the angle of the shoulders and depth of the armholes.

To calculate increases or decreases along a sloped edge, you need to do a little more math. Let us say that you are working out a dropped sleeve that is 15in wide at the top and 8in wide at the bottom. Still working to the same gauge, this makes it 82 stitches wide at the top (number rounded down from a fraction to the nearest whole even number), and 44 stitches wide at the cuff. Subtract the wrist width from the top width: 82 - 44 = 38 stitches to play with. That number divided by 2 (for paired increases) gives you 19 pairs of increases.

If the sleeve is 17in long, then it will be 119 rows long overall. If there is a rib cuff that is 2½in deep, the length of sleeve available to work shaping in will be 101 rows. So 101 ÷ 19 (the number of increases) = 5 (number rounded down from a fraction to the nearest whole number). So you will increase at each end of every fifth row until you get to 82 stitches, knit six rows and bind off.

If you wanted to have a longer section of straight knitting at the top of the sleeve, then you could increase on every 4th row to 82 stitches, then knit the last 25 rows straight.

Work out the whole design methodically, area by area, plotting out the shapes as you go, and it will be easy to see if you make a mistake.

WRITING A PATTERN

Even if you are writing up a pattern for your own benefit, it's good to take thorough notes, otherwise you can come back to it in a year or so wanting to knit it again, and have no idea how to interpret the cryptic instructions you once thought were so clear. And if you are writing up the pattern for others to use, you need to make it really clear or risk howls of complaint.

The first point to make is to always, always keep a notebook with you when you are working on a pattern and write down every single row you work. Don't think that you will remember exactly what you did, because that only leads to frustrating counting and re-knitting.

Take a look at patterns that you have found easy to follow by other designers and see how they have set things out. Are there abbreviations you prefer? Or ways of referring to repeats or rows that you find easy to understand? Make a list of what you like and keep it on hand, and update it every time you find something new. Soon you will build up a personal library of phrases and that will make writing up new patterns quick and easy. (You'll find a list of abbreviations on page 63, and a list of useful terminology on page 64.)

Decide on the measurement and weight system you prefer (imperial or metric) and stick to it. Conversions are usually not perfectly accurate, so swapping between the two systems can lead to trouble. The same applies to the system you use for needle sizes (see page 22 for a conversion chart).

Start a pattern by listing out all the materials and equipment needed to make the project. Include needles, yarn, any other tools (blunt-tipped needle, stitch holder, etc), and any embellishments or fastenings. Then list the size of the finished project.

List the gauge you worked out for the design, stating the needle size, the yarn, and the stitch pattern used. And list any abbreviations that aren't completely standard.

Write out every separate piece of the pattern under the appropriate heading. Start each piece with how many stitches need to be cast on and work methodically through the rows until you reach the bind-off. Remember to put in when to change needle sizes, if appropriate.

Take particular care when writing up shaping so that the reader knows exactly where to increase and decrease, and which methods to use (see pages 80–97).

If you are including color knitting, state what technique should be used. And if there is a chart, make sure you include a key listing exactly what each colored block or symbol means.

Don't forget to include instructions for finishing the project, even if it seems quite obvious to you as to what goes where.

And be consistent; if you describe something in a particular way on one occasion, then describe it that way every time. The clearer and more consistent you can make things, the easier your patterns will be to follow.

CALCULATING YARN QUANTITIES

You need to work out how much yarn to buy to knit up your design, and while this does require some math, the sums are simple. And it is much better to know that you have enough than to make a wild guess, run out, and discover that the dye lot is no longer available…

The first step is to work out the area of the piece, for which you need the width multiplied by the length. So let's start with an example of a scarf that is planned to be 9in wide by 47in long: 9 x 47 = 423in in area.

Then you need the area and weight of your gauge swatch; let us say that it is 5 x 5in, so 25in in area, and it weighs ¾ ounce, which will be expressed in the sum as 0.75.

Divide the area of the project by the area of the swatch: 423 ÷ 25 = 16.92.
Multiply that figure by the weight of the swatch: 16.92 x 0.75 = 12.69.

So you will need 12.69 ounces of yarn.

If the yarn you want to use is sold in 1¾ ounce balls, the ball weight will be expressed in the sum as 1.75.

Divide the weight of yarn you need by the ball weight: 12.69 ÷ 1.75 = 7.25.

You must always round up the figure you get from this sum to the nearest whole number, so in this instance you will need eight balls of yarn to knit your scarf.

Exactly the same principles apply if you are calculating quantities for a garment, such as a sweater, but you will need to work out the total area of all the pieces. The easiest way to do this is to draw a pencil rectangle around each of the graphed-out shapes at the widest and longest points. Work out the area of each piece, then add all the areas together. Divide the total area by the swatch area and multiply that number by the swatch weight to ascertain how much yarn to buy.

The extra amount of yarn that has been added in to the calculation by turning the shapes into rectangles should be enough for small extra details such as ribbed cuffs and a neck band, but if you are adding larger pieces, such as pockets, then you should add those into the area calculation.

Finally, it is always a good idea to buy one extra ball of yarn, just in case.

DESIGNING FOR PEOPLE & PLACES

There will always be both practical and creative decisions to be made during the design process, and it's important not to lose sight of whom or what you are designing for. A cashmere baby bib won't wear well, and a vivid purple pillow may be too much in a pale living room, no matter how much you love the color.

DESIGNING FOR ADULTS

I have talked about designing flattering styles to suit women's shapes on page 264; here I would like to talk about the more practical elements of designing knitwear for adults.

I learned how to compile patterns the slow and hard way. I was lucky enough to be mentored by Lesley Stanfield, the Knitting Editor at Woman magazine, who, when I brought in my knitted-up design, would gently point out a better way of decreasing around a neck!

Most of my information came from poring over commercial patterns to see how they were done, and this was particularly useful when it came to grading other sizes. When I first started designing, the fashion at the time was for generous sweaters basically made up of rectangles for body and sleeves. This made it easier to pattern-write, for which I was very grateful, but the styles I loved to wear were the fine knits of the 1940s era. As I knitted them up for vintage pattern books, I was introduced to tailoring and shaping that has stood me in good stead for the type of knits I still like to design and wear.

For me, the easy part, and sometimes the most exciting part, is the initial stages of thinking about the idea and putting it down in my sketch pad. My workings will invariably show complex ideas where cables run effortlessly into ribbed bands, or branch off around V necks; everything is possible on paper. Unfortunately, too often what seemed like a great idea at that stage proves a little more difficult when I start to swatch with my chosen yarn!

Everything now depends on the swatch. The pattern repeat and gauge will inform whether the initial measurements of your design are going to be possible, and for me proportion is everything. When working from a commercial pattern, if your gauge is off the finished project will not have the same measurements as the original design and that will inevitably lead to disappointment: a couple of inches difference in the width or length can make the difference between a stylish knit and a frumpy one.

The same applies to a design of your own; you may need to compromise your original concept in terms of measurement in order to use a particular stitch pattern if it consists of more stitches or rows than you would have ideally liked, or change the stitch pattern. You may also have to rethink the weight of a yarn if your stitch pattern repeat works better in a finer yarn where you have more stitches to accommodate it. If you are designing for yourself this will probably have less impact than if you are working on a commercial pattern, because grading different sizes can throw everything up in the air!

The shape of the garment may also depend on the stitch pattern. A shaped set-in sleeve may not be possible because the shaping will interfere with the pattern, and you may decide that a square set-in style—where stitches are bound off initially and then the armhole is worked straight—is preferable, or even a dropped shoulder.

Check the neck depth, too, as your preferred depth may come at an unattractive point; for example, if it was going to be on a cable cross row it would distort the neck shaping. If necessary, adjust the depth and then compensate if you need to by changing the back width so that the neck opening will still be the same.

Practicality and wearability come into the equation as well. For example, a generous sweater in width and length should have an equally generous armhole depth, not just for style but because otherwise the garment will pull uncomfortably under the arm and at the sides.

If you are unsure about proportions, measure your favorite existing knits (see pages 266–267); it is an infallible method for getting things right.

DESIGNING FOR BABIES

For me, there are few things more enjoyable than designing for babies and children. This is mainly because the resulting photography is always so charming, but also because it imposes restrictions of scale and wearability that I find interesting.

The thing I rapidly found out when I had my first child, Will, is that style isn't everything. The knits I had made for him before he was born looked great to my mind, but after struggling with a fretful baby who didn't take kindly to being dressed and undressed, I had to have a rethink.

It is even more important with baby clothes that they are practical and comfortable. A baby can register outrage if a too-tight neck is pulled over its head, so we have a pretty good idea of what the problem is, but we can't always be sure what might make an infant uncomfortable; it could be a button fastening on a back neck opening or a too-thick seam. It is always better to be safe than sorry, so try a practical checklist before you embark on a baby design.

In my experience cardigans or jackets are preferable to sweaters, unless the sweater has an envelope neck or button fastenings on the shoulder. I love a crossover, ballerina-style tied at the side; easy and quick to fasten. Jackets only need a few buttons at the top and they help create a more flared style that is perfect for wearing over diapers! You can emphasize the flare by decreasing from hem to armhole, or working a garter stitch side-vent at the bottom of the garment rather than ribs.

Think about scale; a color pattern that works on an adult garment can overwhelm a smaller one, so keep everything as simple as possible. One of my favorite designs from my own collections is a hooded A-line jacket with rolled hems and one button. Worked in stockinette stitch, it has fully fashioned decreasing at the sides to add some detail to its simplicity as a garment. Knitted in a cashmere-blend yarn, it ticks every box: soft and gentle fiber against a baby's skin, shaped to fit over a diaper, edges that curl up so there are no tight hems against plump wrists or legs, and a hood to snuggle into.

DESIGNING FOR CHILDREN

Designing for older children may need a little more research, particularly from the recipient of the finished project if it is for a child you know. Older children have definite ideas about what they want to wear and should be listened to!

For those who prefer a sporty style that is similar to the casual fleeces that they are used to wearing, keep the sizing generous. The knitted fabric generally has a heavier feel than children are used to these days, so make sure underarm measurements are deep and the top of sleeves wide. To emphasize the casual look, add a hood (they look great and are practical as well), and a zipper can be substituted for buttons.

Remember, too, that children grow quickly and so it is better to make the measurements over-generous to begin with, so that they get at least two years' wear out of the garment. Another way to get around this issue is to work from the top down so that the body and sleeves can be easily lengthened to accommodate a growth spurt.

For a more feminine look you can use classic styles as a basis for a design, but then add decorative details such as a lace edge or a ribbon trim. Cropped cardigans, shrugs, and boleros are ideal party wear and never seem to go out of fashion.

Lastly, remember fiber first! We all know children who pull a face, tug at a knit, and say it is scratchy. That may not always be quite true, but they are often used to wearing soft, acrylic fibers, so make sure that the yarn you are using is gentle against the skin as well as washable and wearable.

DESIGNING SCARVES

For the new designer, accessories can be the perfect way to get to grips with the number crunching that comes with pattern compiling, at the same time as creating a style. And where better to start than with a simple scarf.

Even a scarf needs to be approached practically as well as creatively; for example, how will it hang, or be worn? A reversible stitch is a fairly safe bet, as some stitches have an unattractive wrong side. Alternatively, some patterns have a tendency to curl at the edge, so a selvedge stitch such as garter (see page 240) can help prevent a wide, generous scarf from becoming too skinny.

However, many of the new generation of knitters that have fallen in love with the craft were enticed in by the variety of "fancy" yarns that were available. Although not a huge fan of these yarns myself (I prefer classic yarns), I can appreciate that the riot of color and texture that they provided offered up fabulous knits that needed hardly any technique other than knowing the knit and purl stitches.

For novice knitters, the obvious project to start with is a scarf, and instead of the rather grim, uneven object of the past, the fancy yarns disguised a multitude of knitting sins: who worried too much about a dropped stitch when it was hidden in a mass of texture created by the construction of the yarn?

This was the beginning of the scarf craze, and so popular was it that manufacturers brought out yarns specifically for them. The yarn could be bought, the scarf knitted up in an evening, and worn the following day. Who would have thought that the humble neck warmer could be knit up in a variety of loops, "eyelash" fringing, and pierrot frills?

OTHER ACCESSORIES

The craze for scarf yarns created an interest in all hand-knitted accessories, which are the perfect way for the beginner knitter to get to grips with new techniques.

A simple slouchy beanie can be whipped up in next to no time just knowing how to cast on, knit, purl, and decrease. A cowl is the perfect way to learn how to use a circular needle. A plain scarf means you can concentrate on perfecting your technique—how to hold your needles, checking your gauge—while a striped one is useful for practice in changing colors and sewing in ends.

Hats come in a variety of styles—personally I love a beret or beanie. A beanie with a cast on that curls over is a simple one to start with; the thumb method of casting on (see page 36) is preferable as it has more elasticity than others and so will fit around more head sizes. A beret can go from preppy charm to floppy bohemian by increasing and decreasing more stitches, and if you don't want to tackle gloves then hand or arm warmers make a stylish alternative.

I have designed many bags over the years, from cotton beach bags to smart handbags. A simple tote constructed from two rectangles is the easiest to make, with eyelets at the top to thread through and gather up with a cord (see pages 115 and 208–209). For a more structured tote, a strengthened circular base will create a tube shape and the eyelots can be reinforced with metal rings. I prefer even a simple shape to have gussets at the sides, which can then be extended to form straps that can be lined with fabric or iron-on curtain stiffener. A beaded clutch with a contrast satin lining makes a beautiful evening bag.

Any chapter on accessories would not be complete without mentioning socks! When I first started traveling to the USA for work back in the 1990s, I was amazed at the American knitters' passion for sock knitting, as this was something that was usually only seen done by older knitters in the UK at that time. However, I soon started to appreciate the charm of hand-knitted socks; durable, practical, and portable, so great for knitting on the go.

I am not sure which came first, the interest in sock knitting or the availability of amazing sock yarns. Historically, sock yarn was a wool mix with a good percentage of nylon to prevent the stitches wearing away where feet and shoes rubbed. Now there are beautiful yarns that are good enough to be used in fashion garments, with many being self-striping or color-shaded: the flash of a well-turned ankle can cause as much excitement as it did in Victorian times, if for rather different reasons.

I love texture in socks, so personally love to create Aran patterning in the traditionally fine yarns—so that neat cables run up the leg in long or over-the-knee socks. Unless I am designing sofa socks, I prefer to keep the foot in stockinette stitch, so that they can be worn easily in shoes. Comfort is key, so knitting in the round on double-pointed needles is preferable to a flat sock with a seam, except for baby socks where the number of stitches is small and you will need to use two needles. Remember that socks stay on a baby much more easily than bootees, even if they may not be quite so cute.

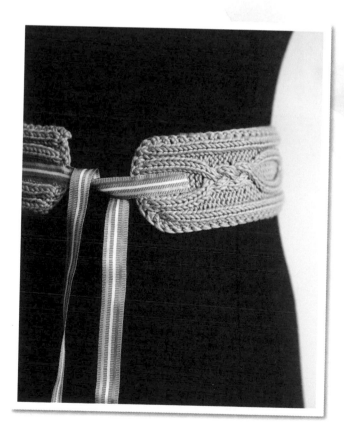

HOMEWARES

One of the most exciting developments in knitting has been the explosion of interest in projects for the home. For knitters, homewares often have the same function as accessories; they are an easy way to practice techniques without having to think about complicated shaping.

A simple rectangle can become the basis for many homeware projects. Work a chunky-weight cotton yarn using the yarn double or triple on extra-large needles and you can create a great rug. Line a strip of knitted fabric with iron-on curtain stiffener, attach ties at each end, roll it up, and you have somewhere to keep your magazines. A modern take on the Victorian antimacassar for the back of an armchair is a length of knitted fabric—such as garter or seed stitch—edged at one end with a pretty lace trim; antimacassars may not be needed now to prevent gentlemen's oiled hair from staining the fabric of the chair, but they add some decorative interest to a plain piece of furniture.

As a designer I love working with "stories," and home projects are ideal for themes. Here are some suggestions:

For creamy or white rooms, simple cables (see pages 122–123) in a crisp cotton yarn can look beautiful.

Lace-knit (see pages 136–140) pillow covers over a gray fabric lining look fresh.

For a summery, nautical look, try pillows and throws in white and blue stripes, or knit a rug in a chunky denim yarn used double.

For rooms that need a splash of richness, try a Santa Fe style. Throws and pillows in wool and wool blends, with Navajo motifs using the intarsia method (see pages 176–179) in geometric patterns in rich, warm shades—terracottas, turquoise, and ochre—will look stunning; add fringing to enhance the look. The same style can also be adapted for a Middle Eastern theme, with patterning taken from kilim rugs.

If you want a pop of color to brighten up a dull room, try art galleries for inspiration. Look at the paintings of Piet Mondrian or the paper collages from Matisse, and use them as starting points for your designs.

BLANKETS

Whether you call it a blanket, a throw, or an afghan, and whether you make it large enough for a king-size bed, or small enough for your puppy, a blanket is a great blank slate for the budding knit designer.

Blankets have always been popular of course, and there is nothing quite as cozy as snuggling down under one on a sofa. I usually start with my blanket draped stylishly (I hope!) over the back of the sofa, but always end up with it draped over me, even in the summer.

Blankets are a great way to use all your gauge squares and practice stitch pattern samples. I always edge my swatches with garter stitch so that they don't curl, and not only then can they be kept neatly, but it also makes it much easier to measure stitches and rows over a flatter square without pressing (which can distort the gauge). This also means that should you wish to create a blanket from the swatches, you have great edges to sew together.

With my love of texture it will be no surprise that I love Aran-knit throws, either with simple panels of cable, or with a patchwork of stitches. I particularly like mixing classic Guernsey and Aran stitches together in squares or panels so that there will be a landscape of texture, which can include cables, bobbles, and lace. This means that—as some of the stitch patterns will pull in more than others—I need to work out increases and decreases carefully where necessary to make sure that the fabric doesn't pucker and look uneven.

Afghans and throws create a great opportunity to personalize a project; I often initial a baby blanket or embroider the date of birth.

PILLOWS

Can you ever have too many pillows on a sofa? They are rather addictive to knit once you get started, but fortunately if you do make so many that there is no room on the sofa for you, then the surplus can go on beds!

Pillows work well using texture or colorwork. On my sofa at the moment I have a scattering of cabled pillows, and Union Jack, and spot and zigzag intarsia ones. If you want a fresh, summery look, then a lace stitch in a cotton yarn is perfect; on the pillow inside I like to use a fabric cover in a contrast shade that will show through the knitted lace. A quick fix is also to work a knitted square that can be sewn onto the front of a well-loved existing pillow to give it a new look.

Not all pillows need to have a knitted back; floor pillows are perfect for visitor overflow or small children, but fabric is sturdier if there is going to be wear and tear on floorboards. On a basic pillow cover I prefer an envelope-style button fastening on the back, as it looks neater than a zipper inserted along the edges. If you are knitting a stockinette cover in one piece (so making a long rectangle that will wrap right around the pillow), then for a sharper edge where the front becomes the back, work a knit row on the wrong side to form a ridge, as for a garter fold hem (see page 242).

TROUBLESHOOTING

11

The beauty of hand knitting is that it is organic and very personal to each knitter, but a downside of that is that it can be very easy to make an error. Losing concentration for a second can lead to mistakes, but nearly all problems, if caught quickly before too much work has been completed, can be easily corrected.

DROPPED STITCH ONE ROW DOWN ON A KNIT ROW

It is very easy to drop a stitch; it can slip off the point of your needle, or you can find that you haven't completely worked a stitch on the row below. This is easy to remedy, but you need to act quickly before the stitch drops too far. Keeping a safety pin handy with your knitting bag is useful so that you can put a pin in to hold the stitch loop while you are getting ready to pick it up.

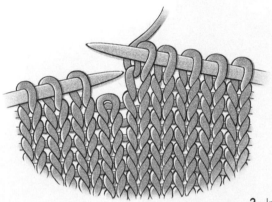

1. Make sure that the loose horizontal strand that runs between stitches is behind the stitch that has been dropped. This strand will be picked up and re-made into a stitch.

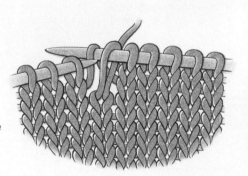

2. Insert the right-hand needle into the front of the dropped stitch and under the horizontal strand running behind it.

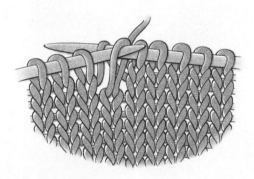

3. Insert the left-hand needle into the back of the dropped stitch on the right-hand needle and lift this stitch over the horizontal strand. The strand has been picked up and made into a stitch. However, the stitch is on the wrong needle and is facing in the wrong direction.

4. Insert the left-hand needle into the front of the picked-up stitch and slip it onto the left-hand needle ready to be knitted.

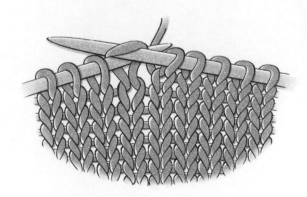

DROPPED STITCH ONE ROW DOWN ON A PURL ROW

The same principle applies to picking up a dropped stitch on a purl row, you are merely working on the other side of the fabric. If you find it more difficult to negotiate the bumpy fabric of reverse stockinette, then carefully turn the work and pick up from the knit side.

1. Make sure that the loose horizontal strand that runs between stitches is in front of the stitch that has been dropped. This strand will be picked up and re-made into a stitch.

2. Insert the right-hand needle into the back of the dropped stitch and under the horizontal strand running in front of it.

3. Insert the left-hand needle into the front of the dropped stitch on the right-hand needle and lift this stitch over the horizontal strand. The strand has been picked up and made into a stitch. However, although the stitch is facing in the right direction, it is on the wrong needle.

4. Insert the left-hand needle into the front of the picked-up stitch and slip it onto the left-hand needle ready to be purled.

DROPPED STITCH MULTIPLE ROWS DOWN ON A KNIT ROW

If a stitch has dropped down a few rows before you notice it, then the unraveled stitches form a ladder. The best way to pick up the dropped stitch is by using a crochet hook, but if you don't have one handy it can be done with a knitting needle, although it is trickier.

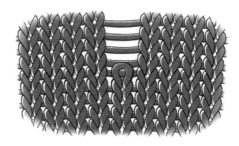

1. Make sure that the lowest of the loose horizontal strands that run between stitches is behind the stitch that has been dropped. This strand will be picked up first and re-made into a stitch, then the ones above will be made into stitches in turn.

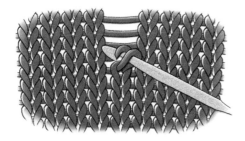

2. Put the crochet hook into the front of the dropped stitch and under the lowest horizontal strand. Pull the strand through the stitch: it has now become a stitch and you have picked up one row. Continue in this way, picking up each strand in turn, until you have reached the top. Insert the left-hand needle into the front of the final picked-up stitch and slip it onto the left-hand needle ready to be knitted.

DROPPED STITCH MULTIPLE ROWS DOWN ON A PURL ROW

The same principle applies as on a knit row (see above), but you are working on the other side of the fabric. If you find this method awkward, turn the work and, with the right side facing, follow the instructions for dropped stitch multiple rows down on a knit row.

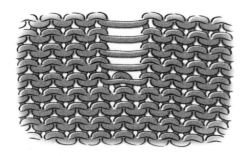

1. Make sure that the lowest of the loose horizontal strands that run between stitches is in front of the stitch that has been dropped. This strand will be picked up first and re-made into a stitch, then the ones above will be made into stitches in turn.

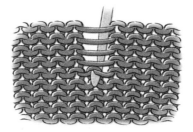

2. From the other side of the work, put the crochet hook into the dropped stitch and under the lowest horizontal strand, as shown. Pull the strand through the stitch: it has now become a stitch and you have picked up one row. Continue in this way, picking up each strand in turn, until you have reached the top. Insert the left-hand needle into the front of the final picked-up stitch and slip it onto the left-hand needle ready to be purled.

DROPPED STITCH ON AN EDGE

The stitch that often gets dropped is the first one on the needle, because it is always the loosest. The pick-up method is slightly different to that used to pick up a stitch within a row, and you work on the right side of the fabric whatever the row about to be worked is. You will need a crochet hook to carry out this technique.

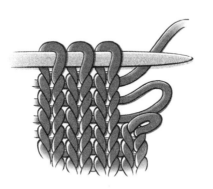

1. When an edge stitch drops down a few rows, a large loop of yarn appears for every two rows dropped. These loops need to be picked up and re-made into stitches.

2. Insert the crochet hook into the dropped stitch and catch the large loop of yarn. Draw a loop through the dropped stitch, but only a loop that is the size of a stitch; don't pull the whole of the large loop through. You have re-made one stitch.

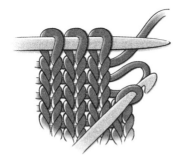

3. Catch the large loop again and draw a second loop through the stitch on the hook; this is the second re-made stitch and the last one to be made from the large loop. If there is more than one large loop, re-make them all into stitches in this way, making two stitches from each large loop.

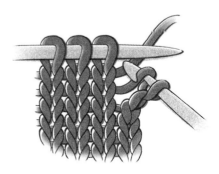

4. At the top, the final re-made stitch is made from the working yarn. Pull a loop of it through the stitch on the hook, then place this last stitch onto the needle, making sure it faces the right way (see page 302).

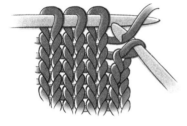

UNRAVELING STITCH BY STITCH

If you have made a mistake on the row you are currently working and there are just a few stitches to unravel, then doing that one stitch at a time is the best and safest method. This is a very simple technique and learning to do it properly will save you a lot of time in the long run.

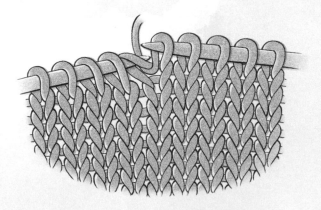

1. On a knit row, insert the left-hand needle into the front of the stitch below the first stitch on the right-hand needle. Drop the stitch off the right-hand needle and pull the yarn free. Unravel each stitch in this way.

2. On a purl row the same principle applies as for a knit row, but you insert the left-hand needle into the front of the stitch looking at it from the purl side. Drop the stitch off the right-hand needle and pull the yarn free. Unravel each stitch in this way.

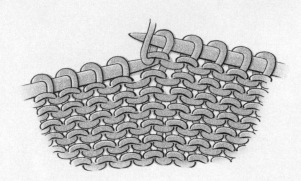

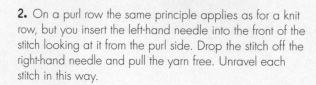

UNRAVELING SEVERAL ROWS

If there are several rows to unravel because you have worked too many rows, or you have spotted an error further down the piece, it is quicker to unravel a few rows at once rather than unpicking each stitch.

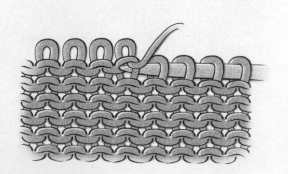

1. Take the knitting off both needles. Slowly and carefully pull out the yarn to unravel the stitches until you reach the row with the mistake in it; it doesn't matter if this is a right-side or a wrong-side row. Then hold the knitting in your left hand and a knitting needle in your right hand. Insert the needle into the first stitch below the unraveled loops and pull the yarn free. Continue in this way until the row with the mistake in is unraveled and all the stitches are back on the needle.

UNRAVELING TO A LIFELINE

If you have to unravel several rows, but you are worried about dropping stitches and not being able to easily pick them up again, or about unraveling too far, a lifeline is the answer. Use a piece of smooth waste yarn that is about the same thickness as the project yarn.

1. Thread a blunt-tipped sewing needle with a length of waste yarn that's longer than the knitting is wide. Pass the needle through the right-hand leg of each stitch in the row you need to unravel to, being careful not to split the yarn with the needle.

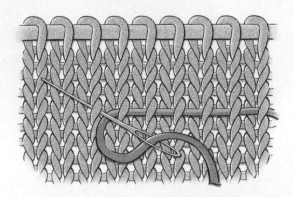

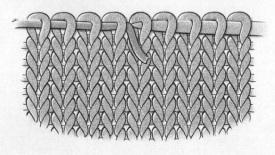

2. Then take the knitting off the needle and pull out the yarn to unravel the rows. The lifeline will prevent rows unraveling beyond it, and will hold all the stitches facing in the right direction.

3. Following the path of the lifeline, slip each stitch in turn onto a knitting needle, pulling out the waste yarn as you go. Be sure to put the stitches back on the needle in the right direction, so that the working yarn is at the tip of the needle, ready to work the next row.

TO A CIRCULAR NEEDLE

If you have a circular needle the right size and length, you can thread that through the stitches instead of a lifeline. Pull it through so all the stitches are on the cable before unraveling the rows, then you can work the next row straight off the circular needle onto a knitting needle.

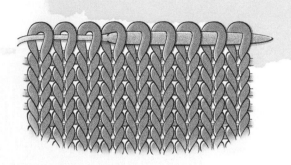

TWISTED STITCH ON A KNIT ROW

Dropped stitches can be easily twisted. When you have picked up a dropped stitch the final stage is to make sure that you have put it back on the needle in the correct way. If you miss doing this, you can easily correct the twist as you work the next row.

1. If you think of a stitch as having two legs that straddle the needle, then the right-hand leg should always be in front of the needle and the left-hand leg behind it. Here, you can see that the third stitch from the tip of the needle has the left-hand leg in front, and so the stitch is twisted.

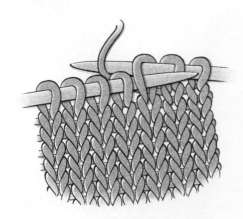

2. Knit along the row to the twisted stitch, then knit that stitch through the back loop (see page 77). Doing that will turn the stitch around the right way as you work it.

TWISTED STITCH ON A PURL ROW

The same principle for dealing with twisted stitches applies to the purl row. Twisted stitches—when they are not deliberate, as they are in some stitch patterns—need to be corrected as they will show on stockinette fabric.

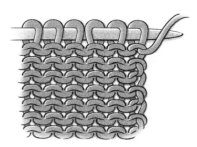

1. As with a knit stitch, the right-hand leg of a purl stitch should be in front of the needle and the left-hand leg behind. Here, the third stitch from the tip of the needle is twisted.

2. Purl along the row to the twisted stitch, then purl that stitch through the back loop (see page 77). Doing that will turn the stitch around the right way as you work it.

EXTRA STITCH ON A KNIT ROW

A common problem for beginners is that because they are unfamiliar with how stitches are formed, they often end up with one extra stitch on a row than they should have. Often it will have been created at the very start of the row. So take extra care to work the first stitch properly.

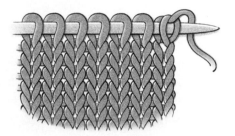

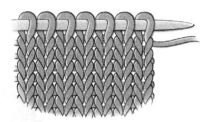

1. On a knit row, if the working yarn is pulled over the top of the needle to the back, then the first stitch is distorted and two strands appear. It's easy to knit into both of these as though they were separate stitches, and so increase by one stitch.

2. To prevent this, always make sure that at the start of a row the yarn is pulled down at the front of the work, and then taken backward, ready to knit with.

EXTRA STITCH ON A PURL ROW

The principle for addressing the extra stitch at the beginning of a purl row is the same as for a knit row. If after using this technique the edge stitch on the row below looks baggy, you can ease the excess out of it in the same way as for fixing baggy stitches (see page 305).

1. On a purl row, if the working yarn is pulled over the top of the needle to the back, then the first stitch is distorted and two strands appear. It's easy to purl into both of these as though they were separate stitches, and so increase by one stitch.

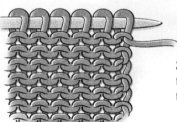

2. To prevent this, always make sure that at the start of a row the yarn is pulled down at the front of the work, ready to purl with.

INCOMPLETE STITCH ON A KNIT ROW

This is another common way in which beginners inadvertently make extra stitches. An incomplete stitch is made because the right-hand needle is inserted into the stitch and the yarn is wrapped around the tip of the needle, but then the stitch is slipped rather than being worked and the yarn that was wrapped around the needle becomes a strand lying over the needle. This then gets worked into on the next row and an extra stitch is made.

1. Here, an incomplete stitch was made when the fourth stitch from the right was worked on the previous row. The incomplete stitch was made on the purl row, but you can fix it as you work the knit row that follows.

2. Knit to the incomplete stitch. Insert the right-hand needle into the back of the stitch on the left-hand needle that was slipped rather than worked on the previous row. Lift this stitch over the strand lying across the needle and drop it off the needle. The stitch has now been completed and is facing the right way on the left-hand needle, ready to be knitted.

INCOMPLETE STITCH ON A PURL ROW

On a purl row, an incomplete stitch is made in the same way as on a knit row. The result looks rather like an unwanted yarnover followed by a slip stitch.

1. Here, an incomplete stitch was made when the fourth stitch from the right was worked on the previous row. The incomplete stitch was made on the knit row, but you can fix it as you work the purl row that follows.

2. Purl to the incomplete stitch. Insert the right-hand needle into the front of the stitch on the left-hand needle that was slipped rather than worked on the previous row. Lift this stitch over the strand lying across the needle and drop it off the needle. The stitch has now been completed and is facing the right way on the left-hand needle, ready to be purled.

FIXING BAGGY STITCHES

Baggy stitches can happen to most knitters, even very experienced ones. They sometimes just seem to occur for no reason, but it's usually because a stitch has been knitted more loosely than the surrounding ones.

IN STOCKINETTE STITCH

Before you block a piece of stockinette stitch knitting, lay it flat and check it over. If there is an occasional looser, baggier stitch, you can use a blunt-tipped sewing needle to redistribute the excess fullness over the stitches either side so that it isn't noticeable. Simply slip the needle under the leg of a stitch to one side of the baggy stitch and gently ease it until one side of the loose stitch is flatter. Then do the same on the stitch to the other side.

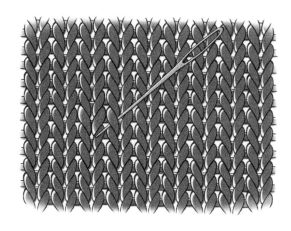

IN RIB

When knitting rib patterns with two or more knit stitches together, the left one of the group can be baggier. This is caused by the way the yarn wraps when changing from a knit to a purl stitch. Here, you can clearly see that the last knit stitch is larger than the previous two. You can try simply knitting the last knit stitch of each group more tightly, but it can be difficult to do this consistently. Alternatively, knit the last stitch through the back loop (see page 77). The twisted stitch won't show much in a rib pattern and can look better than a baggy stitch. When purling the same stitch, wrap the yarn clockwise rather than counterclockwise around the needle.

IN CABLES

When working cables in stockinette stitch on a background of reverse stockinette, you can end up with unsightly long strands on the left side of the cable, particularly where the cable twists. As with baggy rib, this is caused by the way the yarn wraps when changing from a knit to a purl stitch. To tighten the strands, try working the purl stitch after the cable very firmly. You can also try purling this first background stitch through the back loop.

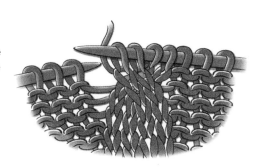

FIXING UNEVEN STOCKINETTE FABRIC

Uneven knitting can sometimes happen due to inattention, but often it will be to do with your technique for holding the needles or the yarn, or both. Because it can show up and spoil the look of stockinette fabric in particular, it is well worth trying various ways of fixing the problem as soon as you are aware of it.

UNEVEN STITCHES

If your knitting is very uneven, then the most likely cause is the way in which you hold the needles and yarn. If you hold the needles like a knife (see page 32) and you let go of the right needle when wrapping the yarn around it to make a stitch, then your gauge will be uneven. Similarly, if you are holding the yarn awkwardly, it may not be tensioning smoothly through your fingers (see pages 30–31). Experiment with different methods and knit swatches to perfect your gauge and make your knitting more even.

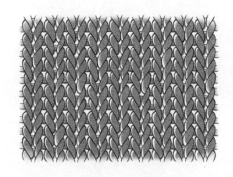

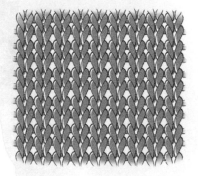

UNEVEN ROWS

For some people there will be a noticeable difference in size between the stitches on knit rows and those on purl rows, with the purl row stitches being bigger. If you have this problem and practice does not cure it for you, then try working the purl rows with a smaller needle. So if the pattern asks for size US 7 needles, then cast on and work the first knit row using those needles. Then swap the free needle for a size US 6 needle and purl the next row with that needle in your right hand. Carry on knitting and the smaller needle will automatically be in your right hand on the purl rows.

ONE LONGER EDGE

This usually happens because the yarn is not tightened at the end of the knit rows before turning the work to start the purl rows. Get into the habit of deliberately tightening the last knit stitch in a row, and make sure that you work the first purl stitch in a row firmly.

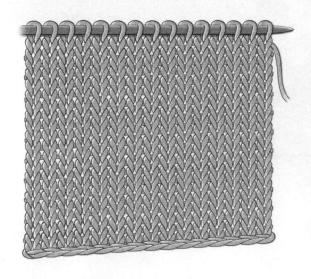

SHORTENING KNITTED FABRIC

If you have worked a large piece—such as the front of a sweater—and it is too long, but armhole or shoulder shaping at the top means you can't just unravel a few rows, you can shorten it in the following way. The technique adds a grafted row, so take this in to account when working out how many rows to shorten by.

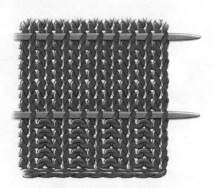

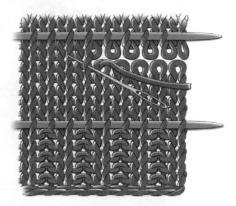

1. It is easiest to use this method on stockinette, so if there is rib—or another stitch pattern—at the bottom of the piece, then shorten it above that. Thread a knitting needle through the right-hand loop of every stitch in the row at the top of the rib. Thread another needle through the right-hand loop of every stitch in the row at the top of the section you want to take out.

2. Cut the first stitch of the row two rows below the upper needle and then unpick the stitches in that row using a blunt-tipped sewing needle. Use the sewing needle to unpick the row of loose stitches below the upper needle and secure the tail of yarn on the back. Unravel the rows down to the lower needle. Graft the two pieces together (see page 228) with the unraveled yarn.

LENGTHENING KNITTED FABRIC

As with shortening (see above), this works best on stockinette fabric, so work above a rib or other border stitch pattern. Remember you will need extra yarn, so make sure you have enough before you cut the knitting.

1. Thread a knitting needle through the right-hand loop of every stitch in the row at the top of the rib. Thread another needle through the right-hand loop of every stitch two rows above. Very carefully cut through a stitch in the middle of the row between the two needles and use a blunt-tipped sewing needle to unpick all the stitches in that row. Secure a tail of yarn on the back of each piece.

2. Join in new yarn and work the extra length wanted onto the needle holding the rib. Then graft (see page 228) the last row of the newly worked section onto the stitches held on the upper of the two original needles.

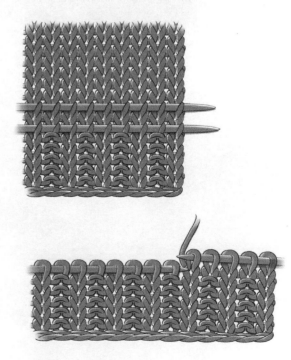

CORRECTING COLOR PATTERNS

If you have made a mistake in a color pattern, you can correct it without having to re-knit the whole piece using the same principle as for shortening fabric (see page 307). Another way of disguising small errors in color knitting is to use duplicate stitch (see pages 192–193) to embroider over the wrong-colored stitch, though this can make a visible bump in the fabric.

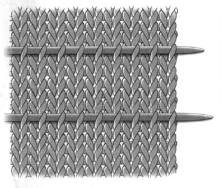

1. Start by finding a single-color row above the row with the mistake in: in this example the single-color row is four rows above the incorrect row. Thread a knitting needle through the right-hand loop of every stitch in the row above this single-color one. Thread another needle through the right-hand loop of every stitch in the row below the mistake.

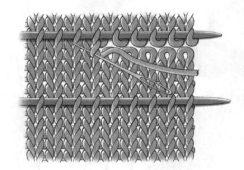

2. Cut a stitch in the single-color row and unpick the stitches across the row.

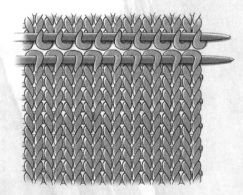

3. Unravel the stitches back to the lower needle. Re-knit the section, working the correct color pattern until you reach the row below the single-color one.

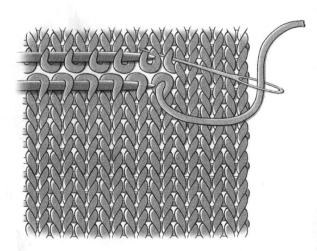

4. Using the single color yarn, graft the two pieces together (see page 228) to complete the color pattern correction.

CORRECTING CABLE PATTERNS

If you discover that you have crossed a cable in the wrong direction after you have worked a considerable amount of the piece, you can correct the mistake using the method shown here rather than having to re-knit the whole piece. This can be quite a fiddly procedure, so work slowly and carefully to avoid unraveling any more stitches than is necessary.

1. Have prepared a couple of short lengths of waste yarn threaded into blunt-tipped sewing needles. Cut the center stitch of the row where the cable crosses. Working carefully, unpick the stitches, leaving the ends of yarn loose on either side. Quickly thread a length of waste yarn through the live stitch loops to prevent further unraveling.

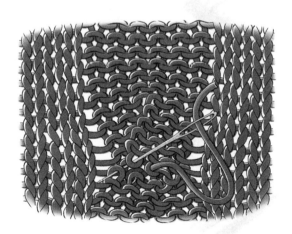

2. Lift up the lower stitches, which will become the top stitches when the cable is re-crossed to run in the right direction. Turn the work over and on the wrong side and using matching yarn, sew the original stitches together, taking out the waste yarn as you do so. Sew in the loose ends. If they are very short, you can sew them to the stitches on the back of the cable using matching sewing thread.

MENDING SNAGS

The golden rule for snags is never to cut them off. If you do so you are effectively cutting a stitch and the knitting will unravel surprisingly quickly and a hole will form.

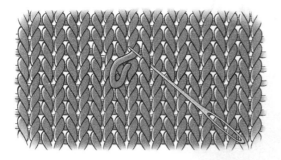

1. If stitches either side of the snag have pulled tight, use a blunt-tipped sewing needle to gently ease the snagged yarn back into them and to re-shape them. If the snag is small, you may be able to completely eliminate it this way.

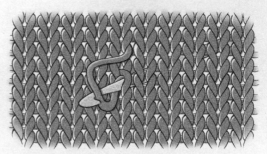

2. However, if you still have a snag loop, slip a crochet hook through the stitch from the back and pull the loop through to the wrong side. If need be, sew the loop to the back of the knitting using matching sewing thread.

MENDING HOLES

If the yarn has actually broken and a small hole has formed, you will need to graft a new stitch to prevent the fabric unraveling further. It is a good idea to keep a small amount of the yarn you used for any project, just in case repairs are needed.

1. Start by stabilizing the hole and sewing in any loose ends of yarn to stop them unraveling further. Thread a blunt-tipped sewing needle with a length of the yarn the project was knitted in. Secure the yarn on the back, beside the hole. From the back, bring the needle through the center of the stitch at the top right-hand side of the hole. Take the needle into the front of the stitch below, then out from the back of the next stitch to the left.

2. Using the grafting technique (see page 228), work across the hole, following the path of the original stitches to duplicate them and close the hole.

DARNING

This is the technique required if a larger hole has formed. It can be used to darn invisibly or to add vintage-style decorative detail. There are various methods of darning, but this is one of the simplest. It is shown here in a contrast color for extra clarity.

1. Start by stabilizing the hole and sewing in any loose ends of yarn to stop them unraveling further. Thread a blunt-tipped sewing needle with the darning yarn and work running stitches in a square around the hole. Work at least half a stitch outside the hole.

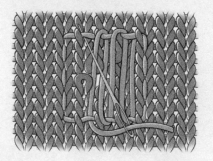

2. Starting in one corner, take the yarn across the hole, under one of the running stitches, then back across the hole and under another running stitch. Pull it taut enough to keep the fabric flat, but not tight enough to pucker it. Span the entire hole with stitches in this way.

3. Then work back and forth across the hole in the other direction, weaving the needle alternately under and over the spanning stitches. On each row the yarn should go under the strands it went over in the previous row, and vice versa.

4. Continue darning until the strands are as densely woven as required. Fasten off on the back.

RESOURCES

Debbie Bliss has her own brand of hand-knitting yarns that range from from lace-weight up to super-chunky. The yarns, designs, and color palettes are selected by Debbie.

Debbie Bliss's ranges of knitting accessories, homewares, and gifts can be found online at www. debbieblissonline.com where you can also catch up with her latest news on her blog. In the real world you can buy her homewares at Debbie Bliss Home, 36 Orford Road, Walthamstow, London E17 9NJ. Follow Debbie on Facebook debbieblissonline / on Twitter @debbieblissnews / on Instagram debbieblissknits / on Pinterest debbieblissnews

Worldwide distributors of Debbie Bliss yarns: contact regional distributors for local stockists.

USA
Knitting Fever Inc.
315 Bayview Avenue
Amityville
NY 11701
USA
Tel: +1 516 546 3600
Fax +1 516 546 6871
www.knittingfever.com

CANADA
Diamond Yarn Ltd
155 Martin Ross Avenue
Unit 3
Toronto
Ontario M3J 2L9
Canada
Tel: +1 416 736 6111
Fax: +1 416 736 6112
www.diamondyarn.com

UK
Designer Yarns Ltd
Units 8-10 Newbridge Industrial
Estate
Pitt Street
Keighley
West Yorkshire BD21 4PQ
UK
Tel: +44 (0)1535 664222
Fax: +44 (0)1535 664333
www.designeryarns.uk.com
enquiries@designeryarns.uk.com

AUSTRALIA/ NEW ZEALAND
Prestige Yarns Pty Ltd
PO Box 39
Bulli
NSW 2516
Australia
Tel: +61 02 4285 6669
www.prestigeyarns.com
info@prestigeyarns.com

GERMANY/AUSTRIA/ SWITZERLAND/BENELUX/ DENMARK
Designer Yarns (Deutschland) GMBH
Welserstrasse 10g
D-51149 Köln
Germany
Tel: +49 (0) 2203 1021910
Fax: +49 (0) 2203 1023551
www.designeryarns.de
info@designeryarns.de

BRAZIL
Quatro Estacoes Com
Las Linhas e Acessorios Ltda
Av. Das Nacoes Unidas
12551-9 Andar
Cep 04578-000 Sao Paulo
Brazil
Tel: + 55 11 3443 7736
cristina@4estacoeslas.com.br

CHINA
Lotus Textiles
22 Zhonghua Wst
Xingtai
Hebei
China
05-4000
stella@lotusyarns.com

FINLAND
Eiran Tukku
Mäkelänkatu 54 B
00510 Helsinki
Finland
Tel: + 358 50 346 0575
maria.hellbom@eirantukku.fi

FRANCE
Plassard Diffusion
La Filature
71800 Varennes-sous-Dun
France
Tel: + 33 (0) 3 85282828
Fax: + 33 (0) 3 85282829
info@laines-plassard.com

HONG KONG
East Unity Company Ltd
Unit B2, 7/F Block B
Kailey Industrial Centre
12 Fung Yip Street
Chai Wan
Hong Kong
Tel: + (852) 2869 7110
Fax: + (852) 2537 6952
eastunity@yahoo.com.hk

HUNGARY
Sziget Store Kft
2310. Szigetszentmiklos
Haszontalan dulo 34
Hungary
Contact: Janos Nemeth
janosnemeth@mol.hu

ICELAND
Storkurinn Ehf
Laugavegi 59
101 Reykjavík
Iceland
Tel: + 354 551 8258
Fax: + 354 562 8252
storkurinn@simnet.is

ITALY
Lucia Fornasari Distribuzione
Via Castellamonte, 9
Banchette (TO) 10010
Italy
Tel: + 39 345 566 5568
www.lavoroamaglia.it

MEXICO
Estambres Crochet Sa De Cv
Aaron Saenz 1891-7
Col. Santa Maria
Monterrey
N.L. 64650
Mexico
Tel: + 52 81 8335 3870
abremer@redmundial.com.mx

NORWAY
Gjestal, House of Yarn AS
Hunnedalsvegen 1150
4333 Oltedal
Norway
Tommy.Eide@gjestal.no

POLAND
Amiqs
Ul Michala Aniola 8
Bielawa
05-520 Konstancin Jeziorma
Contact: Marcin Ratynksi
Tel: + 48 60 641 001
marcin@ittec.pl
www.amiqs.com

PORTUGAL
Knitting Labs
Rua Professora Virginia Rau 10 3c
1600-673 Lisbon
Contact: Mrs. Maria Luisa Arruda
Tel: + 35 191 728 1659
luisa.arruda@knittinglabs.com
www.knittinglabs.com

SPAIN
Oyambre Needlework Sl
Corcega 371, 2o
08037 Barcelona
Spain
Tel: +34 (0) 93 487 26 72
Fax: +34 (0) 93 218 6694
info@oyambreonline.com

SWEDEN
Nysta Garn Och Textil
Hogasvagen 20
S-131 47 Nacka
Sweden
Tel: + 46 (0) 708 813 954
www.nysta.se
info@nysta.se

BOOKS THAT I REFER TO INCLUDE:

A Treasury of Knitting Patterns
by Barbara G Walker
(Schoolhouse Press)
A Second Treasury Of Knitting Patterns
by Barbara G Walker
A Third Treasury Of Knitting Patterns
by Barbara G Walker
A Fourth Treasury of Knitting Patterns
by Barbara G Walker
Charted Knitted Designs
by Barbara G Walker

75 Knitted Floral Blocks by
Lesley Stanfield (Milner)

The Knitter's Stitch Collection by
Lesley Stanfield and Melody Griffiths
(Search Press)

*The Ultimate Sourcebook of Knitting
and Crochet Stitches: The Harmony
Guides* (Collins and Brown)

Knitwear Fashion Design
by Maite Lafuente (Promopress)

9 Heads by Nancy Riegelman
(9 Heads Media)

*How to Draw like a Fashion Designer:
Inspirational Sketchbooks – Tips from
Top Designers* by Celia Joicey and
Dennis Nothdruft (Thames & Hudson)

*Entrelac: The Essential Guide to
Interlace Knitting* by Rosemary
Drysdale (Sixth & Spring Books)

*Patterns for Guernseys, Jerseys and
Arans: Fishermen's Sweaters from the
British Isles* by Gladys Thompson
(Dover Publications)

If you see them in second-hand shops,
Odhams Practical Knitting Illustrated

ONLINE RESOURCES

Ravelry
A community site and yarn and
pattern database.

Blogtacular conferences

Pinterest
Create online moodboards and find
inspiration for projects.

Instagram
Take a picture or video, and if you
want to you can choose a filter to
transform the look and feel of it.

KNITTER'S GRAPH PAPER

These sheets of proportional graph paper can be photocopied for your own use. See pages 65 and 282 for more on using this specialist type of graph paper.

2:3 RATIO GRAPH PAPER

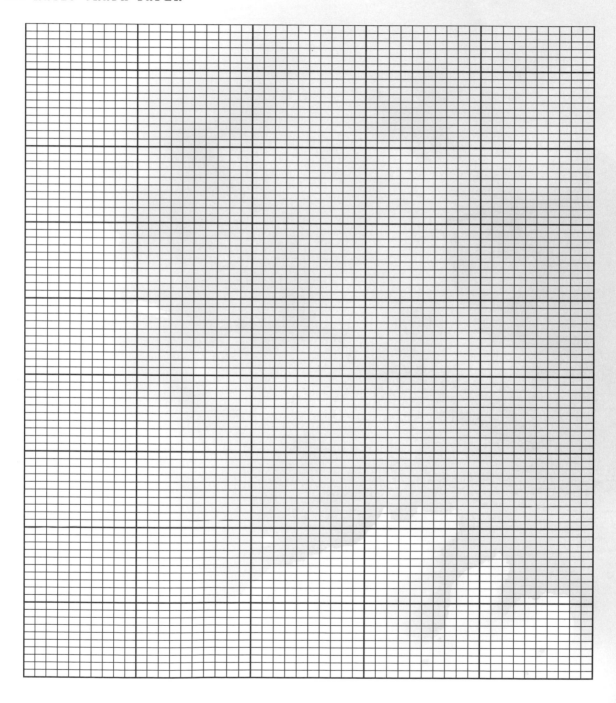

4:5 RATIO GRAPH PAPER

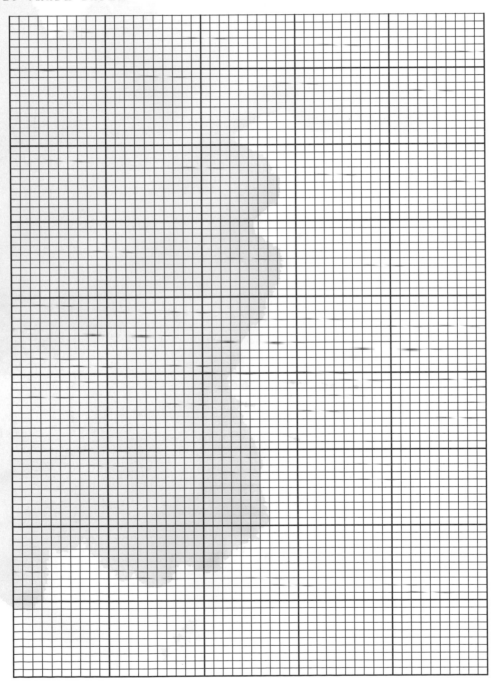

INDEX

LARK
New York

An Imprint of Sterling Publishing Co., Inc.
1166 Avenue of the Americas
New York, NY 10036

LARK CRAFTS and the distinctive
Lark logo are registered trademarks
of Sterling Publishing Co., Inc.

This Lark edition published in 2015 by Sterling Publishing

First published in 2015 by Quadrille Publishing Ltd

Text © 2015 Debbie Bliss
Photography by Kim Lightbody
Illustration by Cathy Brear
Design by Gemma Wilson

ISBN 978-1-4547-0926-8

Distributed in Canada by Sterling Publishing
c/o Canadian Manda Group, 664 Annette Street,
Toronto, Ontario, Canada M6S 2C8

For information about custom editions, special sales, and premium and corporate purchases, please contact Sterling Special Sales at 800-805-5489 or specialsales@sterlingpublishing.com.

Manufactured in China

10 9 8 7 6 5 4 3

larkcrafts.com

If you have any comments or queries regarding the instructions in this book, please contact us at LarkCrafts.com.

AUTHOR'S ACKNOWLEDGMENTS

I would like to thank the following people for their contribution to this book.

Kate Haxell To say that *The Knitter's Book of Knowledge* would not have been possible without Kate is an understatement. As project manager and editor, her generous collaboration and exhaustive sourcing has been invaluable, and her enthusiasm and patience endless.

Lisa Pendreigh My fantastic commissioning editor at Quadrille, who first approached me with the idea of a knitting techniques book.

Teresa Conway Who diligently applied her proof-reading skills to the text and check-knitted her way through the book.

Rosy Tucker My colleague who waved her red pen over text and diagrams when I had brain fade.

Kim Lightbody Whose beautiful photography and styling make the book such a joy to look at.

Cathy Brear For her painstaking work on the detailed and lovely illustrations.

Gemma Wilson For her stylish and thoughtful book design.

My thanks to all the knitters who have so generously shared their skills with me over the years.